Praise for 12 (

MW01139929

"What a powerful book! [...]
within and guide us to discover our own inner wisdom. Reading the
12 Golden Keys is like listening in on a conversation between our self
and Soul in search of clarity. It's honest. It flows. And it inspires."
 – Janet Matthews, co-author of *Chicken Soup for the Canadian Soul*

"The 12 Keys gives you the tools to unlock blocks and move toward a
more fulfilling and prosperous life."
 – Jodi Smith, JLS Entertainment

"M. J. Milne's book is a primer on how to find our way through the
daunting world of the twenty-first century. Exercises, personal stories
from all over the world—everything to make it as easy as possible to
follow the path to conscious freedom."
 – Clélie Rich, poet, editor, and member of *Room's* editorial collective

"This book is just what our current world situation needs—a way to
bring inner and outer practical shifts in this time of large scale world
change. Read it now to have the solutions you will need to usher in
a profound, new, and powerful way to live–regardless of external
conditions."
 – Satyen Raja, author of *Living Ecstasy*, Founder of WarriorSage.com

"An innovative approach to higher consciousness. The Keys give access
to the subconscious in a way that accelerates your transformation."
 – Nancy Shipley Rubin, psychic & counselor, RubinEnterprises.info

"M. J. Milne's book inspires me to pay more attention to my spiritual
growth—knowing I'll reap priceless benefits. Her anecdotes illuminate
the book's very practical information about how to experience the
power of Soul. I highly recommend *12GKs*."
 – Jeane Manning, author of *Breakthrough Power*

"M.J. Milne's book is a powerful toolbox for tackling the challenges of
a world in transition, and the perfect catalyst to reignite your spiritual
quest. The Keys unlock the door to those secret worlds we long to
enter."
 – Michael Harrington, author of *Touched by the Dragon's Breath*

"The 12 Keys provide exercises and tools necessary to live a joyful
life. They teach us how to get in tune with our inner selves."
 – Babe Gurr, recording artist, *Chocolate Lilly*

12 Golden Keys for a New World

Unlocking the Door to Conscious Freedom
❧ Change Your Life, Change Your Planet ☙

M. J. Milne
Author of *Universal Tides*

Blue Heron Productions
North Vancouver, Canada

Library and Archives Canada Cataloguing in Publication

Milne, M. J. (Marilyn J.), 1948-
          12 golden keys for a new world : unlocking the door to conscious freedom--change your life, change your planet / M.J. Milne.

Includes bibliographical references.
ISBN 978-0-9739654-1-4

          1. Spiritual life--New Age movement. 2. Self-realization.
I. Title. II. Title: Twelve golden keys for a new world.

BP605.N48M557 2010   204   C2009-900307-4

Editor: Karla McMechan
Layout: RichWords Editing Services, Vancouver, BC
Cover design: M. J. Milne, Eva-Maria Schoen, and Jerry Leonard
Author photo: Michael O'Shea

Published by Blue Heron Productions,
North Vancouver, Canada
Website: 12goldenkeys.com; or, universaltides.com
Email: info@12goldenkeys.com
10 9 8 7 6 5 4 3 2 1
First Edition

For my family and all the shining Souls
who touch my heart and show me
what it means to Live to Live.

I have one small drop of knowing in my soul.
Let it dissolve in your ocean.
—Rumi

12 Golden Key Symbols

 First Key — You Are the Key

 Second Key — Follow the Blue Light

 Third Key — You Are a Key Guardian

 Fourth Key — There Is No Limitation

 Fifth Key — Through the Eyes of Soul

 Sixth Key — Live to Live in Spirit

 Seventh Key — Lighten Up to Light Up

 Eighth Key — Love and Gratitude Are Key

 Ninth Key — Go with the Flow

 Tenth Key — Let Go and Dream Travel

 Eleventh Key — Share the Magic

 Twelfth Key — Be a Spiritual Warrior

Key to Icons

Explanation of icon images used in the text

 Key Exercise: The Star points to the primary exercise for you to use when practicing each Golden Key; located at the end of each Key chapter.

 Key Tip: This Key marks helpful tips for practicing various aspects of a Golden Key.

 Spiritual Experience: The Third Eye marks an experience where the author was able to see through the eyes of Soul and receive spiritual guidance.

 Spiritual Wake-Up Call: The Butterfly indicates an experience while wide awake that alerted the author to pay attention.

 Spiritual Warrior Code: The Spiritual Warrior indicates a wisdom code to live by; it complements the Golden Key in which it appears.

 Story from the Heart: The Hands of Light icon points to a story of how divine love opened the heart.

Contents

KEY CHAPTERS:

Preface

WELCOME. The inspiration for *12 Golden Keys for a New World* (*12GKs*) first came through while rewriting my novel *Universal Tides®* (*Utides* for short). The idea for *Utides* came to me in a dream, and after handwriting a 500-page first draft, I promptly placed it in an old trunk in the basement. I stumbled upon the story 25 years later, and recognized its prophetic relevancy for today's world. Compelled to update *Utides*, the evolving 12 Keys appeared!

It's best to go at your own pace. Start by reading over each Golden Key, and do the exercise at the end of each chapter. Stay with a key until it becomes a part of your spiritual toolbox, ready to use at a moment's notice. Each key includes bulleted points, and sometimes I refer back to these points numerically, e.g., 1:2 means the First Key, point 2. This allows you to go back to review. Also, words in the Glossary are written in **bold** type the first time they appear.

Toward the end of each chapter are wonderful stories written by others, illustrating the key's meaning. See "Meet the Contributors" for their biographical information.

You are about to make your own personal history of spiritual experiences. I encourage you to follow your own inner guidance. It is important that you use your gifts of intuition, inspiration, and spiritual illumination. Seek and you shall find your own truth—and keep choosing love over fear.

Live to Live,
M. J. Milne

12 Golden Keys
for a New World

INTRODUCTION

There is but one history, and that is the soul's.
—W. B. Yeats

THERE ARE 12 GOLDEN KEYS that unlock gateways to secrets hidden inside of you. Fear is the gatekeeper that blocks your passage. As you unlock each door, you gradually enter a state of **conscious freedom**, a state of awareness that allows you the freedom to create and choose how to experience your life, dissolving fear. Conscious freedom leads you to the realization of who you truly are—**Soul**, a consciously aware being here for experience—and what that means in the grand scheme of things is life-altering. There is something more to life—being Soul. The rest is an illusion, an illusion of your own making, and you can change it, if you wish. As you do, you will begin to realize we are one planet, one spirit, and one family, breaking free of conditioned beliefs. Thus, your life journey is truly a spiritual quest. This book is designed to help you become who you are intended to be. It is meant as a practical guide for personal and planetary transformation through conscious freedom and the power of Soul.

The **12 Golden Keys** came through while rewriting my sci-fi, new-age, survivalist novel *Universal Tides: Barbed Wire Blues* (*Utides* for short). Little did I know that the theme of **Universal Tides**—the fall of Man and the rise of **Spirit**—could actually happen, depending on our choices! While helping the characters, the 12 Golden Keys also helped many readers gain inner insights, and they began using the Keys to ask Soul all of life's most intriguing questions—and getting answers!

... she tried the little golden key in the lock, and to her great delight it fitted! Alice opened the door and found that it led into ...
—Lewis Carroll, *Alice's Adventures in Wonderland*[1]

The character Alice in Lewis Carroll's *Alice's Adventures in Wonderland* learns that very few things are impossible. Although a fiction story, I believe it's true, and there are three primary steps to discovering that truth.

First, the Keys unlock the secret gate of ageless wisdom that leads inward into the worlds of Soul. Life is a wonderful adventure, but there is something more. Your inner life is a buried treasure, along with secret life codes in your DNA.

Second, with the gate unlocked, allowing your passage through, the Keys explain practical ways to learn the ancient science of visionary sight. The secret knowledge they impart is how to access your authentic self (Soul) every moment, connecting you with God, **Divine Source**, or Spirit, or whatever you wish to call It. Throughout our world there is a growing phenomenon, a subtle revolution that is changing your human consciousness. You and millions of others are developing your spiritual sight, partly by opening your inner eye or **Third Eye**—the seat of visionary sight. With this inner knowledge you view everything through the eyes of Soul. By using the inner guidance of Soul you can plan ahead, knowing your purpose, envisioning and manifesting your life.

Third, the path is now before you and the 12 Keys show you how to travel on your journey. We are on a spiritual quest for survival. The word "spiritual" simply means you are in pursuit of your personal development. To become spiritual means to live in the present moment, fully conscious and content; and to be content you need spiritual freedom, meaning to be more aware of the presence of Soul in your life. We all need contentment and to live consciously each moment. That is our quest. We are on a quest to find our truth, passion for life, and contentment in turbulent times. For me, contentment is the ability to give ourselves permission to be who we are, being grateful for our mistakes because they are opportunities for growth.

A Spiritual (R)evolution is the Solution

We are on a quest during a time of **Spiritual (R)evolution**. Every good and pure quest needs a mission, a map, and a guide.

The mission offered here is for you to discover who you really are and to reclaim responsibility for your own life so you can Live to Live® and **Help Others Help Others**. *12 Golden Keys for a New World* is your map, and the exercises provided will help you to co-create your life. Know that you are not being asked to believe in anything outside your own direct experience. This book acts as a practical guide, giving you exercises to create your own history of experiences, to open your perception and unlock new doorways for your unique growth and transformation. You create your own truth every moment, in the present.

The 12 Golden Keys are non-denominational, universal truths connected to ancient teachings that are in harmony with all life. The belief that we are in harmony with one another and the cosmos is the oldest form of faith. Seeing our place in the universe with new eyes, we realize once again that we are a part of everything. This belief is the original simplicity that can open our eyes to the planet-wide Spiritual (R)evolution. The simple cosmic secret that we are Soul has been inaccessible to the majority of us on this planet. When the breath of Soul is gone out of your body, Soul has moved on. I invite you to accept the quest, to activate secret codes, to begin to transform your life and experience moving into a **new world** view, shifting gears.

An Evolutionary Quest

We are each on an evolutionary quest, embarking on a new adventure in the **Age of Consciousness**. What is **consciousness**? It is the state of being conscious. It is your personal identity compared to your surroundings. How conscious are you? Are you asleep and a follower, or are you half-asleep and in the process of waking up to the outer and inner worlds? Or are you wide-awake, conscious of the planet and beyond? When consciously awake, you are co-creating.

Consciousness is light, and we are composed of light within a vast energy field, called zero-point energy, hyperdimensional space, biofield, the living matrix, or, what I call, **Living Energy**. As we expand into a higher level of consciousness, we also vibrate at a higher level of light, able to hold more information.

Our personal vibration and frequency, which is partly influenced by our emotions and thoughts, is linked to the life-sustaining field of Living Energy and can, quite possibily, influence Earth's cycles. Our conscious state continually changes, grows, and develops through our experiences. Every moment something new is added, like in a movie, revealing the development of the characters and story as a whole. Just when we think we know what lies ahead, the character reaches a turning point, and the entire direction of the story changes. Life is change. Everything is in flux, including the cells in your body. However, up until now, *Homo sapiens* have been stuck on the evolutionary ladder.

We have been asleep on Mother Earth for eons, but now something evolutionary is happening. Something that hasn't happened since the first aquatic creature took its first step onto dry land over three billion years ago. At the edge of an ancient shoreline, the ocean teemed with a bounty of marine life. Envision one little fish, gently nudged by the tide over the boundary between ocean and land, slithering up the beach, abandoned as the tide withdraws, but it survives and others follow. This one gigantic evolutionary step changed the Earth forever. Once again, we are about to take an evolutionary leap across a boundary and be forever changed.

> *The day will come when, after harnessing space, the winds, the tides, gravitation, we shall harness for God the energies of love. And, on that day, for the second time in the history of the world, man will have discovered fire.*
>
> —Pierre Teilhard de Chardin[2]

I believe that each of us has secret life codes embedded in our DNA. These current codes and the energy imprints from our past lives affect our present life. The codes also setup a domino effect for how our life can evolve. It is choice that changes everything. Each secret code, or God particle,[3] ignites a certain set of predestined chemical reactions to circumstances that move into play for us to experience and learn from. But the outcome is our choice. How we accept and handle free will and choice is through the ancient wisdom of Soul.

Every generation is born with the most current genetic

drift, or current adaptive DNA. But now something amazing is happening! All of us are entering a new evolutionary consciousness, together. Even Souls who live in parallel dimensions are affected. Or, perhaps you do not believe Souls live elsewhere? Eventually, it's something we'll all discover. You're about to learn how to consciously use your spiritual sight (Third Eye) to access a new evolutionary awareness. Our worlds are converging, and we are all shifting on the cellular level in order to step across the boundary. What waits on the other side? Could there be beings of great wisdom who watch our progress and wait for us to evolve? Or are we about to discover, as did the Inkan Elders, that "we are the ones we've been waiting for"?

Many are inwardly sensing this major transformative change, called variously the Changing Times, Shift of the Ages, or **Great Turning**. The shift is within ourselves and is an evolutionary shift of consciousness. Author and activist Joanna Macy, who coined the term "the Great Turning," states: "The Great Turning is a name for the essential adventure of our time: the shift from the industrial growth society to a life-sustaining civilization."[4]

Today's great minds in anthropology, astronomy, quantum physics, astrophysics, biophysics, bioenergetics, frontier biology, holistic medicine, the indigenous traditions, and world religions are feeling the shift, as are many of you, realizing that we are more than just our physical body. Personal investigation can lead you to hundreds of books and DVDs with supportable truths that offer a bridge between scientific and spiritual thought. The 12 Golden Keys given here can assist you during these Changing Times of the fall of aggressive man and the rise of Spirit by offering a gateway through to this new paradigm. We have come to a critical crossroad for the future of our planet and we will have to change the way we live. Whether or not we take the leap forward depends on our choices. The Spiritual (R)evolution has begun, introducing a new world consciousness.[5]

Ancient Survival Keys

This new world consciousness is anchored in ancient survival keys; however, most people are unaware of these 12 Golden Keys which lead to the inner worlds of Soul, beyond our physical universe, and thus, it's still a secret. But that is about to change. The 12 Golden Keys can unlock the secret wisdom of Soul. This secret way to truth is real and has been practiced for many eons by our ancestors, the "Ancients."[6] But the possibilities of Third Eye spiritual travel and the process of developing your spiritual senses have been kept from you, suppressed for reasons of power and greed. Now, herein, the secret way is at your fingertips!

I honestly don't know how I would survive in today's world without a Soul-to-Soul connection with Divine Source. Many of you are also in touch with inner resources, whether you call it connecting with your higher power, the Holy Spirit, your guides, angels, guardians, masters, or being aware of synchronicities and listening to your **intuition.** You are also becoming aware of the amazing and often difficult changes happening in our world. Difficult, yes, but consider the possibility that, before you were born, you signed up to be here. There is a reason you are here. Find that reason and you discover your life's purpose and destiny.

The 12 Golden Keys of illumination are keys to survival in these Changing Times and, also, keys to the **Otherworlds**— heaven and beyond into parallel worlds. The 12 Keys act as stepping stones, guiding you on your quest to find your path, your mission, your truth. The choice of path is always yours. Choose a path that resonates with your heart; meaning, choose the path that makes you feel fulfilled and allows you to live from an **awakened heart,** in touch with your inner self known as Soul. One's heart is either open (awake) or closed (numb). When your heart is awake, it means your heart is full of love, consciously aware of the love that is all around you. By choosing to practice these twelve survival keys, you can unlock your secret path to the wonderful worlds of Soul, thereby discovering the keys for living your life's purpose, a way to raise your consciousness above this physical plane, and eventually moving from a social consciousness of separation to a Soul consciousness which leads to an organically organized, sustainable community—your evolutionary quest and mission.

Legend of the New Human

Our story begins long ago in the jungles of South America in the time of the Maya and Inka, and in other parts of the ancient world, such as Tibet, China, India, and the Southwest, USA, where indigenous peoples, at different times, received and safeguarded a message for us, a prophecy. The basic core of this message is:

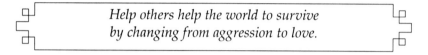

Help others help the world to survive
by changing from aggression to love.

Their prophecies do not predict the end of the world as some people have reported, but this did not come from the Maya; it's about our evolution of consciousness. All indigenous people are coming together to help one another. In 2006, Mayan Elder Don Alejandro and his wife Elizabeth Araujo traveled to meet Sri Bhagavan of India who is loved by over a hundred million people. An important exchange took place between the spiritual traditions of the West and the East. The indigenous Elders of all groups believe that "This is the time to share sacred indigenous wisdom, prophecies, and old traditional knowledge to help mankind survive."[7] Survival means shifting gears to a global, holistic viewpoint based on sustainable cooperation.

The Inka Prophecy states that when the condor and the eagle reunite and fly again, wing-to-wing, it will signal the end of separation and conflict on the planet, bringing about the beginning of healing and reunion, and the coming together of a unified community and a new planetary perspective or a change in consciousness.

The ancient Inkan Empire was the largest nation on Earth in pre-Columbian America. During the latter days of the twentieth-century, the last 600 individuals of the Laika or Q'eros Indians of Peru, the descendants of the Inka, reappeared in the physical plane. Alberto Villoldo, Ph.D., of the Four Winds Society has trained with the Q'ero shamans for many years and has played a key role in bringing their beliefs to us.[8] According to legend, in 1950 the Q'ero appeared at a feast where thousands, including the Elders of several indigenous groups, had gathered. When the Q'ero arrived, wearing ponchos emblazoned with the royal emblem of the Sun, the sea of people parted to let the Q'ero pass. The Elders recognized the emblem and knew the Q'ero were the last original descendants of the Inka or Children of the Sun.

"We have waited for you for five hundred years," said one of the Elders.

The Q'ero people were isolated from the world for a long time, and the importance of their return heralded the beginning of their prophecies. The legendary Laika responded that the evolution into a new human is upon us now and that they are here to assist us as we grow into a new species of human being.

On Becoming *Homo Luminous*

We are being called upon *en masse* to consciously recreate our lives. If we're unable to be as a caterpillar and transform into a butterfly, we will miss the opportunity to become *Homo luminous* and be forced to remain the more aggressive *Homo sapiens*. Fortunately there is a way, an awakening that is already encoded in our cellular structure. This evolutionary change is happening, in part, through a process of cellular change. Once you know the simple yet transformative 12 Golden Keys and learn to connect with Spirit, you will be able to adapt to the changes, and trigger innate secret codes automatically.

We are beginning to understand what it means to be *Homo luminous*, the new human. We are learning how to receive energetically rather than mentally by opening our hearts with love and a detached compassion (i.e., not of the emotions). We are beginning to activate, exchange, and dialogue with the matrix of the Living Energy, or what Villoldo calls the "**Luminous Energy Field**" (LEF).[9] This is the evolutionary leap we are now called upon to make.

People from all walks of life are now experiencing profound spiritual awakenings. The new perspective offers a release from fear and the discovery of a newfound sense of contentment. In short, this is living a life of conscious freedom with an awakened heart, awakening Soul to the reality of living consciously every day. It's the nature of our becoming that is forging a new spirituality and, thus, turning the legend of the new human into reality.

The 12 Golden Keys can teach you about your intuitive, inner spiritual gifts. It is said that the seventh sense is enlightenment, being at one with the cosmos. It is an entrance **portal** to the divine worlds, using a practice that you are about to learn called conscious **dream travel** or soul travel.

Conscious dream travel and the 12 Golden Keys are based partly on the science of focused intention, dialoguing with the hyperdimensional energy continuum currently being investigated in Quantum Physics. Recent experiments demonstrate the possibility of a bridge between our outer and inner worlds.

We connect subconsciously with each and every person we come in contact with, no matter where we are at the time. We connect on a non-physical Soul level. When your spiritual eye is open, you will see yourself and the people around you in spirit form, from Soul's vantage point, usually located in another dimension beyond our 3-D world. What you converse about depends upon the past lives and the karma you had experienced together and your mission. You are about to learn how to do this as you master the 12 Golden Keys.

The Matrix of Energy

We will be talking about energies, so here is a little background in quantum theory. Quantum physics is easily researched through books in your local library and, also, in films.[10]

Max Planck, the father of quantum theory, gave a speech in Florence, Italy, in 1944 describing a "matrix" of energy, the container holding our universe.[11] Quantum physics tells us that matter is densely packed light. Planck described a universal field of energy that connects everything in creation, basically saying that we are immersed and awash in a force (Living Energy) as a fish is awash in water. Author Gregg Braden calls this the

"Divine Matrix."[12] To me, if it were a computer, this divine matrix would be the operating system and everything in our world would be the software or computer programs. So when I talk about changing our state of consciousness, I'm talking about changing the computer software, not the operating system.

The ancient alchemists once called this matrix of energy "the luminous energy body." Alchemists believed this hyper-dimensional sphere was around every animal, planet, and everything in the universe. Villoldo believes that the LEF is a golden light energy which can transform and heal the body, changing the way we live our lives.[13] American chiropractor and author Eric Pearl also speaks about a continuum of energy that's comprised not only of energy, but of light and information.[14] Richard Bartlett of Matrix Energetics teaches how to use an energy field and a consciousness; but it's not a technique, it's a consciousness shift.[15] Others believe that in quantum time our thought and intention changes our quantum reality and, thus, the field of unlimited creative potential (or LEF); and yet, there is a divine plan.

It's as if an enlightened thought form has appeared through igniting a secret life code (the God particle) and, simultaneously, has touched the field and rippled through it, becoming a wave that affects everyone in our present day by creating the coming of a different world. This new world consciousness consists of systems based on sustainability, grassroots collaboration, harmony, the awakening of an egalitarian society, and a new trust in mutual cooperation and interconnection. Our tumultuous times are caused by the sweeping away of the old to allow for new ways.

Quantum Science has proven that this divine life current exists. Members of the New Energy Movement and quantum physicists are aware of this new energy paradigm. It is a new science using the universal energy. British New Energy researcher John Davidson writes: "This is a wave that many of us are jointly riding, and which is simultaneously breaking, apparently independently, in all parts of the World."[16]

The Mayan Elders spoke of great changes to Mother Earth's vibrational frequencies and her energy field and how we must accept these new planetary energies. Because our bodies will be changing and shifting with the new energies, we need to learn how to access these energies, to accept them, to allow them to free-flow through us, to keep the flow moving as the worlds merge and open portals for us to step across. Not so farfetched when you consider how many ancient civilizations have already utilized this energy field.

Why Is This Happening Now?

Astronomers tell us that every 26,000 years our sun is in alignment with the very center of our galaxy. The ancients knew that at certain times during the cycle of precession of the equinoxes, the earth-sun-galaxy relationship allows the influx of a multi-dimensional light energy, the Photon Belt, which could trigger a transformational leap in mankind. These crossing-points were known by the ancients as "gates."

Don't be overly concerned about this alignment information, because life is about the now, and how we live our lives *now*. Yet it is important to note how many people believe that, during the time when the path of the Earth's Sun is in alignment with the galactic core (the crossroads of solstice), new informational energies will be transmitted to our species and to our cells. Scientists have proven that the human body contains approximately 80 to 100 trillion cells. Around sixty-million body cells die and rebuild every minute, which means about every eight years we have a new body. These new energies from the Photon Belt are also changing our cellular makeup and we are gradually becoming *Homo luminous*, **Beings of Light**, joining the cosmic community.

In *Touched by the Dragon's Breath*, Michael Harrington says:

> This planet of ours is entering a spectacular band of multi-dimensional light known as the "Photon Belt." We first touched the edge during the Harmonic Convergence [August 17, 1987].... Earth is graduating from the third dimension.[17]

I believe we have entered an era where our focus is on an Age of Consciousness. I'm not talking about a spiritual la-la-land. In astrological circles, it is known as the Age of Aquarius which represents a universal humanism, meaning: No one outside yourself is going to save you except you, and by first discovering your inner connection you can then, if you choose, go on to help others and the planet by doing service. Your consciousness is evolving. We are evolving creatures on the evolving **new Earth** where our state of consciousness and acceptance is changing from a negative viewpoint of greed, anger, aggressiveness, and closed hearts, to positive wonderment, community, and awakened hearts, in a new world age.

The new world will eventually lead us to a community mindset. I discuss this in the Eleventh Key, under the heading "Be an Earthkeeper," explaining that a sustainable community needs to consider environmental, social, and economic impacts.

This is why the simple, yet wonderful 12 Golden Keys are here—to get us ready! It is very evident that we are in a time of spiritual renewal. I am hopeful that your inner awareness of these 12 Golden Keys will come as a spark in the night and you will instantly light up! It is time to light our lanterns of truth to shine into the darkness.

The (R)evolutionary Grail of Divine Love

During the twelfth-century Age of Chivalry, warriors were tested for skills, mettle, and prowess, but they also had to live by a code, helping others less fortunate. As a global community living in the Changing Times, we will have to do much the same. Just as the Age of Chivalry was about romantic love, this evolving new world is about divine love, changing from a fear-based society to love and from separateness to community. Thus, our mission is to Help Others Help Others, as friends helping friends, creating a global egalitarian circle of love and understanding. The Spiritual (R)evolution using the amazing power of divine love is our current solution.

The twelfth-century legend of the Holy Grail teaches us that we are here to learn our spiritual lessons and to pass each test one by one. So choose the best possible situation for yourself in which to learn about divine love, forgiveness, gratitude, compassion, and giving back to the whole. Expressed in these pages are 12 Golden Keys to truth that will help unlock the gateway to the secret path that leads to the knowledge of your true heavenly origin as Soul. The secret path to heaven is here, now, and the keys to a more meaningful life are at your fingertips!

You are now ready to begin the legendary quest. I now present the 12 Golden Keys for your spiritual assignment, enjoyment, and exploration.

> *Coming out of the gate, was a knight in armour carrying a golden cup in his hand. He held his lance, his shield and his horse's reins, in his left hand, and the golden cup in his right.*
> —Chrétien de Troyes, *Perceval, or The Story of the Grail*[18]

FIRST KEY:
YOU ARE THE KEY

1. You are the Key! You hold the key to your spiritual essence —Soul.
2. You have individual creative potential and co-create your own world; thus, you are responsible for everything in it, including overcoming fear. But more than that, your personal world and the people in it are the result of your inner intentions.
3. By knowing yourself through inner and outer Soul messages, you will discover your purpose for being on the planet at this moment in time. You will discover what it is you must fulfill in order to go forward.
4. Have faith in who you are. When you realize how much infinite spiritual power you have, that you can literally co-create your life, take charge of your reality, do anything, go anywhere in the world, be anything you want, the universe opens up for you.
5. Break free to live free, listen to your inner guidance, be flexible, and learn conscious dream travel.[19]

(1:1 to 1:5)

THE FIRST KEY REVEALS that you have the keys to manifest your life. It is a universal key and its spiritual power is for all beings, as are all the Keys. To change your life and your world, you shift your energy and attitude. Older locks have a set of tumblers opened by a special cut on a key. When the correct key is used, the lock's tumblers shift and click into place and open the lock. In much the same way, the 12 Golden Keys unlock a gateway to manifest and change your life, guiding you to take your place within the new world state of consciousness. The Inka and Peruvian Q'ero call our transition "the age of meeting ourselves again," a time when "the veil will dissolve" between worlds, as the New Zealand Maori predict. The Keys give you personal survival tools to help you prepare for life on a new Earth, and they unlock secrets to living a more spiritual life. By practicing the exercises included in each Key, you can discover an inner connection to your true self, Soul, and Source (God), the originator of life. This chapter explains how to practice the ancient science of visionary sight by knowing Soul, the life breath. When you communicate with your personal oracle, Soul, you begin to live from a place of spiritual power. You can ask Soul anything!

Discover the Secrets of Soul

One day the Creator gathered all of Creation and said, "I want to hide something from the humans until they are ready for it. It is the realization that they create their own reality."

The eagle said, "Give it to me, I will take it to the moon."

The Creator said, "No. They will go there and find it."

The salmon said, "I will bury it on the bottom of the ocean."

"No. They will go there too."

The buffalo said, "I will bury it on the Great Plains."

The Creator said, "They will cut into the skin of the Earth and find it even there."

Grandmother Mole, who lives in the breast of Mother Earth, and who has no physical eyes but sees with spiritual eyes, said, "Put it inside of them."

And the Creator said, "It is done."

This wonderful Sioux Indian story helped me to understand that my true identity is Soul, and I am not my body. I was also taught that I don't *have* a Soul, I *am* Soul. Like an eternal inner-galactic Being of Light, you are a true child of the universe(s) and are able to co-create your life.

We are now ready to re-discover that we are an extension of the creative and intelligent life force, capable of using it to create our lives. However, we need to change our reference point from our head to our heart, or from our ego to our divinity. This is the world shift that is taking place today. In other words, are you walking with Ego, or are you walking with God, your heart wide open? As our new world emerges, be aware every moment which side of the road you walk upon. And to help you change your reference point, you'll come upon new terminology in this book. Like ripples in a pond, nothing is static, everything is moving, everything is vibration, and the old needs to move aside for a brand new perspective, viewing everything through the eyes of Soul.

Our guidance comes directly from our inner resources. Once we learn how to tap into our higher vibrating Soul consciousness naturally and easily, we no longer need outside tools. Why? Because we have our own spiritual toolbox. As we practice using the Keys, we vibrate stronger energetically, and we become capable of finding solutions that are in alignment. We receive clear messages that give us personal ways to solve any problem. The exercises herein help you learn how to access your inner resources—how to ask Soul.

> *Prophecy can come through in the dream state, or it can come through what I call the Golden-tongued Wisdom—where something in your daily life suddenly pops forth. It's as if golden light surrounds it and gives you whatever you need just at that moment.*
> —Harold Klemp, *The Language of Soul*[20]

Listen for Soul Messages

How do we listen for Soul messages? To practice the First Key, you open yourself to inner and outer Soul messages. The two major aspects in this chapter are *outer* messages that act as wake up calls and *inner* Soul messages. Both are invaluable spiritual tools to take charge and co-create your life.

Eileen Caddy (1917-2006), author and co-founder of the Find-horn Foundation, a spiritual community, education center, and ecovillage in Scotland, opens her heart and listens to a little voice inside for "teachings of grace." She said, "One day, I went into a room, what one calls a sanctuary, to pray in silence. I was right in the middle of my serious monologue when suddenly I clearly heard a voice speak to me and to say: 'Be still and know that I am God.'"[21]

Many of you already have this ability to listen to "teachings of grace" or inner messages from your higher self—Soul. Here's a story to illustrate what I mean.

Destination Hawaii

Out of the blue I thought of a friend I hadn't seen in months. As soon as I had the inner nudge, I immediately called him and he answered. He was amazed I got him at home because he was always on the road selling fitness equipment and rarely in town. Realizing the synchronicity, we met for coffee.

On my way to the coffee shop, a high-pitched electrical hum buzzed in my inner ear, and I knew I was to pay attention to something. I saw a billboard sign. On the billboard a word jumped out at me, the word "destination." Within the next block another word jumped out at me, this time from an ad on the side of a taxicab: "Hawaii."

I wondered, "Am I *destined* to go to *Hawaii* soon?"

At the coffee shop my friend and his little daughter arrived. She had a paper finger game to play. I think it's called the Fortune Teller game; you make it out of paper and slip it on your fingers, then choose a number and quickly move your fingers to the respective spot. Before she lifted the little blue flap of paper to tell me what was underneath, I knew the word would be "Hawaii" and told her so. She quickly looked under the flap, and the word was indeed "Hawaii." She was flabbergasted, as was her dad. Hawaii was his favorite destination in the entire world, and he talked about wanting to move there many times. Presently, his entire life was in transition; he had no idea what to do. This was a reminder, letting him know that something awaited him in Hawaii—perhaps he would discover a pathway to go forward in his life.

So why wasn't the "destination Hawaii" message meant for me, instead of my friend? It was. There was a double whammy in that Soul message, and a year later I ended up going to Hawaii on holiday. What happened there helped me to piece together my own life puzzle.

"Destination Hawaii" was an authentic experience in the art of spiritual sight. It is also an example of using one's intuition to receive a spiritual illumination. Intuition is an inner knowing about something that is beyond rational mind knowledge; it is a hunch or gut feeling. In the story above, the message was received through listening to an intuitive **spiritual wake-up call**—an inner message given while you are fully awake and conscious, yet able to listen to and be guided by Soul, one's higher self. Soul knows and perceives all things and has a direct linkup to Source. These subtle, synchronistic[22] Soul messages happen all the time; and yet, because we're not focused on them, either we don't recognize them, or we discount them. Receiving and recognizing intuitive Soul messages is not just for a few gifted people. It is everyone's birthright.

Soul—The Breath of Life

When you recognize and practice a Golden Key, it changes millions of cells in your physical body, because the Key activates your mind-body-spirit like a genetic or biological tattoo, a secret life code. By practicing the Key exercises we connect to Living Energy, the universal life force. The connection is through **Soul Energy**, our life force, which resides in each and every being, including plants, animals, and water. Soul may reside in your body temporarily, but it is always connected to Living Energy, and you as Soul maintain your distinctness while standing alongside God. Soul is the process that is used to experience life in this physical realm. Soul is the breath of life. When Soul leaves, the breath is gone, and the body deteriorates. The analogy works something like this:

If God, Living Energy, were the flames of a campfire, then the sparks from the fire would be Divine Source; and when a spark flies through the air and lands on a piece of brush and the brush bursts into flame, this process is Soul's experience. All are a part of the original fire.

When you consciously put your attention on this divine Living Energy, you exchange spiritual information. The information is already encoded inside you. However, as with most things here, in order to consciously know them you must recognize and accept the Key's ancient wisdom. As the First Key says, knowing the Keys will help you know yourself, and by knowing self you will discover your reason for being on the planet (1:3). By living your purpose in the present moment, you naturally balance your life, regardless of the world situation. There is a natural cleansing taking place and you cannot stop it. Instead, find your balance within it.

> *Humankind is being led along an evolving course,*
> *Through this migration of intelligences*
> *And though we seem to be sleeping,*
> *There is an inner wakefulness*
> *That directs the dream,*
> *And that will eventually startle us back*
> *To the truth of who we are.*
>
> —Rumi[23]

Message from the Elders

 Here is another example of receiving an outer Soul message. A while ago I was a passenger on a crowded bus and experienced a spiritual wake-up call. There was only one seat left, next to a Canadian Aboriginal. He said he was traveling to Campbell River on Vancouver Island where he'd lived for twenty-five years. He also told me he was of the Kwakiutl tribe.

I said, "Isn't that interesting, because I just left an international conference where I met five Kwakiutl dancers." Both of us were amazed. I mean, how often do you meet Kwakiutl dancers! We both laughed.

This synchronistic event from Spirit helped to break the ice. He realized our meeting was special, and that he was meant to impart something for the benefit of my spiritual growth, and I to him: a sort of karmic sharing.

He started to explain that he had just left a meeting of the Elders of his tribe. At the meeting they told everyone that within the next few years more and more people will be seeking Spirit, and that they (the Natives) must be ready.

I looked at him and said, "I am also on a spiritual path and our Elders are telling us the same, that we must be ready."

He looked at me, amazed, and said, "Then we will work together."

I nodded "Yes" without knowing how or why.

That was twelve years ago. Twelve is known as a magical number because, for most of us, a new cycle begins every twelve years. Today I am indeed assisting in the world's preparation for spiritual change and also listening and writing about knowledge from the world's Elders. From this conversation I received a personal Soul message by way of a conscious spiritual wakeup call. By that I mean a message from Soul given in the light of day when you are fully awake and conscious. From this Soul message I realized that we are indeed heading toward a Spiritual (R)evolution—a revolutionary evolution of the way we see ourselves and our connection with the universe.

> *I believe that to meet the challenge of our times, human beings will have to develop a greater sense of universal responsibility. Each of us must learn to work not just for his or her self, family or nation, but for the benefit of all mankind. Universal responsibility is the real key to human survival.*
>
> —His Holiness the Dalai Lama[24]

Conscious Dream Travel—Break Free to Live Free!

The First Key (1:3) says: "By knowing yourself through inner and outer Soul messages, you will discover your purpose for being on the planet at this moment in time." The two conscious dreams above are examples of receiving outer messages. Here is an explanation about how to receive inner messages and **break free to live free.**

By using an ancient technique, Soul may transcend the human body and "travel" into the different worlds beyond the physical veil. Conscious dream travel, both inner and outer, expands our present perspective to encompass the worlds of what some might call heaven—the worlds of Soul. In one form or another, for centuries, dream travel has been used in aboriginal cultures around the world. It is a universal technique for living consciously.

Through conscious dream travel it is possible for you to see the bigger picture of life and sidestep what others might fall headlong into (Fifth Key). It will assist you to leap across the void, so to speak, if you stay in the present moment and pay attention to your subtle inner nudges or Soul messages. I have always called this ability to journey within by following one's inner guidance, inner dream travel—although, while doing it, one is conscious of what is happening. Others call it being sensitive to energy, clairvoyant, telepathic, precognitive, a remote viewer; having extra-sensory perception (ESP), out-of-body experiences, using your sixth sense, or your ability to soul travel;[25] or also, spirit walking, astral projection, or lucid dreaming. No matter what it's called, it is breaking away from conditioned responses and tapping into the divine matrix of Living Energy.

To keep it simple: Follow those inner nudges!

By listening to the inner breath of Soul and focusing on the First Key, taking responsibility for everything in your world, you will discover your passion and life purpose and know what it is you must fulfill in order to go forward. However, the world outside of you is full of conditioned responses, an illusion; the true world is inside you. Therefore, to heal the world, you heal yourself. You hold the key.

Use the First Key and the technique of conscious dream travel to open the door to the messages of Soul and break free from limitations. When you realize how much infinite power you have as an individual, and that you can do anything, go anywhere in the world, be anything you want, endless poss-ibility is available to you (1:4). First, you need to break free from all types of conditioning, because what you pay attention to is what you become conscious of. To break free to live free, listen to your inner guidance, be flexible, and learn conscious dream travel (1:5). It is the process of receiving guidance for finding solutions to life's problems.

Your Energy Fingerprint

Everyone receives Soul messages every day, whether we call them chance meetings, synchronistic events, conscious dreams, or spiritual wake-up calls. The keys to spiritual living are about living life as a sacred journey, where we recognize and are devoted to our divine purpose. In simpler words, your life has meaning.[26]

Author Darlene Montgomery wrote, "There is a story which tells how in a particular African tribe, before each child's birth, the mother climbs to a place on the side of a mountain and waits. She listens for a song, a song which is for her child, and is of his or her life force. This song is to be sung by the tribe at the child's birth and at important points throughout his life and at his or her funeral. I once heard a speaker talk about God's fingerprint, how each of us from our conception as Soul has a unique energy fingerprint which is unique to us and is unlike no other."[27]

This energy fingerprint is connected to our God particle, or the secret life codes within each of us. The responsibility to discover our own energy fingerprint is perhaps our spiritual purpose in this lifetime. Just as the Kwakiutl man helped me to find my new path as a messenger and co-worker with Spirit, so too, can you use the Keys to unlock your true path.

How to Dream Travel

How do we dream travel to unlock the secret path to conscious freedom and the power of Soul? The way to consciously practice inner dream travel is the art of spiritual sight and illumination; it is a way of dream walking, "walking" out of your physical plane body to enter a different state of consciousness. The Australian Aboriginals call it "entering the dreamtime."

At the end of this chapter there is an exercise for you to use. Until then, the easiest way to practice soul travel is to shut your eyes and listen to your breathing. By doing this you are instantly in the present moment, where no distractions enter your safe zone. Life has accelerated, the world is spinning faster, and everyone is a little hamster on the wheel. Stop! Sloooow down. Take a deep breath. Simply breathe. Listen to your breathing. Close your eyes and listen. Take a few moments throughout your day and feel the breath of Soul—your heartbeat. When you go inside, leaving the outside world behind, do you hear a gentle sound in your inner ear? Focus on it and let it take you out of yourself. Continue listening to your breath for a few minutes and connect with the breath of Soul.

This is a good exercise to develop your focus. Keep focusing on your breathing, and see tiny sparks of light on your inner screen. Soon, with practice, one of those lights will unlock and turn into a portal. While focusing, some people even get the tingling sensation of this portal opening in the middle of their forehead, like a camera lens. Now come back refreshed. Open your eyes. This is a simple exercise to re-balance and spiritualize your energies.

Why Learn Dream Travel?

The benefit to experiencing dream travel on a regular basis is to assist you in handling change and chaos in your life in order to find contentment. These are two things in this life that you cannot escape. Inner dream travel will teach you how to handle every problem or dilemma. It is the process of receiving guidance for finding solutions to life's problems. It's your inner guidance that connects you directly to Source and assists you in your life.

To use this technique you need to ask yourself: "What do I need to realize that would move me closer to my goals, and along the way, closer to my spiritual purpose?"

Every one of us has a way to discover our own inner guidance. It doesn't matter what religious denomination you are; we can all seek our own guidance. We can all tap into divine wisdom. If you are someone who does not believe in a higher power, then what made you pick up this book? Coincidence? Synchronicity? Or, your alignment with inner guidance, which comes directly from Soul, the real you?

By learning conscious dream travel you can take charge of your life by handling change and chaos, and major turning points in your life. Let's say your boss comes in and tells you he's sorry but he's going to lay you off, starting tomorrow, and he won't change his mind. When you catch your breath you'll realize you have two responses: (1) You react like a victim and blame; (2) You accept what has happened as a positive step, knowing what's waiting for you around the corner could be even better. And then use conscious dream travel to see your new direction.

After all, why else has this happened to you? So why not power up and think up? Thought is a many-mirrored prism with hundreds of sides or facets. You want to choose the most beneficial one. Why not take the responsibility to think positively and view the experience from the highest facet and send it love. Be your own best benefactor. You are the Key.

Your personal world and the people in it are the result of your inner intentions. By sending the person or circumstance love, it also bounces back to you. When talking about divine love, there is only one meaning to the words "I love you" and divine love does not hurt. "I love you" is an international phrase that, when said, cuts through negative energy like a sword through butter. Saying those words silently to another changes the energy between you.

Why ask: "Why did this have to happen to me?"

Ask instead: "Why did I create this experience and what am I supposed to be doing instead?"

There is a subtle difference between these two reactions. Can you see it? In the second one you realize that there is a divine purpose behind whatever has happened. There is something else you're supposed to be doing. Your life is a series of connecting links, and if you're living in a state of conscious awareness, nothing happens that you don't already intuitively know about. Below are two examples of accepting turning points.

Focus on What's Best, Go to What's Next

Life has lessons galore to help us grow into wise spiritual beings, to prepare us for our next phase and, like Christopher Columbus, our safe passage into a new world age. As a personal example, when I was a music-band publicist, using my skills as a grassroots marketer, I was given an opportunity to reframe my life. When the band members decided they wanted to do their own publicity, I chose to turn it into a positive opportunity.

Conscious dream travel helped me to see the wonderful opportunity that my departure from working with the band presented. I began to realize how I had been forgetting about my own dreams. Self-care suddenly became important. Looking at the big picture, my inner self, Soul, moved me into a position where I could concentrate on my writing. By doing an inner dream travel exercise and asking "Why did I create this experience and where is it leading me?" I was told to focus on the next step. I was given an opportunity to learn about the positive force associated with practicing self-responsibility. I learned to focus on what's best and go to what's next!

Jason Turns His Life Around

 There are millions of stories about life-changing turning points because people took responsibility for their own life, and they happen every day. I was recently privileged to hear a story from an acquaintance of mine, an important example of positive willpower and love.

Jason's father was injured in World War II in the North Atlantic. The Navy ship was attacked and blew up, and he was airborne, falling hard on to the sinking hull. His pancreas was damaged beyond repair and eventually removed by surgeons. Every November 11th his father would take great care to shine his medals and clean his Navy uniform in order to join in the Remembrance Day parade. It became an important marker in his father's life. But his life became a slow downhill health battle, complicated by alcoholism and diabetes.

For years Jason endured his father's deteriorating health and occasional violent drunkenness. Finally, a few years before his death, he joined Alcoholics Anonymous (AA) and quit drinking. The day he quit was on a November 11th down at the local Legion. None of his drinking buddies, also war veterans, believed him when he vowed to never take another sip again. But he kept his word. AA had helped Jason's dad quit for good, although physically it was too late to turn around his degenerating body. The young son, only seventeen, watched his father die horribly, gasping for breath in an oxygen tent. From then on, every November 11th, he held a special remembrance of his father, not only as a war veteran, but because that was the date his father took responsibility for his life and quit drinking.

Unfortunately, when he lost his father, Jason developed his own relationship with alcohol and even with drugs such as heroin. Jason said that the two primary reasons he did drugs were to have fun and to have sex; but heroin didn't do it for him. He discovered it acted as an anesthesia, blocking his sensations, so he quit that drug immediately. Alcohol was another matter; he had fun on alcohol, and even though he was a handsome lad, he still needed several drinks to be brave enough to approach girls. After his dad died he started to drink habitually and it lasted throughout his twenties and into his thirties, almost ruining him—until he reached a turning point.

At age thirty-three, he met someone who had recently kicked his habit by joining Alcoholics Anonymous (AA). Jason didn't like where his life was headed—he was turning into his father, the bad parts. Jason remembered how AA had helped his father overcome a lifelong destructive cycle and decided to join. That was thirty sober years and one stumbling block ago. He'll never forget the date of his turning point decision to go to his first AA meeting—November 11th—the day that had meant so much to his father.

Eventually, Jason became a successful real estate agent, taking responsibility for his life choices and turning his life around. By integrating his fears and limitations into his life and dealing with them, he was able to raise his consciousness and move forward.

A Dream Travel Journal

You are about to enter a very active and conscious dream life. It might help to keep a journal of your spiritual insights, writing down your waking Soul messages and your inner adventures. It can be a notebook, a special journal, or a digital document, as long as it's exclusively for your spiritual experiences. It's easy to forget spiritual insights, so it's important to write them down. If you wish to recall them months or even years later, then you'll have a record to verify the experience.

Also, write down anything out of the ordinary, such as a sign I received on my way to the meeting with the music group. I still hoped we could stay together as a unit, but pulling out of my driveway to go to the meeting, I saw a huge sign in the middle of the road. It read, "ROAD BLOCKED." I got the message and moved on. This was a practical guide.

Usually the signs are not as obvious as this one. Or are they? Anything is possible when you pay attention! Why not find out for yourself? You can ask Spirit to show you clear signs along the way by using everyday practical things in a way that you understand. I certainly understood the symbol of the road sign. Know that Source or Living Energy is already there. Living Energy is the matrix in which we live; it is everywhere.

Legend of the Spiritual Illuminati

The First Key unlocks a spiritual power that can be used by all beings. So why are we not taught about this infinite spiritual power in school or elsewhere? What if I told you that the secret way into becoming luminous beings, or new humans, is the true Illuminati of legend? We are the people of the light, the Illuminated Ones. Our amazing abilities have been suppressed, perverted, forgotten, and hidden from us for eons. But now, we are finally waking up.

The word "illuminati" is derived from the Greek, to illuminate, and refers to the Luminous Energy Field (LEF), the energy from Source, composed of Living Energy. For thousands of years, ancient mystics and healers have believed that our physical bodies are surrounded by a luminous egg or sphere of energy. This energy is shown in old religious paintings as an angelic halo and is sometimes called the aura or auric field that protects us. Angels in Renaissance paintings are actually images of Living Energy in Soul form. According to Tibetan and Hindu masters, the entry and exit points in this protective energetic field are known as chakras.

Light is the first manifestation of Spirit. Our Soul Energy also manifests in our realm as light. Light is information. Raised on the television series *Star Trek*, many of us are familiar with the healing light tools used by Dr. McCoy, the chief medical officer on the Starship *Enterprise*. Perhaps the knowledge of how to use this LEF, our protective angelic aura, is the secret of everlasting life. So flip the switch ON and light the secret codes within.

FIRST KEY STORIES

Here are two stories that illustrate the First Key. They offer a unique insight into ways people just like you realized they are the key that opens doors in their own life. In "Meet the Contributors" at the end of the book there is biographical and contact information for each story contributor.

Author Michael Harrington follows his inner guidance even while playing baseball, being responsible for key moves in the game of life and learning an important life lesson.

The Play
By Michael Harrington

It wasn't just my most memorable moment of the College World Series; it was the most memorable event in an entire baseball career. I've replayed it countless times in my mind, trying to understand why it has held me spellbound for over thirty-five years.

I've often wondered if my teammate, Ron, felt the same transformational impact of the play as I did. Only a simple glance of mutual respect passed between us afterwards: "Good job."

Ron was the catcher at Linfield. I was a timid freshman on a team of veterans well on their way to the 1971 NAIA title. In fact, only a single obstacle stood in the way—a Tennessee team threatening to end our quest with a late-inning rally. A leadoff double in the eighth had left them in an enviable position in a 7-7 game. In all likelihood they would score. But fate intervened with the play.

It was the boldest, yet most dangerous call anyone could make. I doubt that Coach Rutschman, with his years of experience, would have called for it. But Ron was our leader, our All-American. To my disbelief, I heard his calm voice over the dull background chatter calling for it NOW—the pickoff play from the catcher to the rookie shortstop.

Had Ron seen complacency in the runner's eyes? Had he forgotten that in sixty games we had only attempted the play a handful of times, and never with success? Had he forgotten that I'd made two errors earlier in the game? Didn't he know that disasters usually happen in threes?

An errant throw could sail past second base into the outfield, scoring the runner. There was also a chance of hitting the runner as he slid back in. The odds of picking him off, even with his aggressive lead, were, in my estimation, 100-to-1.

My heart raced as I flashed Ron the agreed-upon sign of confirmation. The pitcher, Vince, glanced back anxiously, not at the runner dancing off second, but at me. He was asking, "Do you know that the national championship is riding on the outcome of this play?" Unfortunately I did.

A pitch-out was called. Nervously, I held my breath as Vince finished his delivery. In a single, graceful motion Ron caught and released the ball. I found myself on "soul time," watching an insignificant white blur approach at nearly seventy miles per hour, insignificant to everyone but those in this stadium.

Ron's throw was perfect. The look of horror in the runner's eyes said it all. The tag caught him nearly a foot off the base. We held them scoreless that inning and went on to win the game 9-8 in ten innings.

It was the play that shifted the momentum that sultry night in Phoenix and earned us the championship. Ron and I knew it; Vince knew it, too. Somehow the play instilled in me an unqualified feeling of success that even winning the title could not eclipse.

At every turning point in my life, the play revisits me. "Buck the odds," it says. "Go for it." For thirty-five years it has inspired me in secret. Why the urgent need now to write it down? What turning point is this on the road of life?

As I lie awake listening to the wind testing the new maple leaves outside my window, I hear a faint, yet familiar voice from deep inside my being. "Call it," it urges gently, yet insistently. "You can do it. Call the play."

‼‼★‼‼

Author and Atlantis Rising *magazine journalist Jeane Manning's story illustrates the First Key. When you realize how much divine power you have, that you can co-create your life with responsibility, you will have activated the First Key's secret code.*

Finding My Unique Way to Serve Life
By Jeane Manning

This experience was about trust, and finding my unique way to serve life.

My turning point came in 1987. Previously I had met an inventor, Bill Muller, who introduced me to a new energy-research field which has potential to clean up our world, make oil wars and power grids obsolete, and enable regional economies of energy abundance. Mainstream media labeled the field "free energy" and ridiculed it as "impossible perpetual motion."

"But I don't claim to have perpetual motion machines," the inventor protested. "I just have a super-efficient magnetic motor/generator."

However, he named his company Pran Technologies. "*Prana*" describes a universal background energy, a life force. Concepts such as *prana* and *chi* were dismissed by western scientists, but the inventor could see no other source for whatever continually replenishes the field around a permanent magnet. Later, others would turn to quantum physics and its "zero-point quantum fluctuations of the vacuum of space" to explain what energizes their unusual energy converters.

All that was a far stretch from my university degree, Sociology. But I'm a journalist with insatiable curiosity and driven to use this lifetime productively. When I learned about the international underground of "free energy" researchers, I decided to write a general book for the public about this fascinating subculture with all its drama.

The problem was that I lacked a strong belief in the importance of my possible contributions. This fact surfaced when I saw my scientist friends preparing to attend a conference in Hanover, Germany. The Pran Tech inventor, Bill Muller, was invited to speak, along with other inventors and scientists whom an author should interview if she was to write a book about quantum-leap new energy systems. The meeting would gather leading lights of the field internationally; I wasn't even a minor techie. Being unemployed at the time, I also lacked travel funds.

The Muller family made their travel plans and enthused about the scientists they would be meeting. The conference would attract an audience of nearly a thousand, mostly engineers.

One night my perspective did a complete turnaround. Suddenly I heard an insistent message in my head in authoritative tones, "The only thing stopping you from going to Hanover is your belief that you don't belong there!"

I paid attention, since I had begun to study a spiritual path and was learning to listen for inner guidance. My thinking shifted. If that's the case, then how might I get there?

Everything fell into place easily. My eldest son lent me the airfare. When I returned after the conference it became obvious how I could quickly repay him; I opened the *Vancouver Sun* and saw a classified ad for a community newspaper editor in a town where I had connections.

I got the job, wrote the book, served on the board of the New Energy Movement (NEM) and co-founded NEM Canada. Those grassroots organizations, when allied with other world-changing initiatives of the people, could help bring about a more conscious civilization on Earth. Listen to those inner nudges from Spirit!

⤳⤳✦⤳⤳

FIRST KEY EXERCISE

How to Master the Keys

 Each of the 12 Golden Keys has one primary exercise at the end of every chapter. It is best to commit to a specific time each day, for example, just before falling asleep, or before getting out of bed in the morning. I have found first thing in the morning works for me, mostly because I'm still in the dream state and relaxed, but the choice is yours. In fact, when I was a bus driver I used to do a contemplation (one type of **spiritual exercise**) in the car in between my split shifts. Practice this focused exercise for fifteen minutes a day—it is the basis for all the exercises we will be using. The next exercise, at the end of the Second Key chapter, expands and builds on this basic one.

Everything in this book is meant as lightly scattered seeds along a trail and is offered as guidance toward new perspectives, but it's up to you to trust in where the path leads you. Follow your own heart. No one can tell you "This is truth!" because it's *their* truth, but not *the* truth, or *your* truth. Be your own witness and experience the 12 Keys for yourself. First learn to stand apart so you can see your own truth, and then come together in community to share.

Be Present in the Moment

Using the breath of Soul to be in the present moment, we are able to access inner wisdom.

1. Find a quiet place and turn off all distractions (music, radio, TV, computer, etc.). I once lived in a noisy neighborhood and used earplugs—they work too. Get comfortable by sitting or lying down.

2. Take a few deep breaths while thinking about something that instantly opens your heart, whether it's a loved one, a child, a pet, or something that makes you smile, bringing love into your heart; or read an inspiring passage from a book. If your heart is closed or you're angry, spend a little more time on this step.

3. Now think about who or what is looking out from behind your eyes. Who are you, in there, in the present moment? Put your attention and focus on your breath. Soul is the witness to your life. Breathe. Even when you think you are alone, the breath of Soul is there. Soul is watching you read this, waiting for your attention. You are about to listen to the voice of immortal Soul. Breathe.

4. Now close your eyes, and ever so lightly place all your attention on your breathing. Focus on your breath. Let go of the outside world.

5. Sometimes there will be flashes of light on your inner screen, or a tiny pinpoint of light. Watch the lightshow and lose the sensation of your physical body. Listen to your breathing. You are Soul, a being of divine love; and it is possible to see your true beingness on your inner screen.

6. When you are ready, open your eyes and come back. Write in your journal any discoveries you experienced.

SECOND KEY:
FOLLOW THE BLUE LIGHT

1. Follow the Blue Light! Travel to the inner worlds of Truth. Close your eyes and gently focus on your breathing and the inner spiritual worlds.

2. Why wait until you die to know the Otherworlds? What we call death is simply walking through a gateway; it is a shift into higher consciousness. The Ancients[28] used the trilithon gateway in megalithic temples to pass through to the Otherworlds. The Egyptians used the Third Eye. We will use an inner pinpoint of light, known as the Blue Light or Blue Star, as our gateway or portal.

3. The Blue Star is a portal to Soul, or that which is the true self. You are Soul, an eternal Being of Light. Soul has free will. Soul is your protector, prophet, and beloved. Communicate with your personal oracle, Soul, and begin to live from a place of spiritual power, consciously aware of Soul's visionary messages.

4. Soul and Soul Energy consist of light and sound energy from Source or Divine Spirit. Light is sound; sound is light. Both lead you to God. This divine light lights your pathway; the sound calls you home.

5. Ride the Blue Star and reclaim contentment to live life as Spirit intended. Be fearless of fear. The way to conquer fear is with love.

(2:1 to 2:5)

THE SECOND KEY SAYS TO FOLLOW THE BLUE LIGHT and go into the inner spiritual worlds. The adventure begins by following a pinpoint of bright light. In this chapter you will learn about the Blue Star, the sounds of Soul, inner dream travel, and be introduced to the Otherworlds.

The symbol of the Second Key is a triangle of self-knowledge. The three sides of the triangle represent three major steps to conscious freedom:

Three Steps to Conscious Freedom:

1. Take responsibility for your life.
2. Love yourself & others unconditionally.
3. Be fearless of fear.

All three are connected. If you rid yourself of nothing else, rid yourself of fear. The way to conquer fear is with love, and through love of self you will discover you are worthy. But first you must take responsibility for your life, the First Key.

The Light and Sound of Soul

What is the **Blue Light** or **Blue Star**? Some believe the pinpoint of blue starlight seen with our inner eye comes from our aura, affecting us internally and externally. In world mythology and religion, the color blue symbolizes spiritual clarity. Others believe that the Blue Star is connected to the core of the Earth's magnetic field. There are also influences on the magnetic field in our bodies from the solar flares, gamma-ray bursts, and charged particles in the solar wind between the Sun and Earth. This phenomenon is known as "magnetic reconnection."

The Blue Star is the most prevalent image of inner guidance, and is actually a white pinpoint of light surrounded by blue. Inner spiritual travelers also experience the brilliant white light surrounded by yellow, pink, purple, and other colors, depending upon where they are in the inner worlds. Each time you see this inner light or hear its vibratory frequency, practice the Second Key and follow where it leads.

I sometimes see a pinpoint of bluish light while going about my daily chores. It flashes in front of me at the most appropriate times. Instantly I know I'm supposed to pay attention because I'm about to receive a Soul message—or a warning!

Many times throughout the day we miss opportunities when Soul is trying to reach us, for example, trying to tap us on the shoulder to introduce us to people who will give us a helpful life tip, whether these people are aware of it or not. Every time I witness the flash of light and do not stop and take notice, I miss an opportunity to communicate with Soul.

On the Buses—Example of How to Use the Blue Star

 One day I was sitting in a coffee shop reading the newspaper, scouring the employment classifieds, searching for a job. Having recently quit university due to one of life's traumatic turning points I needed to find a job quickly, either that or not eat! My paintings weren't selling and, although I could always move back home with my parents, I knew the time had come to make my own way in the world.

As I got to one advertisement a tiny light flashed about three times before my eyes, or in my eyes, I couldn't tell. This little light had happened at other times in my life, but not as bright.

I asked the man sitting at the table beside me, "Did you see that flash of blue light?"

He looked at me strangely and replied, "You've been staring at that newspaper too long. Or else you need to see an eye specialist."

"It's a six-pointed blue star. I think it's trying to tell me something."

The man looked at me like I was nuts, quickly collected his things and left.

Then the tiny blue light flashed again on the same classified ad. The ad was from the city's public transit company, wanting to hire bus drivers. I wondered, "Me, a bus driver? But I don't know the first thing about it."

I kept reading the large ad and discovered they would train

me and pay for my Class 2 Driver's License with air brakes. With this training course I could also be a long-distance truck driver, which usually costs $10,000. I already had my Class 2 from living up north and driving a dump truck around an isolated gold mine. But it didn't seem to count because, driving in the middle of a forest, about the only thing I could have hit was a bear.

I decided to go to the interview; little did I know it would change my life!

That morning something woke me up earlier than usual and I was out the door by 5:30 a.m. I knew I was supposed to go NOW, no questions asked. So there I was at 6:00 a.m. freezing in the cold and standing in front of the bus depot for an interview that was three hours away. There were ten burly men in the line-up in front of me. And here I was, a 5-foot 2-inch woman.

They laughed at me and said, "Forget it! You'll never get the job. They'd have to put blocks on the pedals."

But I stayed, and I waited, and more men arrived to stand in line. By 9:00 a.m. the line went around the corner and around the block and back again – about 1,000 people showed up. I was the first woman in the line-up. I looked down the long line and saw a few other women, but that's all. It's strange but never once did I question myself and think I shouldn't be there.

I was interviewed, wrote a test, and, passing that, I was asked to return for a second interview. For this second meeting I wore a skirt and heels.

At the meeting, my interviewer was the head boss. He wanted to interview me himself because, as he said later: "A woman had not been hired by the bus company for fifteen years."

He showed a short video on how to drive a bus, including how long the bus was, and how to turn a corner using the laws of physics.

Afterwards he asked, "Do you think you can do that?"

"Of course," I said, "Absolutely." But I wasn't sure at all.

Then he said, "Follow me." And he took me out into the bus yard and said, "Get onboard. You're driving."

My mouth dropped open. I sat in the bus seat and I froze. My high heels kept slipping off the pedals. The steering wheel was huge. There were buttons and gadgets all over the dash. I felt like a rookie pilot in *Battlestar Galactica*.

Then I saw it. A little blue light flashed in front of my eyes. It calmed me and I knew everything would be all right. I put the diesel bus in gear and gingerly pulled out. Eventually I made it around the block without hitting a parked car. But the interview was not over yet. The VIP interviewer took me into the bus yard to a trolley bus and told me to watch him. At the back of the trolley bus he pulled on two cables and they snapped and got stuck.

Then he turned to me, "Get them unstuck. I want to see if you're strong enough."

I couldn't imagine doing that, I mean, I could barely pull them. Then the little blue light flashed again, but it flashed on a bus billboard sign that read, "Nike. Just Do It!" Another sign to let me know I could do it.

I remembered the instructional video and pulled with all my might, releasing the cables. They snapped into place and I passed the interview. I did it, thanks to the blue light giving me the confidence I needed. From that day onward, I loved my job as a bus driver.

It wouldn't be until a year later that I discovered what that blue light was and how I could use it in my life. I realized it had always been with me, but I never paid attention.

Art of Inner Dream Travel

Here are a few techniques on using the inner light (Blue Star), an inner sound, and a special word to sing quietly to yourself to help you focus.

The art of inner dream travel is doing a spiritual exercise which connects you with Source, the universal life force, and develops the power of advanced spiritual sight. First, find an energetically restful place for yourself, a sacred space just for you, or with a group of like-minded people.

Your Third Eye is located between your eyebrows in the middle of your forehead and behind your eyes in the area of the pineal gland. Peek at it gently with your eyes closed, looking for a pinpoint of bright light. It is sometimes seen as the Blue Star and is an inner portal, a gateway that opens into the Otherworlds. You will learn how to access this portal. In Buddhism and Hinduism the Third Eye is a symbol of enlightenment; in Indian tradition it is the eye of knowledge, the teacher inside; in ancient Egypt, the Eye of Horus or All-Seeing Eye. In the Bible, it is the lamp or the light: "The lamp of the body is the eye. If therefore your eye is good, your whole body will be full of light." [Matthew 6:22][29] They are all referring to the ancient science of visionary sight.

Create an image for yourself. Imagine that Soul "travels" through the portal of the Third Eye, much like characters in J. K. Rowling's *Harry Potter and the Goblet of Fire* touch a boot-shaped port key to travel to different locations. Also, in the television series *Star Trek* they say, "Beam me up, Scotty" when standing in the transporter, a device that converts objects and people to energy and sends that energy to another destination. In similar ways, when you access your Third Eye portal, you (Soul) travel to another destination or state of consciousness.

If that worries you, please consider this: Soul has protection because you are an individual spark from Source, God, the Great Goddess, the Great Spirit, the Jedi's Force, or whatever words fit your world view. Source creates everything and that includes the negative as well as the positive. Although you do indeed manifest your world, Soul has the protection and guidance of Source known as Living Energy, which is always to your benefit. Also, there is a sound to help you, which is explained in the next section.

But first a word about Isis. This wonderful wisdom of the Third Eye has come down to us from ancient Egyptian times. We owe the goddess Isis our respect and gratitude for sharing her sacred secrets, gathered by her scribes from many ancient lands, perhaps even Atlantis and Lemuria. The ancient seers were proficient dream travelers whose advice was sought after by the military and politicians of the time. The book of Hermetic philosophy, *The Kybalion*, tells us that many nations have borrowed her secret doctrines—nations such as India, Persia, Chaldea, Medea, China, Japan, Assyria, ancient Greece, and Rome. All of these and more have borrowed that which the Hierophants and Masters of the Land of Isis so freely provided.[30]

The 12 Golden Keys have no affiliation with any religious path, group, or spiritual teaching or philosophy; and yet, they are all of them all at once. Everything comes from everything. The 12 Keys are meant for your personal illumination and investigation.

What Is the Inner Sound?

We talked about the inner light of Soul, but there is a second element. The Second Key includes the "sound" of Soul. Soul consists of light and sound energy from Source (2:4). Tuning into a sound frequency is an excellent way to help you travel out-of-body into a different consciousness.

In physical terms, the sound ignites the pineal gland, located between your ears and behind your eyes. This important gland is affiliated with the secret life codes within the physical body. Perhaps the grid of EMFs (electromagnetic frequencies), now so prevalent in our world, is affecting the pineal gland, because more and more people are hearing this inner sound from Source energy. Some people experience what is called simply, "the hum," a particular vibration that seems to be an outer sound. Whereas, I have a certain ringing in my ears, which usually sounds like an electrical hum and yet it is not tinnititis. The sound has always drawn me into a dream travel experience.

I also recall another sound from my childhood in a recurring dream. A bee would buzz around my head constantly, and I remembered that in my sleep I tried to swat it away. Except the bee was inside my head on the inner planes. I didn't realize at the time that the buzzing sound was an echo from an inner world. There are many other sounds from the inner spheres, such as the wind or ocean waves, or the owl's hooting. All sounds have an underlying message, which depends on the energy you are mastering and on which dimensional plane you reside at the time. All are the voice of Soul.

The ancient Greek Pythagoras, in the sixth-century BCE, used the term "music of the spheres" to describe the many sounds in our cosmos, which we also pick up in our inner ear. The ancient Vedic scriptures of over 3,000 years ago talk about the "vibration of ether" which comes from the celestial realm.[31] Modern day Indian music known as Raga Sangeet is based on this sound current. In contemporary times, Sant Kirpal Singh (1894–1974) described *Sant Mat* as a synonym for the yoga of the Sound Current, or more simply *Shabd Yoga*, a meditation technique originally practiced in northern India, that also uses the term *Light and Sound Current* to describe the connecting link between human beings and God.[32] Shabd (Sanskrit for "The Word") or Inner Sound Current can be heard by the inner ear.

According to psychologist and Mayan priestess Dr. Eugenia Casarin, "We have been moving in the same pitch or tone for quite a long time, but now we will transfer onto a much higher pitch. For this transformation, however, for this change in time and age, all of humanity needs to have attained an equal level of consciousness. This means that we need to enter into an expanded level of consciousness. If you wish to be in harmony with heaven and earth, you need to be in harmony with all there is—and with all the others. We need to accept that everyone is unique, without judging them. Each individual is the way they are. Let us respect that!"[33]

Choose a special word to sing, one that can relax you, so that you can, as Rumi, the thirteenth-century Sufi mystic and poet, said, "Catch hold of the music that lasts through eternity."[34] To help them stay focused on awakening the voice of Soul, millions of people in today's world focus on and sing the ancient and non-denominational words OM and **HU**. Both universal words have the ability to vibrate cells in your body. For our purposes, let's talk about HU (pronounced like the word "hue" or the name "Hugh"). HU is a sacred name for divine love and has been called the most sacred of all sounds. It has also been described as the beginning and end of all sounds. Hazrat Inayat Khan, a Sufi, writes: "The word Hu is the spirit of all sounds and of all words, and is hidden within them all, as the spirit in the body. It does not belong to any language, but no language can help belonging to it. This alone is the true name of God, a name that no people and no religion can claim as their own."[35]

Jehovah, from the Hebrew *Yahuva* contains the "hu." As does the English word *human*: *hu* means "God" and *man* means "mind." In Arabic, the word, *huma* is divided into: *hu*, "Spirit" and *ma*, "water." These ancient translations remind us that we are God-conscious beings.

The Egyptian and Greek traditions of 5000 years ago used the word HU to refer to God; and the Kabbalah states that HU is the originating sound of the universe. HU is also found in Eckankar, a popular New Age religion of the Light and Sound of God and is used as a form of prayer.

I remember hearing the chanting of twenty Tibetan monks in a local cathedral in Vancouver, BC. It was the monks' first visit to North America. When they were ready, they started to chant in a low, guttural sound that seemed to emanate from the deep recesses of the earth. As they continued, they created the most beautiful sound, and above this beautiful sound at the top of the harmonic pyramid was the overtone of a pristine, high-pitched HUUUUuuuuu.

When you communicate with your personal oracle, Soul, by using the inner sound, you begin to live from a place of spiritual power, consciously aware of what Soul is telling you right NOW. When you access this Soul power, you begin to live from that place, as given in the Second Key (2:3).

Sing a Favorite Word

When you do the exercises in this book you can sing the word HU or use any special word of your choice, such as LOVE, PEACE, OM (AUM), or another mantra, or a Gregorian chant. When I met author and peace troubadour James Twyman, he said he used the word "AH," singing it like "Ahhh," because it's in Halleluiahhh, Yahhhweh, Mahantahhh, Allahhh and other important crossover words. While you sing your word or sound, use your creative imagination to open yourself up to the exercises and resonate with the energy field. This is the infinite creative power within each of us. Once rediscovered, it is a powerful tool toward health, joy, success, abundance, gratitude, and love. It is the creative power at work.

First, you need to get past the busy little monkeys of the mind that will try to distract you. The key is to *feel* yourself rising out of yourself into a dream travel state, dreamwalking into a high state of consciousness. Rise up, dreamwalker! Try the exercise at the end of the chapter.

What Are the Otherworlds?

The Second Golden Key (2:2) speaks briefly about the Otherworlds. By lightly focusing on the Blue Star, we sometimes follow it into different or parallel planes of existence. The pinpoint of light is a gateway or portal into these different dimensions that, for ease of reference, I call the Otherworlds. The light in these worlds shines very brightly because it is purer than our Earth's light. Ride the Blue Star and experience it for yourself!

There are many other ways to experience the Otherworlds. Sufis twirl into a deep trance. Others describe near-death experiences (NDE), where the person usually reaches another plane of existence by traveling through a tunnel of light or over a bridge, visiting different realms. Sometimes the Otherworlds are called "a land where spirits dwell." There are also out-of-body experiences and astral traveling, during which people travel down the street or to another galaxy. All these have been well-documented.

All the information in this book is already inside you. You have probably read or watched science fiction films where the characters travel through Worm Holes or Black Holes to go to parallel dimensions. Mostly these turn out to be horror films that try to scare you out of trying it for yourself; it's not true. The Worm Hole I'm talking about resides in your inner consciousness and never leaves you; it is also the most divine and loving place you will ever visit.

What if all those quantum-leap, science fiction stories about visiting Otherworlds in the time it takes to blink an eye are true? The scientists of quantum physics agree that this is so. In the 1950s, US physicist Hugh Everett III proposed a Many-Worlds Theory as his doctoral thesis. His teacher was John Archibald Wheeler, a renowned American physicist and professor at

Princeton. Everett drew the simple conclusion that one outcome is as real as the next and that the universe splits every time a new physical possibility occurs. For example, a skateboarder shoots onto the dangerous curved ramp and has a near miss, but he lands safely. In a parallel universe, the skateboarder crashes, breaks his neck and dies. Yet in a third universe the boy recovers in the hospital. The scenarios are endless.

Quantum Physicists believe it's similar to taking a loaf of bread and cutting it into several slices, each slice represents a galaxy. Our galaxy is the Milky Way. Each slice is a parallel universe and you can visit the slice next to you as easily as reaching out your arm and entering. To date, parallel worlds have not been proven by a scientific experiment, but don't let that stop you. You have the ability to experiment for yourself. Although scientifically unproven, many of us have experienced alternate realities and dimensions other than our ordinary 3-D world here on Earth. Having personally experienced parallel dimensions, i.e., multiverses, I get a sense that one day everyone will be traveling to them as easily as opening a gate onto a different field.

There are many ways of consciously dream traveling, such as out-of-body experiences, near-death experiences, day-dreaming, out-of-consciousness traveling, and unnamed ways yet to be explained. Many people say they have never actually experienced the Otherworlds or inner worlds, and yet, they do every night—every time they go to sleep. Dreams are a form of walking through the veil into extraordinary realms. Even in bizarre dreams there are hidden messages, secret codes, and usually the appearance of a pinpoint of light is seen, if only we were aware enough to follow it. Following the inner light is also following our dream guides, which you will discover in the Third Golden Key.

❧❧★❧❧

SECOND KEY STORIES

Here are two stories that illustrate the Second Key; both involve the light and sound of Living Energy. Living Energy can appear as a vision, as sound with an audible frequency, as an inner voice, or even as a spirit animal. Soul Energy is in all things and can even speak to you directly, but we need to be ever watchful, as this story from Kay Johnston points out.

The Call
By Kay Johnston

I wended my way around the outer trail at Myrtle Park on automatic pilot as my mind drifted its way around my own inner pathways. Suddenly something flew up at my face from the undergrowth missing me by a couple of inches. Stunned, I stopped in my tracks. The park was absolutely quiet. I could feel eyes piercing my back.

Slowly I turned and scanned the tree branches. There were the eyes. Sitting on a very low branch was an owl. I approached slowly until I was only about twelve inches away. It did not move but continued to stare into my eyes for what felt like hours. Finally I turned away, wondering what this was all about, and continued my walk. I looked back frequently to check, and sure enough it was still there, watching.

I had put the incident out of my mind until the following night when it rushed into the forefront of my mind again. I was reading in bed when the hoot of an owl broke the silence. I got out of bed and went into the backyard and listened to the hooting as it floated out over the watery inlet. He was sitting right above me on a branch, close enough for me to see his large yellow eyes gazing down at me as he continued to "talk."

My skin went into goose bump mode. Two owls in two days had to mean something, but what?

A few days later I had lunch with my friend, Gloria Nahanee, an elder of the Squamish Nation Indian Band. Gloria was taught the old cultural ways and beliefs by her Elders; she continues the oral tradition as a cultural teacher by passing on those teachings to her Nation's youth. I respect her wisdom and knew she would be able to tell me what the presence of the owls meant. She became very still and explained to me that this was not a good omen. In ancient Indian folklore, if you hear the owl call your name it means your death. In this instance, Gloria felt something was coming and it would not be good news, but she did not know what. Well that did not put my mind at rest; in fact my imagination kicked into overtime trying to come up with some logical explanation.

Several days passed without another owl intervention; I began to relax. Foolish me! Two weeks later, I was meeting with clients in my office, as usual, when the phone rang. I ignored it as I have a policy of not answering the phone when I have clients because I feel it is disrespectful. However, a couple of minutes later, our receptionist appeared, saying to take the telephone call—it was an emergency.

I picked up the phone and heard: "Kay, we have the call." It was the voice of my friend Lorraine. I knew immediately what she meant. I must have gone white, as my clients quietly signaled me and left. I nodded and stayed on the phone.

"The call" was to tell us that Maddie, my partner of many years, but no longer my partner, was in danger of dying. Maddie had told us years ago that, if Lorraine and I were ever called at the same time, we had to go to her immediately. The time had come.

Neither Lorraine nor I had been able to get through to the ranch for awhile. We kept getting the answering machine and thought Maddie was being her usual self and taking a break from people. She had been deteriorating and refused to accept care; she was sometimes independent to the extreme.

Surprisingly, the calls to Lorraine and me came from a care worker who explained that Maddie had given her permission to call the two of us and that we would know to come to her. Relieved to hear that she had someone there to look after her, we made plans to drive to her, leaving early the next morning.

After a six hour drive, we arrived at the Lazy Dog Ranch in Enderby, BC, to find only the two dogs and the cats in the house. We drove back down the dirt road to a neighbor's house and asked where she was. He told us the ambulance had taken her into the hospital about half an hour before we rolled into the yard. We jumped back into the car and drove to the hospital to find Maddie unconscious. The doctor told us it was only a matter of time as her organs were shutting down. We spent endless hours talking to her and holding her in the hope she knew we were there. We drove to Vernon, which is about forty minutes from Enderby, to pick up bags of blood for a transfusion, knowing it would not save her, but in the hope that it would allow her a final rally.

At 6:00 p.m. on November 11th she rallied. She woke up to see several of her friends, who had all arrived at the same time, standing around her bed. She sat up and started to chat brightly. She was smiling and laughing, and then she saw the two of us.

Her face lit up and she said, "You are here."

Shortly afterward, she asked me to send everyone else home because it was noisy and she was tired. Dutifully they hugged and said their goodbyes. Lorraine and I stayed with her as she laid back and closed her eyes for awhile. We could hear her rough breathing as we sadly waited. After about five minutes she sat bolt upright, eyes wide open with a smile on her face. I had never seen her eyes so blue. She sighed, layed down, closed her eyes, and died.

We brought her ashes back to her ranch to be spread under the apple tree. I had to do something very important before we spread her ashes. Maddie was very present in spirit as I took her ashes for a final walk around our beloved ranch. She hadn't been able to travel the trails for a long time. We walked every one of our favorite trails on the 160 acres. We talked and remembered the picnics in the snow, Sitka, the Samoyed, joyfully leaping onto Maddie's skis as she came down from the upper meadow, causing them both to tumble with howls of laughter and lots of yipping. We laughed at the cattle, pig and horse stories, the deals we tried to make with the bears about not eating all the cherries, and the coyote about leaving the chickens alone.

We laughed and we cried.

The light was beginning to fade and we headed out of the last trail toward the upper meadow. As I stepped over a log my boot caught in a root and I stumbled, almost dropping Maddie's ashes. Unnerved, I had stopped to gather myself back together when the silence dropped like a blanket. No birds sang; no trees moved; everything was still.

I knew. And I raised my head to find the owl sitting on a high branch. He hooted soulfully as he looked at me, then silently flew away. The birds resumed singing; the air seemed brighter and lighter.

Maddie had gone. She was free.

❧❧✴❧❧

It is said that composers on Earth write music that is a reflection of the greater music of the spheres or that which is created by the motions of the planets. Musician and composer Debra Howell believes that the authentic universal vibration is 432-Hertz (concert pitch), and not the international standardized version of pitch that has been set at 440Hz; meaning all pianos, violins, and musical instruments are calibrated at 440Hz or 440 cycles per second. Instead, Howell tunes her instrument to A=432Hz.

Debra Howell explains how she discovered the 8Hz difference in tuning instruments and how it changed her life.

Tuning into Spirit
By Debra Howell

In 2007, I felt purpose was missing in my life and music. I prayed to Divine Spirit to show me what I was missing and how I could utilize my gifts for the good of all. After being guided to surrender my will to the will of the divine, I became a vessel for Divine Spirit to work through me. Since then I have been blessed with much divine knowledge about our human energy system—the chakras, the universal authentic vibrations, divine music, energy transformation, and my purpose or dharma at this time in my life.

After I performed a ritual, cleansed myself, and proclaimed that I'm a vessel for Divine Spirit to work through me for the good of all, I put my guitar in my hand and received the lyrics, melody, and music for a song called "Love." The following day

I did the same, inviting Spirit to work with me, and I wrote another song. I felt there was something unique about this music and asked Divine Spirit to guide me to the knowledge I needed to know. And that's when my light went on, so to speak. I was guided to understand how the standard tuning of musical instruments was standardized in 1955 to 440hz, and the vibration of this tuning strayed from the more natural universal, earthly vibration of 432hz. I knew it was important to integrate this realization into my music and life.

I repeatedly invited Spirit to work with me daily until I finished a series of songs that wove together into a themed, live, musical performance called "The Key." I began to understand that I was being introduced to a new paradigm with this project, involving the chakras, and that I was writing songs that related to this energy. To help me through the creative process Divine Spirit showed me a chakra tuning system that I do daily to keep my vibrations in alignment with Spirit and the universe. I have since recorded this chakra tuning system and created a guide book for the benefit of others.

According to modern physicists, all reality can be described as vibrations emitting frequencies, meaning that every thought and action give off vibrational frequencies and affect the whole. There are positive frequencies that heal and help the whole to function optimally, and there are negative frequencies that are limiting and promote underfunctioning. The multitudes of human-made negative or manipulative frequencies, which are constantly vibrating, leave a confusion of our truth and disconnection from our authentic nature.

The chakra tuning system and the music I've been shown bring the world true authentic intentions and vibrations to help awaken the global heart, break down the manipulative frequencies, and assist the human race to awaken to its authentic nature.

I believe each one of us has an important role in helping to bring our world to the next level of evolution into the Golden Age (Divine consciousness). You might say we are on a rescue mission to become aware of who we are in relation to this Earth to help make our world a better place. As one person becomes whole, humanity on a collective level is that much closer to wholeness. I pray that before we know it the chakras will be a household topic and we'll all be walking a new Earth finely tuned. I am honored to be a part of assisting in this divine global transformation.

˙SECOND KEY EXERCISE

Ride the Blue Star

Here is a spiritual exercise to contemplate on: learning to follow the pinpoint of light. It builds on the exercise in the First Key. Do this exercise anytime, but it works best if you commit to a specific time each day. Discover what works best for you.

1. Find a quiet place and turn off all distractions (radio, TV, computer, etc.).
2. Get comfortable by sitting or lying down.
3. Take a few deep breaths while thinking about something that instantly opens your heart, whether a loved one, a child, a pet; or while reading an inspiring passage.
4. Close your eyes and sing the word that sounds like "hue," or your chosen word, in a long drawn-out breath, repeating it and rolling it off your tongue in succession.
5. Ever-so-lightly place all your attention on your Third Eye, located between your eyebrows and behind your eyes. Sometimes there will be flashes of colored light on your inner screen, or a tiny pinpoint of light called the Blue Star.
6. Follow the pinpoint of light through time and space by lightly focusing on it. Consider it a portal into another world or parallel plane.
7. Listen for an inner sound. You may feel as if it is calling you to enter Soul's doorway into the Otherworlds. Follow where it leads. Focus for ten to fifteen minutes. If it takes you somewhere, go with it, and sense the movement of your

consciousness as it expands.

8. Once you have entered the Otherworlds, say out loud: "I wish to establish my special place in the Otherworlds." Then start to visualize what your special place looks like. Where is it? Is it a hut in a mountain grove? Is it on a cloud plane, or on the Moon, or in the star worlds? Is it on the other side of Mars or in another galaxy? Is it located in a parallel plane? Your choice is unlimited. But always remember to follow the Blue Star where it leads you.

9. You can continue or you can fall asleep. Upon waking, end the exercise with three or more HUs in a long drawn out breath; and then write your experiences in your journal.

Try this focused exercise for fifteen minutes per day. Keep practicing it, and see where Soul leads. You will amaze yourself!

Next is the Third Golden Key, where
you will learn about the ancient Key Guardians.

THIRD KEY:
YOU ARE A KEY GUARDIAN

1. You are a Key Guardian and a Karma Warrior!
2. You have Key Guardians or ancient spiritual travelers who are your own special dream travel guides, even on parallel dimensions. They are always with you.
3. As a Karma Warrior you are capable of viewing your past and future lives. You play out a different karmic role each lifetime, and you choose the karmic role into which you are born and your secret life codes. You, as Soul, play different characters throughout the ages.
4. There is no point of arrival; you (Soul) are always arriving in the present.
5. When you meet someone, s/he may not be a stranger at all, but from one of your many past lives. More importantly, that Soul is here to profoundly change your life, depending on how open you are to receive the offering. It is a karmic exchange intended for your spiritual expansion.
6. Remain open to receive your purpose and role as a Key Guardian and to be a co-worker alongside the spiritual travelers guiding you.

(3:1 to 3:6)

*Y*OU HAVE A KEY GUARDIAN TO ASSIST YOU, and you are also in training to become a **Key Guardian**. The Third Key represents guardianship and the protective golden shield. Responsibility, protection, and care for others are all part of guardianship. Eventually you will be your own Key Guardian, and with that comes great responsibility. Until then, accept the guardianship of the many spiritual guides, masters, or angels—all are non-physical Beings of Light who pass between our 3-D world and the Otherworlds, into parallel dimensions. These extraordinary beings know what lies beyond the invisible gateway. These special emissaries are masters at going to and fro.

In this chapter you will learn the three aspects of the Third Golden Key: You have a Key Guardian to assist you; you are a **Karma Warrior**; and, you are in training to become a Key Guardian.

Key Guardians

Key Guardians are inner guides or spiritual travelers who protect you no matter where you are. They are always with you, and you need only call upon them. (3:2)

When traveling to distant lands, a travel guide, roadmap or guidebook definitely improves the quality of the journey. A Key Guardian is like a personal travel agent. S/he acts as your inner guide who protects you on Earth and on parallel planes in other states of consciousness and, also, when you exchange energetic information by accessing the Living Energy. We live in an ocean of motion. Everyone exchanges energy, Soul-to-Soul, and your Key Guardian is there to act as a shield. One of the major differences between us and a spiritual guide is their vast ability to receive God's love.

When you enter the Otherworlds, your secret entrance portal is also guarded by a Key Guardian. Nothing can penetrate your LEF unless you allow it. Often, due to our inexperience, we make allowances that may prove dangerous, so your Key Guardian is ever-watchful. When traveling in the Otherworlds with a spiritual guardian, you wear the golden shield of protection.

Later we will do an exercise to find your special Key Guardian. Key Guardians are the divine life current, or Living Energy, and appear to us in many forms. They can be warriors or knights of old, dressed in golden armor, ready to wield a protective sword in your defense. Or they can resemble an elderly Indian woman, wrapped in a blanket, whose power is hidden until you call on her. Or, if your imagination wills it, they can be like Yoda the Jedi Master from *Star Wars*. Or, they can be disguised as a beggar on the street corner. Many people experience inner guides in the form of Jesus and the Virgin Mary, the Christ Consciousness being part of the Living Energy.

> *"I recognize this place. I've been here in one of the dream visions. A plane of light and brilliant colors," she said to herself.... She was standing on the shore of an ocean of light. The sound of a tone filled the vision. The sound was the scene. One note sounded like a thousand buzzing bees, a long note held steady and singing on the ocean of sound and light. Then she heard the sound like the word 'hue', H-U-U-U-U. She finally understood the inner sound. Standing up in the boat and pushing the long pole was a figure, or a Being. Her vision clouded when she tried to see who the figure was. The brightness of the Being's light body blinded her. The overwhelming feeling was that the Being was a guide, or an Angel, or a Master of Light—someone who had mastered the technique of doing what she was doing, of what she called dream travel, and who now wanted to teach her.*
>
> —*Utides*, Chapter 25, p. 153

Meeting Key Guardians

The first time I was conscious of meeting a spiritual Key Guardian in the physical, that is to say the first time I recognized the experience for what it was, I was driving a city bus. I pulled up to a bus stop to pick up passengers, one of whom was a maroon-robed gentleman with a black goatee beard. I didn't think anything of it because he wasn't out of place in the East Indian shopping neighborhood. But he wouldn't board my bus.

Instead, he stood there silently staring up at me. I grew impatient, closed the bus door, and drove off. The second day, and then a third day, he was there again, and the same thing happened.

Finally, after getting my full attention—I was a thick Soul back then—he said to me telepathically, "Isn't it about time?"

His voice entered my beingness, and somewhere deep inside myself I knew what he meant. Isn't it about time I stepped onto a spiritual wisdom path to learn about the secret truths?

A week later, I was led to a spiritual bookstore. As I walked through the door, there before me on the wall was a drawing of the exact same man at my bus stop. I was dumbstruck! I came to learn that this particular spiritual traveler is over 500-years old, from Tibet, and lives on the Earth plane and the inner planes.

One night as I was walking along the sidewalk, a homeless man approached me. He was most unusual because he sparkled with light. The unusual beggar asked me for some change. When I looked into his eyes, I noticed they were lit with a magical light. This was no ordinary street person. It was a test to see if I was paying attention, once again.

Be ever watchful for guardians. You never know where or when they will show themselves, and when they do, it's usually either a test for you, or a quest to follow them on a journey of understanding. They will approach you when you're ready—either in the outer physical world, like the stranger on the sidewalk, or in your inner dream life. It's up to you to choose a Key Guardian to be your main guide and mentor. You can refuse, of course, but do you want to stay where you are forever, or do you want to jump on board the bus and go on a magical mystery tour? The ride could be the most exciting one of your life. Why not hop on and see where you go?

Once you find your inner guide, you will meet him or her in your dreams, or even in your waking life. When you do meet this special mentor, ask him or her to become your guardian, or ask a direct question to a problem you're having. You will know they're right for you if their answers empower you with positive self-responsibility. They are spiritual travelers of the highest order, and you will soon realize there is a golden thread of love and protection just beyond your reach. Find out how to access it by practicing the Third Key.

Be ever watchful for the one who will approach you more than the others. Pay attention to them. S/he will be your special Key Guardian and mentor. So get ready to meet a Key Guardian using the exercise at the end of this chapter. They can take on any form, even a black dog, as I discovered.

The Spirit Guide

I was one of those children who had an imaginary friend. I would sit and talk with my invisible friend for hours. This being was neither he nor she—this person did not have a gender—but for linguistic reference let's use the pronoun "he."

This ethereal being would visit when no one was around. I don't recall ever visually seeing anyone, but we talked, and I felt a presence.

When I started school, I was taught not to talk with him. Every time I did, the teacher would scold me. So during my school years I forgot about my friend.

At age twelve, shortly after we moved into a new home, I discovered a secret hiding place in the attic over the garage. There I could be at peace with myself and play for hours. In the silent stillness where all things become a part of you, I liked being alone. But I wasn't alone. Someone was with me. Soon afterward I lost conscious contact with this presence. And also, like most children, I lost the ability to play in the Otherworlds.

About four years later, I momentarily renewed the contact. At the age of sixteen, I had a passionate interest in art and took oil painting lessons from Mrs. Keen, a wonderful older woman who had traveled the world. She taught me to look at the world and interpret it with a sable brush.

One night while walking home from her painting class, I became frightened. The night was darker than usual, and a negative disturbance hung in the air. I suddenly felt afraid and alone. I remember talking to the night, out loud, asking for protection. That's when I remembered my imaginary friend. It was the first time I ever called for him.

I started to talk with my invisible friend again, and he

appeared in the most non-threatening way. He took the form of a friendly Labrador, a big black dog. He came out of nowhere and walked beside me. I knew it was my spiritual friend because the dog had the same presence. Anyone else would see just a dog, but when you are able to quietly sense a Soul's presence, you feel their authenticity of spirit. The Lab's shiny coat glistened as we walked together a mile and a half, all the way home, never leaving my side. We talked together the whole way, and I read the dog's mind, and he read mine.

When we reached the driveway of my home, I stopped to thank him. I said goodnight and started to walk up the driveway. When I quickly turned back again, the dog had vanished.

My invisible friend had taken on another form to see me safely home. Since that time I have never been afraid of walking alone at night. No matter where I've been in the world, I've always known I have protection. We all have the protection of our spiritual guardians, but we need to remember to ask.

The Light People

In the late 1950s our family lived in the poor part of town. A sawdust burner heated our small post-wartime house. Each month the sawdust truck arrived in the neighborhood, and we kids ran outside after it. The truck went from house to house, and when it got to ours, my two little sisters and I stood in the basement in anticipation. Our concrete-floored basement was a large open space, except for two ten-by-ten-foot rooms. One of the rooms was for the sawdust. The other room was dark and empty.

I'd watch as the long metal arm of the sawdust truck extended through the open basement window like a huge elephant's trunk. Then the sawdust man would yell, "All clear? Stand back!" Then the orange sawdust chips would fly through the window.

Either Mom or Dad would be ready with a shovel to scoop up the sawdust and move it to one side. Sometimes I'd help. At nine years old, my job was to make sure my two little sisters, aged two and three, wouldn't suffocate under the spraying sawdust.

So while my parents shoveled, I helped by guarding my little sisters. It seemed to me as I grew up that I was always guarding them from something. This big sister syndrome taught me to grow up guarding the world; quite an impossible task.

I remember an experience I had in the vacant dark room opposite the sawdust bin. For whatever reason, my mother always avoided that room, never venturing inside. It was an eerie concrete room with an odd musty smell, had no windows and not even a light bulb on the ceiling. Even though I was fearful to peek inside, something always drew me to the doorway.

One afternoon I was downstairs playing with my youngest sister. She was a toddler and barely got around on her own. My mom was busy upstairs making dinner. The door to the sawdust room was open, letting in a shaft of sunlight. The light streamed through the misty dust that always filled the basement. I had been busy greasing my bike in the corner when I noticed my little sister had toddled off. I went in search and found her standing in front of the dark room. The door was wide open.

How odd, I thought. She's too small to reach the door handle to open it. The darkness inside didn't seem to frighten her. She had the curiosity of a two-year-old, but did not cross the threshold.

I stood at the doorway beside her. The room enveloped us with its darkness and seemed to draw us inside. I took hold of my sister's hand, and we stepped across the doorjamb to the other side. Suddenly the entire room flooded with light.

"There's no light bulb, what's going on?" my child's mind asked, hanging on tightly to my little sister's hand.

She wasn't scared. She giggled, quite delighted. So why was I so scared?

The next thing I remember was a light opening and swirling in front of us. In the light were three Beings of Light. They wore white sheaths of light. I thought they were doctors and nurses. I had wanted to be a nurse at the time, and the only people I knew who wore white were doctors and nurses. And yet, the figures were familiar to me. I instantly recalled an invisible friend, someone I used to talk with. Was one of these beings my invisible friend?

We spoke telepathically for awhile, feeling safe. Or did we speak out loud? Unfortunately I can't recall the conversation. My little sister was playful with them. I was somewhat guarded because I was on duty. Then I sensed it was time for my sister and me to leave. I grabbed my sister's hand and pulled her toward the doorway. The white figures were smiling and waving. They were very loving and stood in swirls of light. My sister and I stepped out of the light and onto the other side of the doorjamb. The door creaked shut behind us, and we watched the light underneath the door flash once, and then suddenly go out.

I quickly opened the door again but the room was in pitch blackness—no one was there.

I don't remember ever going into that room again. In a few years we moved from the house. I never discussed it with my sister until years later when we were both consciously on a spiritual path. She had been too young to remember the experience, but did recall a recurring dream. She described the dream by saying, "We were standing at the entrance to a lighted room, and I had ahold of your hand."

I never told anyone what we had seen, not even our mother. Then again, maybe Mom already knew about the Beings of Light in the basement?

> *Their wings were gold. And all their bodies shone*
> *more dazzling white than any earthly show.*
> —Dante Alighieri, *The Paradiso*[36]

Kelly's Guardian Angels

Kelly is a singer/songwriter and recording artist who had an interesting experience following one of her concerts. Kelly was packing up her instruments onstage and chatting with the other band members, when the soundman for the show came up to her. He said his son Jake wanted to speak with her, but was feeling a bit shy.

Kelly said, "Sure, where is he?" and the soundman gestured to a young man in his early twenties standing off to the side of the stage. Averting his eyes, he walked slowly up the steps. Kelly offered a handshake, thinking he was going to say something about one of the songs she sang, or ask about one of the instruments. She waited as Jake hesitated to speak and looked nervously over at his dad.

"Just tell her," his dad said.

So Jake began, "You might think this is weird, but sometimes I see things."

A bit taken aback, Kelly asked, "What do you mean?"

"While you were performing I saw two spirits standing just behind you, watching over your shoulders. They weren't doing anything, just kinda hovering. But I knew they were there for you, maybe to protect you or something."

Kelly said to the young man, "Thanks for telling me Jake. I believe you because I believe in *guardian angels*. Sometimes when I perform, I feel like I leave my body because I'm so nervous and can't always remember performing certain tunes in the concert or what happened. So before I start any performance I ask my angels to help keep me grounded and calm. And the interesting thing is that I wasn't that nervous tonight."

The young man nodded, understanding.

Kelly has also seen several spirit images over the years. She has been alone at home and been suddenly aware of the strong scent of perfume, or the smell of cigars, which may last for a minute or two. Her dog also senses them and will bark at what appears to be nothing at all. She often wonders why they appear to her and if they are trying to tell her something. She never feels threatened by them.

She has had dreams of a kindly gray-bearded man who resembles Leonardo Da Vinci and is very possibly an unidentified spiritual master. But there is also another figure in the same dreams and it is a female guardian.

Kelly said, "I don't know why I am seeing her, as it is yet to be revealed. I'm not in a time of need or crisis, so that is what makes this so intriguing. It seems that most of the stories I've read about visitations from spirit guides occur when someone is in quite a bad state either mentally, spiritually or physically, which I'm not."

Kelly continued, "The female guardian is a blonde woman in her late twenties or early thirties. She has a warm smile and—I think—brown eyes. She disguises herself to suit the different eras. In one dream she was wearing a powdered wig and clothes from Leonardo's time in the Italian Renaissance, and then in two other dreams she wore a modern hairstyle and clothes."

At the time Kelly related this story to me, I showed her a book with drawings of a few known spiritual masters. Kelly flipped through the book, coming upon a picture resembling the female guide in her dream. "Wow! It sure looks like her! It's definitely amazing. She is very similar, except I see her softer and smiling."

I suggested to Kelly that the next time this female spiritual traveler appears, she could ask to be taught how to let go and follow her.

A Dream Technique

The inner guides or Key Guardians are available to you. Look for them in times of adversity, when you need them the most. Or, call on them anytime to ask, "Teach me what I need to know for my spiritual development."

A tip is to do this just before you fall asleep: ask to be shown something in your dream world, or ask a question, so that when you wake up you will have an answer to whatever you need to know. And then slip off to sleep singing your favorite word or the HU. If you sleep with someone else, you can sing it to yourself silently on the inner. It is in those moments just before and after sleep that you are most open to receiving inner truth.

You Are a Karma Warrior

The second aspect of the Third Golden Key states that you are a Karma Warrior, a Soul who has experienced thousands of past lives, and who is learning to unravel karma with responsibility. A. L. Basham translates karma as "deed": "the effect of former deeds, performed either in this life or in a previous one, on one's present and future condition."[37]

Karma is the cycle of cause and effect. Cause and effect are neither good nor evil, they just are. Karma plays hand-in-hand with reincarnation. Many in the western world have long considered karma and reincarnation as an eastern world tradition only written about in ancient Indian and Asian texts. However, some believe they are written about in the secret writings of Christianity, kept hidden in the vaults of the Vatican. A few allusions remain, however, in the Bible, for example, "a person will reap only what he sows." [Galatians, 6-7] And the Golden Rule: "Do to others whatever you would have them do to you." [Matthew, 7-12][38]

The Jewish Kabbalah speaks openly about past lives, as do many other traditions. In fact, Buddha might say, "Karma means you don't get away with anything." Hinduism says, "One should never do that to another which one regards as injurious to one's own self. This, in brief, is the rule of righteousness."[39]

In today's world, the belief in fate or destiny from our past deeds is recognizable in such phrases as, "What goes around, comes around," and "What you put out there comes back to you eventually." By your actions today, you determine your tomorrow. In business, for example, why not earn your livelihood through service to others and not at the expense of others? It's actually easier and more profitable to do the right and honest thing, blending your higher aspirations with your entrepreneurship.

There is also the "knowing effect," where you agree with, or are conscious of, what is happening to you as a result of what you have caused to happen. Most of us know that if we do something against another being, we will pay for it sooner or later. Here is a paraphrase of a popular saying from Vedic Literature of ancient India: Our present destiny is shaped by our past actions and our present actions will determine our future destiny.

The Prophet Mohammed of Islam in *The Farewell Sermon* said it this way: "Hurt no one so that no one may hurt you. Remember that you will indeed meet your Lord, and that He will indeed reckon your deeds."[40]

The Coat of Many Lives

As a Karma Warrior you are capable of viewing your past and future lives. You choose a different karmic role each lifetime. It's similar to slipping on a new coat, the coat of many lives; except this coat is activated with a set of secret DNA codes to help you play out your intended karmic unraveling—your proposed destiny. Of course, destiny can be changed through co-creation and spiritual expansion. You, as Soul, play different characters throughout the ages so there is no point of arrival, because you are always arriving into a new lifetime, and a new adventure. During your umpteen lives, you've met millions of people. The cycle of cause and effect you've created with all these Souls will come back either to haunt or help you, depending on your deeds.[41]

Resolving karma between strangers is powerful. When you meet a stranger in this lifetime, you're probably re-meeting to unravel the past karma between you. You meet to profoundly change one another's life, and this change depends on how open you both are to receive the offering. There is a karmic exchange with spiritual lessons attached. Meeting an old soul-friend enables you to exchange energetic information.

For those who find it difficult to believe in the concept of past lives and reincarnation, that's all right. You don't have to believe it to do it. Just remember to do one kind act a day and then watch how your life changes. You will also realize that it is not what you do that determines your experience in this world, but your expectation.

Knights of St. John

How do we know our past lives? I've recalled many past lives, but this one might interest you. When I traveled to the island of Rhodes in Greece, my instincts told me I had lived here in ancient times. Walking the Street of the Knights in the medieval town, I was able to see the ancient sights, remember the coat-of-arms carved in stone over each doorway, and hear the echoing sounds of horse hooves on the cobblestones. I realized that sometime between the twelfth and sixteenth centuries I had been both a Knights Hospitaller of Rhodes in the Order of the Knights of St. John, and a Knights Templar. I wasn't the only one.

My friend Rae, who was traveling with me, also felt something similar. She said, "I've been here before in another time. I remember a long room with arched columns and to the right of the entrance is a huge stone fireplace as tall as a man. This used to be a hospital and there is a room inside where the fatally injured and sick people were kept. I was a knight, wounded in battle. It's where I died."

Walking inside we saw a long stone hall, tall arched columns, and a huge fireplace the height of a man. I asked Rae how she managed to describe the inside of the Hospital of the Knights before we entered the building.

"I just knew it. My inner voice told me that I'd been here before."

Later on, the knights became known as the Knights of Malta. Among other places, they also established themselves in Rome. During my stay in Rome in 2008, I was led to a famous keyhole in the Villa Malta on the Aventine Hill that houses the Sovereign Military Order of Malta. The secrecy surrounding this enclave is legendary. The Vatican has actually declared the location of the Villa Malta the tiniest country in the world.

Standing outside the tall wooden gate with my friend Dominica, I recognized the coat-of-arms as identical to the one I saw on the island of Rhodes. It was the Cross of Malta, the original emblem of the Knights Templar. There was a definite past-life connection. It is interesting that I should be there with someone whose name means "belonging to God," as did the soldier-monks of the Knights Templar.

The Villa Malta is surrounded by a high stone fence and guarded by two machine-gun carrying guards. The only way you can look inside is through a round keyhole. Looking inside you see a hedged pathway that leads to a view of Saint Peter's Basilica in Vatican City over one and a half miles away. It's startling, because it's a trick of the eye. The hazy reflection makes the dome look closer than it actually is. There's no way the dome should look that large. Are the eyes being deceived? Or the mind?

The cover of *12 Keys for a New World* was created from a photo of this round keyhole. But through the keyhole on the cover, instead of seeing St. Peter's Basilica, one sees the Blue Star which represents divine love, conscious freedom, and the journey of Soul.

It's interesting to note that when viewed from the air the Vatican courtyard is shaped like this gigantic keyhole. And if you were to draw a line around the outside of Saint Peter's Basilica, it is shaped like an antique key, and this key looks as if it is entering the keyhole (courtyard). Therefore, the key is in the keyhole. The symbology of this suggests that the Vatican holds key secrets that, when unlocked, would probably tell us the real history of the last 2,000 years.

Discovering this mysterious keyhole in a locked gate was enough to bring back memories of my life as a Knights Templar. I have since delved deeper into this lifetime—through the "keyhole of Soul."

There is Good Karma

There is what's known as good karma. You might have helped someone in another lifetime, and in present day they repay you for your kindness. That bothersome driver might be trying to slow you down so you don't get in an accident up the road. The neighbor who rakes up your fallen leaves when he doesn't have to, or the teacher who stays after school to help you with your studies, or the barista boy who gives you a free dollop of whipped cream, or the man walking along the street who sees a house on fire and runs in to save a family—these many acts of kindness by unsung heroes are reciprocal, too, paying it forward as you go through life. Have you ever wondered why a hero says they never feel like a hero? Giving of one's self is a humbling experience and a natural payback of karma.

The stories throughout this book are not the kind to make newspaper headlines; rather, they are stories from the heart. You don't have to do a fantastic feat to be an everyday hero and win at life. In helping others, all that is needed is to do it with love. That is the most fantastic kind. To practice good karma, pause and view the world from a perspective of positive wonder, and then live your life by practicing kindness.

Long ago we humans communicated with one another not from the ego mind, but directly from the heart. The heart is where Soul lives. Divine love is unconditional love in action for the good of the whole; it is not emotional love. It is the matrix that holds the atoms together—it is energy. Once upon a time, we accepted and understood our heart-to-heart connection. We could create and heal anything because we were open to a direct connection with the life force and, from that viewpoint, there can only be good karma. In the emerging new world we will need to remember this. As Mayan priestess Dr. Eugenia Casarin said, "Be still and hear again the quiet voice from the heart."[42]

Golden Handshake

 Here is an exercise to release karma between you and another Soul.

- In contemplation, sing a special word five times (a word like HU or LOVE), then go on the inner. Envision a meeting between yourself, the person you're struggling with, and a Key Guardian or inner guide. Notice how each of you is dressed in light bodies; it's your physical body except it is full of the luminous Soul Energy. Soul consists of energy composed of light and sound.
- Conduct the gathering like a meeting and introduce yourself to the Key Guardian and to the person or persons involved.
- Tell the person that you honor the divine love in them, no matter what happened between you or what the situation. You don't have to like the person(s), but you do need to release the karmic attachment through accepting that the divine love in you is also within them.
- Feel what it would be like to accept and receive that they are divine love. Ask for them to also let go of the negative

thoughts they have for you, freeing both of you.
- Send them divine love throughout the process, knowing you're both doing the best you know how to do in the present state of consciousness.
- Ask them to join you in a mutual golden handshake. See it happening through your spiritual eye: take each other's hand in a handshake surrounded by a golden light, each of you saying: "May the blessings be."
- Back in the physical world, each time you see the person or think of them, send them divine love like you did on the inner. Gently keep it in your heart.

It may be hard for you to understand that this simple gesture of a golden handshake can undo an event that took place, say, in the Middle Ages and change a possibly destructive event that could have happened in present time. But it *is* possible. Only you and this other Soul would know. You hold the key to your karmic past, present, and future. As the karma unravels, your life changes because you change, and so does your destiny. This is what's known as "deserved destiny," that of which you have become worthy.

You Can Train to Become a Key Guardian

At the beginning of the chapter we talked about guardianship. This is the third aspect of the Third Golden Key. With learning comes mentoring; eventually you become a Key Guardian to others, or a co-worker, sharing knowledge and doing service. It doesn't necessarily mean you are your brother's keeper, because everyone must learn self-responsibility (First Key, 1:2). The old saying is, "God helps those who help themselves."

Key Guardians are co-workers alongside Spirit, exchanging energy and the 12 Keys with others. In learning to become a Key Guardian we are taught to do kind deeds to serve one another, and in so doing we serve life, giving back to Source. Serving life can be as simple as one good deed a day, listening to a friend's problems, and the giving of one's time to others who are weary travelers on the road of life. By listening and understanding, having no judgments and no attachment, we help one another to grow spiritually.

Guardian of Your Habitat

A Key Guardian is also a guardian of the planet. For us, Earth is a place of passionate possibilities, but in our quest for the ultimate power we appear to be destroying our home. As stewards of our home planet and our community, many of us are waking up to the fact that we need sustainability to usher in the new shift in consciousness. Learning how to tread lightly upon *Gaia* (Mother Earth) has not been our way, and now we're paying for it dearly. Our karmic payback has come due. We are living in a time of rapid eco-change with dramatic earth changes, the collapse of the planetary ecosystems, as well as the collapse of the political and financial systems. What we do affects everyone. We need to lighten our footprint. But we waste time arguing about what has caused us to be in our present dilemma. No one person or group is right when it comes to global climate change and the other events. In other words, we must discover our own truth by going *on the inner*—to seek Soul guidance.

Our damage to the planet is infinitesimal in comparison to the effect our surrounding universe is having on Earth and all the planets in our solar system. Mother Earth has always taken care of herself and knows exactly what she needs to do, and is doing it. We're sensing her changes with our symbiotic connection. Whatever you're being told are the causes—global warming, global cooling, solar flares, an approaching asteroid, a coming polar shift, CO_2, volcanic eruptions—it is still our choice whether to change or continue on the present course.

Another solution is for you and me to be guardians of our habitat and a model for each other of how to live responsibly. The key is to help one another learn self-responsibility (First Key: You Are the Key), taking responsibility for everything in our surroundings. It all begins with us. By being a co-worker, we are helping others help others to awaken our global heart. A wonderful image to visualize is a big red heart and inside the heart is planet Earth. Then say the words: "Hold the world in our hearts, for a global awakening of the heart." Shifting to an awakened heart is what the global earth changes are all about.

Hero with a Heart

Sixty-two-year-old Sandi from Edmonton, Canada, has single-handedly saved over one thousand lives. How? By being a blood donor. After more than 700 visits to the local Canadian Blood Services, she is the second-place female donor in all of Canada.

Sandi began as a casual donor in the 1960s at the University of Alberta. Then in 1968 she was involved in a major car accident and needed an eight-pint blood transfusion.

"I bled to death, basically, and woke up alive," Sandi said. "I almost died in the emergency room. There was no pulse or blood pressure for a period of time, and I required eight pints of blood. I also had an out-of-body experience. I could see it all from the vantage point of the ceiling, and saw my body on the operating table—the nurses and doctors running around and shouting, my sister and friend in the waiting room—but I had a feeling of calmness, and was an objective observer."

After her recovery, she realized there was, and still is, a huge need for blood.

"It's actually plasma they take. They make it into multi-products, sometimes for burn victims. I'm not afraid of being poked with needles, so I go once a week. They take my blood, and then give me chicken soup and cookies. That's my story and I'm sticking to it!" she said. "It's a way you can directly impact somebody else's life. If you could help save a life, why wouldn't you?"

The Magic of Sharing Music

Many people who do small acts of kindness realize it's a great way to keep their own hearts open, while also helping others to help others. Singer Kendra Sprinkling lived in San Francisco in the 1980s which opened her eyes to the effects of the mysterious disease that was wiping out vast segments of the population, and she was later given an opportunity that changed her life.

Back in Vancouver, she was asked to perform in an HIV/AIDS fundraiser called *Starry Night*. At that time, the musical revue was produced by David Harrison, but sadly, David succumbed to AIDS in 1995. Kendra decided to carry on the job of producing and directing *Starry Night*. Kendra and a small group of interested people set about creating an incorporated foundation and The Shooting Stars Foundation was born, with Kendra as the founding executive director. [shootingstarsfoundation.org]

"You know how they say the happiest people are people who have a mission. I feel blessed. I feel privileged and blessed to be doing what I am doing. I just have a commitment to working as long as I can to raise money for AIDS," Kendra said.

Since its inception, the foundation and the many performers, musicians, technicians, and volunteers, have produced over two hundred events and raised thousands of dollars for HIV/AIDS causes. Just one example of how a small group of dedicated people can help change someone's life for the better—helping others help others.

Spiritual Warrior Codes

A **Spiritual Warrior** is someone like yourself who has the courage to go on a quest for the divine consciousness within and to discover Soul—the Grail of legend. The Twelfth Golden Key asks you to be a Spiritual Warrior. Before we reach the Twelfth Key, I'd like to explain about the Spiritual Warrior Codes because a few of them match up with the Golden Keys.[43] They consist of codes of life similar to those of Ancient China, the Age of Chivalry in the Middle Ages, the days of the Knights Templar, and also, in the time of King Arthur and the Grail legends of ancient Britain.

The world needs Spiritual Warriors who use the power of Soul instead of aggression. In verse 69 of the Tao Te Ching it says: "by being armed, but with no weapons, great battles may be won."[44] Spiritual Warriors are also guardians of the planet.

Here is one of the codes for the Third Golden Key, and it's the most important one. If you choose one code to live by, choose this one.

Help one another.
By example, act and deed, each of us can
make a difference.

A New Spirituality for a New World

There is a growing movement to be guardians of the Earth as in **eco-spiritualism**—a new life-sustaining ecological and spiritual philosophy for the planet. With the influx and assimilation of new energies, we are creating a new world, and all of us need to take part in the transformation, creating a new worldview. It is a profound journey that we are on together. In his book *A New Earth: Awakening to Your Life's Purpose* (2005), author Eckhart Tolle uses the words "new earth," as do other authors. Revelation 21:1 says, after the apocalyptic destruction of the Earth, "Then I saw a new heaven and a new earth." According to Tolle, the new heaven is a new consciousness; the new earth is the outer manifestation of the transformed consciousness.[45]

Out of our new consciousness arises our new world. What will be the outer manifestation of our inner changes? One result of the transformative new consciousness is a community attitude, assisting one another in assimilating the new energies and the new state of consciousness, changing and rearranging our world from aggressiveness and closed hearts, to a hopeful egalitarian state of mind based on awakened hearts. The earthly changes are bringing in an era of sustainable cooperation. As a planetary species, we have never been here before, or have we? Why not be among the first to learn how to embrace humanity in the new age of cooperation?

Gifted healer and master herbalist Reverend Hanna Kroeger was known as the Grandmother of Health, a holistic pioneer of the 20th century. She healed many people with the old herbal philosophies of Europe, and by using the dream state to discover certain remedies. Hanna Kroeger told her students, "I cannot do it alone. You must help one another. You, you, and you must and can do it." Her two mottos for life were: "Help each other" and "Help one another." Whichever way you write it, it amounts to being a guardian of your habitat on planet Earth. Hanna knew that in helping others, we also help ourselves and, thus, the cycle is sustained.[46]

In 2009, don Miguel Ruiz, author of *The Four Agreements*, asked his readers: "Help me change the world." He writes on his website: "The goal of changing the world is finding an equilibrium between generosity and gratitude—which is an expression of real love."[47]

As of this writing, there are two million children in Africa affected by HIV/AIDS. Fifty million children in the USA do not have medical insurance and cannot see a doctor. Ninety-nine million people worldwide are starving; and there is half as much farm land for growing crops than there was forty years ago. According to the United Nations, by the year 2050, over four billion people will be water-scarce. These statistics of starvation, lack of water, poverty, and AIDS cases can overwhelm the average person. One of us can help, but many of us together can change the world. Regardless of our karmic boundaries and rationalities, a **compassionate heart** is important for our personal spiritual expansion. Therefore, our mission is this:

> *HELP OTHERS HELP OTHERS*
> *LIVE TO LIVE ~ LIVE TO GIVE*

Summary of the Third Golden Key

- You have a Key Guardian, a spiritual traveler who protects you.
- You are a Karma Warrior, learning to unravel karma and to take responsibility.
- You are in training to become a Key Guardian and a guardian of your habitat.

❧❦✱❧❦

THIRD KEY STORIES

Here is a story that opens our eyes to the world around us. Of course, it's not necessary we leave our own neighborhoods to affect change and to Help Others Help Others. For me, this next story demonstrates that if I have a calling to help the world, I shouldn't be afraid to act.

Six Plastic Cameras
By Susan Standfield

Susan Standfield from Vancouver, Canada, mailed six plastic cameras to a remote town in Northern Kenya. What she received back changed her life.

Disabled orphans took pictures of themselves at play at SHERP, the Samburu Handicap Educational Rehabilitation Program outside Nairobi, founded and managed by Grace Seneiya. Susan was so impressed with the beauty and quality of the photographs that five months later she packed two suitcases, her ATM card, and left for Africa.[48] Fed up with charities that do more harm than good in Africa, she wanted to prove that trade was a far more powerful tool than aid for alleviating poverty.

"Fifty percent of the 6.2 billion people on earth live in poverty. I chose to believe I could use the gifts life handed me to somehow reverse these huge numbers," she said to me in an e-mail. "The first time I connected with young people living in poverty was in 1991 when I went to Fiji with my first camera. I lived with a family in a small village and taught the kids how to take pictures. I then got the idea to send cameras to Africa in 2003. The real reason I do this is because, when my mum died in 1986, my dad gave me a camera; it really helped me heal—so I know cameras can help other vulnerable kids."

"In 2006 I partnered with a Kenyan woman, Mary Wanjiru, and together we started SHINDA: Africa's Youngest Brand. SHINDA, a Swahili word meaning *conquer*, empowers African youth through their own consumer brand. They create T-shirts that are made from 100% recycled fabrics and feature art created by youth. The product line now includes hand-knit sweaters, girls' dresses, and fabric shopping bags. The SHINDA studio also runs youth projects including the creation of a new Reality

TV show and an environmental clean-up project on the Nairobi River. Everything our business does is designed to offer young Africans opportunities to harness their talents and contribute to the positive economic growth of their local economies."

"My idea was not just to give these young people the opportunity, but also to equip them with development skills and business training to be able to go on and form enterprises," explains Stanfield.

Susan Standfield's for-profit business model was designed to generate revenue for young Kenyans using the unique cultural skills they already possessed. Their motto is TRADE, NOT AID; they promote self-sustainability and value-added manufacturing for Africa.

"My story is important because I ended up a changed person—coming from the West, I didn't understand Africa. Now I do, and my business is designed to work in every way to Africa's advantage; something the rich countries need to accept and nurture if we want a world that truly is fair. It is the only work I have done for three years and the biggest dream I have ever had the courage to believe in."

Following the violent political events that began at the end of 2007 in Kenya, I contacted Susan Standfield to ask if there was anything she wanted to add. I was surprised to learn she had not left Nairobi and, at the risk of her own life, had decided to stay. She writes:

Now more than ever the kids need SHINDA. Despite having been robbed of everything valuable I own, and then the election violence, I decided to stay here, following my dream. There is a story I would like to add that is a big part of why I stayed.

A few weeks ago I was walking along the street, and a street kid approached me for money, a little child tied to his back. I was stressed and late, so I crossed the road to avoid him, but then I heard him say, "Mama Susan." *Mama* is the common prefix added to any woman's name as a sign of affection.

Walking to him I asked him, "Have we met before?"

He said, "No, but all the kids know who you are because you help us."

I straightened his collar and wiped the dirt off his face and told him to be careful with the small change I gave him—a wrinkled dirty 50-shilling note that would likely only get the two of them home on a minibus. He had a 50% chance of getting beaten and robbed if the wrong person had seen what I gave him.

I never know what to feel in those moments other than absolute humility. I am so lucky I got a chance to live amidst people experiencing poverty and I am so grateful I am able to understand this whole painful puzzle from the inside out; so at least I can try to explain how easy it could be to change, if the world really wanted to. The only thing the world needs to do that will immediately alleviate poverty—and it won't cost a dime—is to have the desire to do so.

Everyone spends so much time on the HOW of poverty and not the WHY. The only reason why 50% of our world suffers from poverty is because the other 50% allows it. It's a social problem that stems from the promotion of scarcity, mostly by large corporations who suck huge amounts of wealth out of many of us collectively.

Remember that game Musical Chairs? Where everyone wins except one kid? It's the most awful game to teach children because it leaves them with the sense there isn't enough for everyone—but there is.

I know my opinion is correct because I used to live on the other side of poverty; I was part of the wealthy elite rich of the world. Very few people in that world have the courage to begin to let those ideas go for the sake of others' gaining. We have forgotten how to share. If we truly started sharing of ourselves and our wealth, things would start to change very rapidly.

ॐॐ✶ॐॐ

As Karma Warriors, our karmic past is sometimes revealed to us in mysterious ways, such as in dreams. Many of us lived in violent times. Sometimes we can see how a catastrophic event from a past life affects us now. Musician and singer/songwriter Rae Armour had a lucid dream which she believes came from being persecuted in a past lifetime.

Dream: An Ancient Lifetime
By Rae Armour

In my dream I was with a group of twelve peasants who were hunted down by Roman soldiers. We were not wealthy, but our connection to Spirit was very strong. We knew if we were caught we would be tortured and killed. The Romans called us traitors because we didn't follow the religious doctrine of the time. We were the last vestiges of those who followed the teachings of the ancient science of light and sound. We were also aware that it was just a matter of time until we were found.

As we hid in an underground bunker made of stone walls and stone benches that ran the perimeter of the room, we began to quietly sing HU, an ancient love song to God. Above us we could hear the clatter of soldiers as they ran through the streets. We continued to HU softly. We knew we were going to be going home to God very shortly.

Although I knew that death was imminent, I felt a sense of calm that was mixed with trepidation. My heart was pounding, and at the same time I had the sense I was exactly in the right place, with Souls that I had known for lifetimes.

Then, the doorway hatch to our hiding place was lifted, and light flooded the small cell where we huddled together. The soldiers had found us. The last thing I remember of this dream was looking up and seeing the fully armored legs of the Roman soldiers as they descended the staircase.

This dream happened to me for a reason: to teach me not to be afraid in this lifetime. No matter what is happening in the world, I am more able to handle it—as long as I keep my connection with Spirit and my heart open. When I become afraid I need to remember this dream of remaining calm in the face of death. Soul is eternal. I have returned and have reconnected with some of the Souls who were with me in the bunker. This realization reminds me how joining together helps us live through hard times. And when I find myself in fear, I know it is my mind trying to control me. When I'm in the presence of love, I am in touch with Soul. There's no need to hide. The outer chaos is an illusion; what is real is the connection with Spirit.

The dream also reminded me that strength is not measured

in numbers or by what society holds to be true. After all, there were a hundred Roman soldiers against a group of twelve. More against the few does not mean it's right or true. I also learned to appreciate the struggle of minorities who continue to be persecuted and to respect their truths rather than live in fear of their beliefs.

Our relationship with Spirit is measured by the connection of one's true heart to the divinity that is omnipresent. It's not found in the churches, books, or dogma; rather, it is in every living thing.

❧❦★❧❦

Adding to your good-karma tally can be as easy as performing one kind act every day. Just ask Janet Matthews who contributed this story about the grace that comes from giving:

Sunset on Grouse Mountain
By Janet Matthews

I knew what I wanted to do on my last night in Vancouver before leaving in the morning. I would take a cable car up Grouse Mountain and enjoy the spectacular views in time to watch the sunset from the peak. The previous year I had spent three months here recovering and healing from a traumatic experience. Vancouver had become a special place for me, reviving my health and spirits with its sea to sky beauty.

Wanting to travel light I grabbed some bus fare and a ten-dollar bill, stuffed it in my pocket and hurried out the door. On the main street I found a bus stop and began to wait. But an hour passed with no sign of a bus. Eventually I realized it might now be too late to enjoy the sunset as I had envisioned. I was ticked off at the bus line, very disappointed and hungry. Spotting a convenience store across the road, I decided to grab a snack.

As I left the store, lo and behold, along came the bus. I raced across the road, ran up the bus steps, the door closed, and off we went. Alone on the bus, I chatted with Bill the driver about this and that, what I was doing and why. The whole experience began to take on a surreal quality as we carried on up the mountain. By now I realized I probably didn't have enough money to complete my pilgrimage because I had spent it on the snack. I asked Bill if he knew how much the cable car cost, and he confirmed my fear—seven dollars up and back. I had only four left.

When we reached the Grouse Mountain parking lot, Bill handed me a transfer and told me it would get me back on the bus when I was ready to come down. It was then I told him I wouldn't be able to go up the mountain, because I only had four dollars left.

"How much do you need?" he asked, "Three dollars?"

When I nodded yes, he reached into his pocket and handed me three dollars, saying, "Take it, my treat. I'm not attached to it; it's only money." He brushed aside my mild protests and confusion and insisted.

The entire experience seemed to be dreamlike, outside of life, like a paragraph that's been highlighted with a yellow marker. I gratefully accepted the money, descended the bus and, waving to him, hurried to the cable car.

When I reached the top I found a place to perch just as the sun began to set. I'd made it. As I sat there enjoying the spectacular view out over English Bay and the setting sun, I thought about the special gift I had just received. I knew that Bill had, from his point of view, only given me three dollars. But from mine, he had given me my evening on Grouse Mountain. I was very grateful and filled with awe.

I wondered, did I now karmically owe him something? Or had I earned this gift somehow, and it had come out of my own good karmic bank account? Upon reflection, I decided it was both. I knew I needed to repay this gift, but also knew I'd probably never see Bill again. Right there, I decided to watch with eagle eyes for an opportunity to pass on this gift from the universe to someone else who was in need.

Back home in Toronto, my life went back to its normal hectic pace, but the memory of the gift remained with me. One day a few months later, the opportunity I had been watching for occurred.

I was at Sears to buy some vacuum cleaner bags. Standing in

line at the checkout counter in front of me was an elderly woman purchasing a pink nightgown. The clerk rang her through and asked her for fourteen dollars. The woman slowly dug out her money and began to count out her bills. When the bills were gone, she began with shaking hands to count out the quarters and dimes, then the nickels, and then the pennies. I watched with dismay as she ran out at thirteen dollars.

The woman, embarrassed and defeated, was about to give up when I reached into my wallet and said to the clerk, "Here's a dollar, is that all you need?"

"Sure, that's fine." The clerk finished the sale, put the nightgown in a bag and handed it to the woman.

The elderly woman was overcome with the experience, and I knew just how she felt. To me it was only a dollar, but as far as she was concerned, I had helped to give her the new nightgown she needed. It felt good giving back. Maybe that's how Bill had felt back on the bus.

She looked up at me with gratitude and said, "Oh, thank you dear! You are so kind!"

When I replied, "You're very welcome," she said to me, "God will bless you for this!" Feeling a little overcome, I took her hand, and looking into her aging eyes I somehow managed to say, "He already has, believe me, he already has."

THIRD KEY EXERCISE

Meet Your Key Guardian

This exercise gives you an example of how to discover a Key Guardian. Experiment with it to find your own way of doing it. Length of exercise: about fifteen minutes.

1. Turn off all distractions (radio, TV, computer, telephone, etc.) and find a quiet place. Get comfortable by sitting or lying down. Think about something that instantly opens your heart.

2. Close your eyes and sing HU or your favorite word a few times. Then ask to meet an inner guardian: "I wish to meet a Key Guardian who will assist me, and who will show me what I need to know." Focus on your request and continue to sing HU, while going to step three.

3. Listen to the sounds all around you, the birds, the cars, the electrical buzz of the lights, or the ticking of a clock. Begin to hear the sound of one inner note, it could be a long-drawn-out sound of a flute, or perhaps an electrical hum, or another sound of equal intensity, whatever it is, concentrate on it. Sing HU or your special word quietly.

4. Focus gently on the inner light behind your eyes. Lightly place all your attention on your Third Eye—that place between your eyebrows, just behind your eyes. At times there will be flashes of light on your inner screen, or a tiny pinpoint of light. This is the Blue Star. Follow where the inner light leads.

5. Enter the portal of the Blue Star into the Otherworlds and go to your special place. Visualize what your special place looks like and start to set up shop there, so to speak. What you're doing is setting up residency in the Otherworlds. But always remember to follow the Blue Star where it leads. Let the lights and sounds be in your present moment and help you focus.

6. As you enjoy your special place, or follow the Blue Star, notice that your Key Guardian approaches. What does she or he look like? What is s/he wearing? Does s/he have a name? Let your creative heart expand by giving him or her a gift. Or ask for a special word to use for your spiritual exercises.

7. Do this focused exercise for fifteen minutes a day to meet your Key Guardian on the inner. Open your dream journal and write down or draw a picture of your experience.

FOURTH KEY:
THERE IS NO LIMITATION

1. There is no limitation, except for the limitations we impose on ourselves. We believe they exist, so therefore they do.
2. This is the key of intention; the intend-to key. The epiphany that you can do anything requires that you believe it, and do it, and be it. To get started takes recognition, acceptance, and using the creative imagination. Whatever we put our attention on, we attract. Once you believe it's possible, you can do it.
3. Get out of your own way to take a step forward with action. The Universe stands aside to let anyone pass who is consciously aware of the path they are on.
4. Make a movement by practicing the "as if" or "to be" technique, which will help you be your desires NOW! What you desire already exists. There is an old saying: Your wish is already fulfilled before you ask.
5. Go to the next step, watch for signs, be fearless, pay attention to wakeful dreams, and the synchronicity of events will point the way.

(4:1 to 4:5)

ONCE YOU DISCOVER YOUR LIMITATION ILLUSIONS, you find the courage to overcome them and are then able to discover new creative possibilities. The Fourth Key is the belief paradigm, Law of Attraction, and "as if" principle all rolled into one.

The Sky's the Limit!

The sky is the limit! Do you doubt that? Self-doubt and fear are the padlocks that keep the door to your secret path locked, shutting you off from believing in unlimited possibilities. Spiritual leader and author Harold Klemp says, "There is no limitation except for the limitations you have made for yourself."[49] What we believe, is.

You Can Do Anything You Believe

The discovery that you can do anything requires that you:

Step 1. *Believe* you can, addressing self-doubt, fear and feelings of unworthiness; it helps to set a goal or intention.
Step 2. *Practice,* start to do it by practicing the "as if" or "to be" techniques.
Step 3. *Become* or acquire what you want, for the good of the whole.

The story below illustrates all three steps to living life consciously with unlimited possibilities.

Beyond the Stage Lights

 While producing three annual music concerts, I assisted a group of amateur musicians to overcome their fears, plus my own. I had no experience producing a music revue, but I didn't let that stop me from trying. It became a personal lesson in "acting as if I already knew how," and also, a little secret of mine, living life as an adventure. I quickly booked the venue, a popular community theater, and set about figuring out what to actually do! Taking that leap of faith in oneself is the first step. This bold step worked and eventually the concerts were sold out, but it took six months of planning and a committee of dedicated people. Throughout, I believed I could do it and I acted as if.

On opening night, backstage was mayhem! You could taste the stage fright. Twelve of the twenty performers had never been on stage before. Many people panic when asked to speak in public, let alone sing. So how did these first-timers get the strength to step out of the stage wings and perform?

One of them, who we'll call William, was shaking in his boots! He had the worst case of stage jitters I'd ever seen. He was shaking and running to the washroom to throw up. One of the performers with twenty-five years of stage experience helped to calm everyone by joking and keeping the atmosphere light. This somewhat eased the churning stomachs. But this wasn't enough for William. He still shook in his boots.

William was a talented singer/songwriter, with the potential to become a celebrated performer. Blockages of fear and feelings of low self-worth had been holding him back. He lived his life as a victim in a self-perpetuating cycle, attached to ego and, thus, had feelings of unworthiness. Here's how William learned to get out of his own way and remove self-made stumbling blocks, ways that anyone can learn to move forward in their life.

As the producer, director, and stage manager all rolled into one, it was my job to make sure the performers were looked after and the show ran smoothly. I had to act as if I were the confident captain of a ship full of panicked passengers, or run the risk of the entire ship sinking. I remained calm and began singing HU backstage. Soon everyone joined in. The rolling sound of HU perforated the fear and calmed almost everyone—except William.

He was too nervous to even talk. In fact, I quickly learned that talking about being afraid to perform made it worse. He was next up. I led him to the stage wings, and that's when I learned the secret of overcoming stage fright.

I said to him, "Remember why you are here, to help people open their hearts to divine love." Suddenly, I could see a shift taking place in him.

Focusing on his purpose helped him go beyond his fears. It changed from being about him, to being about them. With his ego out of the way and his mind on the audience's needs, the magic entered. The belief paradigm—the first step—went into action. He addressed his self-doubt, fear, and feelings of unworthiness through integration and emotional honesty. In those few moments before stepping on stage, he captured the potential to live his life with no limitations, believing he could. Think what would happen if all of us lived each moment from our unlimited creative potential, as stated in the First Key (1:2).

In taking the second step toward achieving his goal to perform, William practiced the "as if" technique. Using his creative imagination, he acted as if he already had overcome his stage fright, and he concentrated on the performance, not on himself. The creative energy is a powerful force and so are our feelings. In fact, feeling is as powerful as thought.

The third step was to become his potential. Later on, the Law of Attraction helped William get his first professional gig. He started out small, playing acoustic guitar in a popular coffee shop. The stage fright still existed, but now he had tools to rise above it. Years later, now a celebrated artist, he always sings HU before going onstage, taking a moment to remember that his purpose is to open people's hearts to divine love.

He learned to break ego's cycle, disarming feelings of unworthiness by connecting with Soul. The purpose of singing HU is to link up with our inner wisdom for guidance. This linkup is done by using a spiritual exercise and singing an energy-charged word such as HU. Once this inner spark of divine energy is activated, the ego quiets.

There is, however, another important spiritual law of the universe in the above story. It's called Law of Right Action, to align your efforts with the universe. If I had pushed too hard, or if the concerts were against the universal laws, or pursuing a music career wasn't what William as Soul intended to do in this lifetime, then it wouldn't have happened. It's important to realize that when your life is working for you, you're moving with the flow and not against it, and all is in divine right action.

We will talk more about living in the flow in the Ninth Key.

When you begin to understand Law of Attraction, and you under-stand that which is like unto itself is drawn, then it is easier and easier to understand that you are offering a signal, and the entire Universe responds. And when you finally get that, and you begin to exercise some deliberate control about the signal that you offer, then it really begins to be fun, because then you recognize that nothing happens outside of your creative control.

—Abraham-Hicks[50]

The Law of Attraction—Car Lessons

 Let's say you want to own a car. In fact, you intend on having one within the next six months. When you intend to do something, you act on the intention because intention and expectation of outcome guide your reality. But perhaps you don't have enough money to buy a car. One way to *act as if* you already own a car is to rent one for the weekend, take it for a spin, and experience how it *feels* to be a car owner. Esther "Abraham" Hicks, one of the original teachers of Law of Attraction, calls it the art of allowing, because you allow the vibration of what you want to be attracted to you. You attract the vibration you want. I told this to my friend Terry, and he did exactly that. He rented a brand new red Corvette! Then he got spruced-up and drove around town all weekend.

The next week he started to tally up how much it would cost him to be a Corvette owner. What with car insurance, upkeep and repairs, new tires every year, and the cost of gasoline he would have to find a better-paying job and change his life. Thoughts of a drastic life change accentuated his fears, so he decided not to buy a car.

Terry told himself, "It's too expensive to own a car. I'll take buses and ride my bicycle. Better on the environment, too."

But the Law of Right Action came into play and, intuitively, he knew it was right for him to change his life and move forward—literally. So, every other weekend he'd rent a brand new car and enjoy driving his friends around town, going on long drives and short sightseeing excursions, or just tootling about on a Saturday night. Without realizing it, he was acting as if and practicing the belief paradigm, manifesting a new state of consciousness: that of someone who accepts a new lifestyle.

Soon Terry found he'd spent all the money he'd saved to buy a car! Well, now what? There was a way—something Terry had not even considered. His grandfather was developing cataracts and couldn't see to drive anymore. So he gave Terry his old car. Okay, so it wasn't a Corvette, but it was a classic—a classic, 2.2-liter four-cylinder, 1986 Chrysler Reliant K-car. All Terry had to do was drive him to pick up his groceries once a week, which he was doing anyway. His grandfather even gave him money to pay the first year's car insurance. Terry returned the money after he got a promotion at work—moving forward.

Terry's story is a good example of "acting as if," and of how the laws of Attraction and Right Action work together with your belief paradigm. To paraphrase Albert Einstein: If you want something you haven't had before, you have to do something you haven't done before.

Robert at the White Spot

This story is about realizing that Soul knows best. At the local White Spot restaurant, my server was twenty-two-year-old Robert. When he refilled my coffee cup, I got the nudge to ask him a question. First I asked his permission, and then asked, "As a young man in today's world, what is your biggest worry?" I half expected him to answer: making enough money, keeping my job, war, pollution, etc.

He answered, "To get control of my fear." Fear stopped him from pursuing his dream of becoming an actor. Instead, he'd worked at the restaurant for four years. When he was younger he was extremely shy, even afraid of taking the bus because of all the people around him. But he acknowledged his shyness, which made all the difference. He purposely took the job of a waiter to force himself to interact with people.

"What does the fear mean to you?" I asked.

"I fear making a fool of myself on stage. It's the low self-esteem, no confidence thing. I've acted in theatre before, but fear holds me back. Working as a server is safe."

Then he told me that recently two people at separate times told him he had the X-Factor (charisma) to pursue acting and become successful. What I said next stated the obvious, but to him it was brand new. I said that he, Robert, attracted these two people, and now myself, because he needed to hear this message: that the time to go forward with his dream is NOW. I watched him experience an A-HA moment! By following through on my subtle nudge from Soul, his spiritual eye opened and, suddenly, he could see his road ahead. The point is, I could have said nothing, just, "Thanks for the coffee." But I believe the time has come to connect with others and gently share our wisdom.

So to Robert I say: *believe it, and do it, and be it.* Whatever we put our attention on, we attract. So be aware because your thoughts are dictating what you attract. What are you thinking about? Ask yourself, Do I truly desire that which I am putting forth? Is this really what I want to project into my future? We also need to assist the universe by taking action instead of doing nothing. When you make your decision to go forward, the universe can move with you. You are a powerful Being of Light. Trust in yourself, and the universe opens to assist you.

Spiritual Warrior Code:

We attract what we focus on.
To change your life, change your attention
and your attitude.

Be Careful What You Wish For

Have you heard the phrase, "Be careful what you wish for?" The Mind is a powerful ally because it uses two of the most important tools in your spiritual toolbox: the power of creative imagination and unlimited potential. However, there's a glitch.

The Mind is like a computer. It takes direction from your thoughts—literally! When we think thoughts of fear or despair, rage or murder, Mind doesn't understand that we *don't* want to create these conditions. It thinks that it must obey whatever we're thinking.

Luckily, God installed a safety mechanism called choice. We can choose what to think about. So make sure that what you're thinking is in line with what you want. What you pay attention to is what comes into your life. Your conscious decisions give your life meaning and direction. Also be careful what you believe, because belief can stop you from looking further for more answers; it solidifies your thinking.

The Fourth Key is the key of intention. Intention is mentioned briefly in the First Key (1:2), which says that you co-create your own world: "But more than that, your personal world and the people in it are the result of your inner intentions"—*inner* because what you do and what you think are two different things. Basically, what you do is intend to pull your life wish into this present moment. This is done through little shifts of energy, using the Living Energy Field.

Here is a key tip for applying the Fourth Key.

Manifesting Your Dream

We *experience* miracles all the time, so why not *manifest* them? Acceptance and recognition are key to removing limitations and creating self-made miracles. The Fourth Key says: Recognize and accept that you can do it. Then, move forward with action. But how do you do this?

First, know what you want. And if you don't know, then write down what you *don't* want and beside it, in a separate column, write its opposite. It will help you immensely to be clear. Energy needs to know where to go. Here are three ways of showing the energies where to flow or what to attach to.

1. Create a catalogue for your life

- Imagine a thick catalogue full of images, or even an online store: let's call it "eLife"! Open the picture catalogue and go shopping at your eLife store. If you had unlimited time, talents, and funds what would you choose?

- Start acting as if, collecting images for your catalogue. If you love to climb mountains, envision pictures of mountains. If you want a motorcycle, picture your dream one—the design, color, make and model. If you want to own your own home, go to open houses every weekend. If you want to serve life, look for pictures of ways you want to serve.
- Now, think BIGGER! Instead of climbing the mountain, buy it and develop the land. Instead of one motorcycle, buy an entire fleet of antique motorcycles and sell them. Buy an apartment building in a cheaper area, fix it up, and then resell the strata units. Instead of looking for a job to serve life, start your own enterprise to help alleviate world hunger. Why not? Remember what a powerful being you are.
- When you can visualize what your life can look like, write it down. You can choose to focus on anything, and remember, what you choose becomes your responsibility.

2. Map your dream

From a map you can determine how to get somewhere, because you create a set of directions to remind yourself daily. Some people suggest you be specific, others to leave room for the winds of change to blow through your life. Try both ways. Below is the version I've used.

- Cut out pictures of your dream vision from magazines, and create your dream map by arranging them on an art board, or bulletin board.
- Every day look at your dream board and put yourself into the images. Accept that you already *are* this new vision of yourself.
- Tape other pictures where you'll see them often, perhaps on the bathroom mirror. You can also use an image or write out a description and tape it onto your wallet, like "The family is going to Disneyland." And then every time you go to pay for something, it is there to remind you. Seeing your dream right in your wallet is an excellent way to stop spending

needlessly, and to save up for what you want.

Of course, acting as if doesn't have to involve materialism. We accumulate so much, maybe it's time to sell some of your possessions and manifest someone to buy them. Or to live by giving, by giving something away. For example, you may no longer want to be afraid of life. To be fearless, you act fearless by trying something you've never done before, something totally out of your comfort zone (see the Second Key, 2:5). The more you find yourself taking risks, the sooner you convince yourself to believe you are fearless! There are unlimited uses for the "as if" principle because you have unlimited potential.

3. Create a dream slideshow

If you sit at a computer daily, keep your dreams constantly in front of you with your own digital dream slideshow using the My Pictures section of your computer and/or handheld.

- Create a new folder called "My Pictures-A Dream Map" so it's first in line; or, remove any pictures unrelated to your dream from the top My Pictures folder.
- Create, scan, or download pictures of what you want.
- Turn your screen saver on to run as a slideshow when your computer is idle for over five minutes.
- Set the time to view each picture to fit your personal preferences. It's a powerful tool to have images of your personal dream map scroll in front of you.

Fine-Tuning Your Dream

As you implement these ideas, you'll find yourself fine-tuning your dream map, your plan, so the pieces of the puzzle can fall into place. Our powerful subconscious mind does not distinguish between the reality of not owning your own home and the reality of pretending by constantly envisioning that you do. Therefore, the subconscious mind sees the pictures of a home and begins to believe that you have one. The Law of Attraction starts to draw it to you. The more you envision and act as if, the more your brain accepts this as an actual belief. After all, isn't it true that almost everything you now have began as a thought? Remember the First Key: You co-create your own world. In the end, you are responsible for creating everything in your life.

Stay flexible. Be open to the possibility of how your dream will manifest. Spirit works in mysterious ways. Try not to be rigid about how it will happen. Terry in the Car Lessons story never expected his car to come from his grandfather. It wasn't in his plan, but the plan was open and flexible enough to allow it.

Here is how two people did their vision boards.

A Map for Finding Love

 Gillian recently did a manifestation dream map to find a new boyfriend. It had been fifteen years since her last committed relationship. So she decided to do a dream map and glued pictures from magazines onto a dream board. She was very specific, and included a smiling couple walking along the beach at sunset, a gentle-looking businessman carrying a briefcase, sharing a Jacuzzi with him, and other bring-a-man-into-my-life scenarios. But she forgot to be specific about where he lived.

Not thinking about the dream map, Gillian called a friend of a friend in San Francisco because he had traveled to South America, a place she was going to visit. After a few phone calls, he invited her down for Thanksgiving. She discovered he was the man on her dream board: entrepreneurial—like she is, positive thinking, with a gentle, nurturing nature. They fell in love. And then she discovered that he mostly lived in Alaska!

When we align ourselves to Spirit (Law of Right Action), along with the Law of Attraction, then those little details get taken care of. The relationship didn't work out, but they did become close friends. It happened as it was meant to, because they both learned a great deal about themselves from the experience. It's all good!

Another person's dream map was too eclectic. He pasted everything he had ever wanted in a mate onto a paper art board that he bought from an art supply store. He spent a lot of time in the store, picking out just the right supplies. Then he found himself over at the acrylic paints. He knew nothing about painting, but years ago in school he had liked to draw. He bought the art board, and in a spontaneous moment, some painting supplies and went home to put together his dream map. He cut out dozens of pictures from magazines and pasted them like a crowded collage on to the art board. His dream map was not specific enough for his mind to grasp what he wanted. Therefore, nothing on the board materialized. However, the universe had its own plan for him.

Even though not one thing manifested from his eclectic dream map, while hanging out at the art shop he discovered his love for painting. And now, after taking painting classes in the Impressionistic style, he has become a popular artist. Let go and let God! There is no limitation.

Let Go and Let God—Law of Reversed Effort

I want to mention the Law of Reversed Effort. Basically, if you focus too hard on something, the reverse can happen. Or sometimes, the harder you try to achieve a goal, the further it moves away. While using our imaginative powers, sometimes we strain too hard and that can work against us. For instance, if you try not to think about the noise around you, suddenly the noise is all you hear. Reversed effort means trying too hard to force results, using your will instead of your heart. Have you ever tried to think of the name of the band who sang your favorite song, and the more you thought about it, the farther it hid from you? Later, when you're doing something else, the name suddenly pops into your head! That's an example of the Law of Reversed Effort: when you no longer push against a closed door to make something happen.

There is a fine line between intending something to happen and willing it to happen. In other words, the universe (Source) knows best! What if you keep forcing something to happen and all the while your higher self has something better for you? Intend for something to happen, but try not to be so rigid that you discount the gentle guidance of Soul's wisdom. Find the balance. When you relax, truly relax, let go and find the balance between doing and not doing, it opens your heart to allow Spirit to take the reins, and that is when the magic happens!

When Spirit Calls My Name[51]
(Music & Lyrics by Rae Armour & M. J. Milne © 1997)

—1—
If I could take any road put in front of me
Without worrying at all.
If I could see the pathway clearly
Without wondering if I'll fall,

Then I'd be free to live the life I'm meant to,
The one I chose before I came.
In my heart, I hear the answers,
When Spirit calls my name.
—2—
If I could trust the voice deep inside of me,
The one I haven't heard for awhile,
If I could stop all the hurrying and slow down,
Just stop and listen for awhile.

Then I'd be free to live the life I'm meant to,
The one I chose before I came.
In my heart, I hear the answers,
When Spirit calls my name.…

Take Action and Your Dream Is on Its Way

Your dream is on its way, accept it. We have to open our minds and realize there is no limitation. Open yourself up to abundance and the world opens up to you. After all, your dream already exists. All you need to do is bring your dream in to the present moment. The power of the present moment works only when there is acceptance. Remember what the Fourth Key says about acceptance and recognition (4:2). Recognize that you can do it and accept it into your life. Then, go to the next step, watch for signs, be fearless, pay attention to wakeful dreams, and the synchronicity of events will point the way (4:5).

The Law of Attraction tells us to focus exactly on what we want. But it takes action after planting the seed; so consciously take action and assist the universe. For example, to get rid of debt, you don't continually think about getting out of debt (negative thoughts) because the brain hears "debt" and you'll attract more. Set up an automatic payment plan and then start thinking about abundance (positive thoughts). Debt is the result of past actions, so change your actions, and get a new strategy— like stop spending and start saving. If you sit there and do nothing, nothing will happen! Makes sense, doesn't it? After all, you can't steer a ship that is docked. For the rudder to work, the ship must be moving. So take a step toward your unlimited possibility. Focus on what's best and go to what's next!

Your Waking Dream Symbol

Pay attention and watch for signs when they point the way to unlimited possibilities, because you have universal guidance, if you choose to look and listen. And to help you, here's an exercise I've used many times:

Choose a specific waking dream symbol or an image. It can be anything: a hummingbird, a hockey logo, a specific flower, the image of a popular landmark like the Eiffel Tower, a blue Volkswagen Beetle, or anything you want. And know that every time you see it—whether on a billboard, in a shop window, on television, in a movie, a magazine, or if someone mentions it to you—it's a sign your dream is on its way. Then take a moment to envision what your world will be like when it arrives. This setting up of a waking dream symbol is to trigger a reticular activation to help you focus your attention on your dream. Our brain is conditioned to see things a certain way. For instance, focusing activates your inner mechanism called the reticular activating system, and once you focus on something, all of a sudden you start to see it everywhere.

Eiffel Tower of Power

Here is an example of a waking dream symbol. A few years ago I decided to buy an apartment. Having set up the *intention*, I chose a real estate agent. Then I decided to use the Eiffel Tower in Paris as my waking dream symbol. I set up the waking dream by stating my intention: "If I see an image of the Eiffel Tower inside an apartment it means I am supposed to buy that apartment." I was very specific.

My realtor showed me over thirty apartments. Not one was a match, and none had an Eiffel Tower image or any reference to Paris. But the reticular activator in my brain was turned "ON" and I saw Eiffel Towers everywhere, except inside an apartment! It helped me keep my focus on what I wanted. I almost gave up, thinking it's not time for me to own a home. Then, one day we drove up to an older building. Looking at its age, I said, "No way, let's not even bother going inside." My realtor encouraged me to look, and I'm glad we did.

The older, but sturdy, apartment was huge and had two bedrooms. It didn't have everything I wanted on my exceedingly long list, but it was in my price range, and on a wall was a small lithograph of the Eiffel Tower! But I still wasn't one hundred-percent convinced to buy it. Then the next day I drove back to the apartment building and sat outside in my car. That's when I noticed what was written in French on the entrance door: "Chez Moi" (My Home). Hmmm. Did I get the message? Yes.

FOURTH KEY STORIES

The Fourth Key states that we can do anything by using our creative imagination. We can be successful individuals in thousands of different ways: out in the world, living our day to day life, connecting with others, or sharing our wealth of knowledge.

Ken Hancherow is a true Renaissance Man. He lives on a 96-acre organic farm where he pursues his work in new energy technologies, the alternative health field, the relationship between sound and healing, and the connection between the land and animals. You will discover a few Golden Keys in his story:

Living Life in the Zone
By Ken Hancherow

I try to stay in flow or in harmony with life. It's being in the zone, like a professional sports athlete who achieves a perfect ten through seemingly effortless effort. When you're in the zone you don't realize the passage of time or what you've done. You're in tune with all life at the highest level you can be. It's that moment when you get a shiver up your spine. Dr. Wayne Dyer calls it "real magic." Hockey legend Wayne Gretzky said he had moments when he played hockey where he could see the game from above. He would go where the puck wasn't and it would come to him.

The first time I experienced this *peak experience* I was ten years old and learning how to water ski. My first success getting up on skis was so exhilarating, I couldn't stop laughing with joy—so this is what walking on water is like!

The next time I felt this way occurred while I was singing in the middle of a choir with a symphony orchestra. The sound transported me out of my body, beyond space and time—so this is total awareness! Recently, this happened again during my piano concert at the Glenn Gould Studio. During that improvisational concert I was challenged to take risks, which led me to another peak performance.

Another time, while my partner Anastasia and I were driving all night to a seminar in Minneapolis, something unusual happened. It started to pour, and the windshield wipers stopped working. I could hardly see to drive. At the precise moment when it did suddenly stop raining, there in front of us stood an incredible deer. I slammed on the brakes. The car stopped within a foot of the deer; it remained motionless. We sat there staring at it, and the stag stared back at us. Time stopped. Everything went so quiet. There was a vividness to the air and you could hear a pin drop. We were in some other zone. Then the large stag walked up the hill, stopped, and looked back at us.

A little while later, still feeling "otherworldly," we drove into an unbelievable tunnel of light and colors. We stopped the car and got out to watch. Growing up on upper Lake Superior, I had seen beautiful Northern Lights (Aurora Borealis), but this was beyond them. The light wasn't in the distance. We soon discovered we were *inside* the swirling lights. Both Anastasia and I experienced a sensation of being out of our bodies. The whole sky and even the air around us was a moving dome of colors—so this is being inside the heart of God!

Time had stood still. Later we realized we had been there about twenty minutes and not a car had appeared. As soon as the experience ended, several cars came flying past, and everything went back to normal.

Having these experiences opened my eyes to living in the zone and to seeing the indescribable wonders of life. I now try to live life with passion, trying things I've never done before. I know I'm here to learn my spiritual lessons, and I enjoy living on the razor's edge. For instance, I'm not a farmer, but I bought a farm to create a health retreat and have an organic garden. Many people tell me I'm an example of how we can be caretakers on our own piece of sacred land, be self-sufficient and do it all organically. For instance, I'm studying ways to improve the soil through compost teas, sea minerals, ormus energies, radionics, and also, breakthrough solar and storage technologies to get off the electrical grid. I want to be the best I can be in everything I do, all the while remaining conscious that my true path is learning how to grow spiritually.

It's about taking love to another level, especially with the animals and the land. It doesn't matter how many dogs, cats, horses, cows and chickens you have. Each one is special and gives back the love you give. I try to teach others that we all have a life's purpose and a mission that we came here to fulfill. The trick is that your goals and your outer life must be in alignment with your purpose and your inner life. Then you are in flow!

❧❧�֍❧❧

When you tune in to your inner nudges, the possibilities become unlimited. Austrian-born Elke von Linde had a dream that eventually led her half way across the world to the Yucatán Peninsula, Mexico. She feels that her inner guidance led her to make a documentary film, helping her to realize there is no limitation, and that the universe stands aside to let anyone pass who is consciously aware of their purpose.

Road to the Mayans
By Elke von Linde

I had a dream about freedom and about crossing borders. I felt like a messenger, like an eagle soaring in the air, breaking out of narrow valleys into the endless expansion of the icy sea. There I discovered a ship: an ice-breaker forging its way through packed ice and leaving behind it an open trail—a white road. This is the story of how I discovered the special meaning of the white road in my dream.

I left on a journey to Merida on the peninsula of Yucatán in Mexico thinking I was going to do a film about energetically powerful places and spiritual people. I had studied Art History and Archaeology at Innsbruck University in Austria, where I graduated with a doctorate, and I had wanted to find a way to bring my three passions of film, art, and archaeology into alignment.

Since 1999 I'd been focused on searching for a synthesis of Art History, energetically powerful places, and the spiritual wisdom of the indigenous cultures in both South and North America. Through a special journey to Mexico I was able to meet with indigenous people who were the living representatives of the ancient knowledge—the Elders.

The city of Merida, where we were invited, is known as the White City. I discovered that the symbolic white road of ice in my dream was the white stucco and limestone roads connecting Mayan ruins, known as *Sac be*. It's a Mayan word that stands for our divine union with God and the universe. It is the spiritual evolutionary road for everybody, in addition to the good Red Road or intercommunication road between creatures here on earth. The White Road represents our heart seeking the essence that connects us all. Deep down in our hearts we are all one.

Sac be or *Zac be* also means the Milky Way and refers to a connecting link for communication between the earth and the heavens—a cosmological road. In Peru, the Milky Way is called the Road of Souls, and is the world-tree used by shamans in their ascent and descent.

There are real white roads leading spiritual seekers from one sacred site in the Yucatan to the next one, so all were connected by these roads. Very interesting, because one road purportedly ends up on the beaches of Tulum, and from there it is said they continue to Atlantis and to the Canary Islands, where there are similarities to the Mayan culture.

We originally went there to film something completely different, and then everything changed. How we got to go is interesting. My friend Carolina Hehenkamp, an author who has written books on the Indigo Children, wrote us saying she felt we were meant to be in Merida at a precise time. It was the first time that other cultures were invited to the traditional reunion of elders, priests and shamans in Merida.

Carolina was already working together with the organizer of the meeting, Hunbatz Men, and via a spiritual travel agency here in Germany she organized the trip for us. There was a group of about thirty people involved and they also donated money toward transporting the Elders in Mexico. Another group fresh off a Southwest Pilgrimage to the ancient Anasazi sites in the USA was also there, led by LionFire, the shaman of Hovenweep. And there was Drunvalo Melchizedek with a group there as well. They were keeping the energy of the most outer circle around the event.

Despite enormous difficulties we—our small team of Ines Fröschl-Queisser, Michael Springer, Daniel Loher, and myself— were given the honour of witnessing this very special event: the reunification of the eagle and the condor after 511 long years of suffering and suppression, a symbol of the reunion of North and South America as well as the reunion of the heart and the mind. And also, at the ceremony of the spring equinox at the Mayan temple of Chichen Itza on March 21st, the Mayan Council of Elders, Don Alejandro the head of all Mayan Elders and spiritual leader from Guatemala, and about 250 indigenous

Elders from the North, South, and Central Americas performed ceremonies for peace, joining together their spiritual powers for a world healing.

In the film we show how we were immersed in the Mayan world with their fascinating temple grounds, their unique calendar system, and their mysterious crystal skulls, which we were allowed to hold. However, on site, our small film crew encountered all sorts of obstacles. We had to somehow prove that we were worthy of admittance. Then almost miraculously, the doors opened and everything fell into place. The shamans, all priests who are talking in our film, opened their hearts to us. For centuries their wisdom had been guarded until this special moment when they began to share their knowledge. It felt like the completion of when the eagle (of the North) gains the strength to cross the borders to a new, ancient land, to reunite with the condor in Central America.

The most impressive experience for me was the gathering where we danced, prayed, and chanted together as brothers and sisters with no gap between nations and colours. And heaven answered in appreciation—it rained for twenty minutes in this one place where we were. For me it was the first time I experienced an instant message sent by the elements, by nature, by the Creator. Deep at the bottom of my heart I understood the meaning of the bridge being made between us and Mother Earth. *The White Road: Visions of the Indigenous People of the Americas* became the title of our documentary film because, for us, it represented the road to mankind's future.[52]

FOURTH KEY EXERCISE

 ## Unlock Your Life Dreams

Discover your life purpose, or what you intend it to be, staying open to unlimited guidance.

- Action begets reaction. It is a universal law. Set your intention to what you hope to achieve in the next six months. Choose a goal that aligns with your life purpose, or something you want to change in your life. Write it down in your journal. Remember, there is no limitation.

- When you change your focus from *wanting* something to *having*, a powerful shift in your energy takes place. Why? Because you've changed your thoughts from wishing something would happen, to expecting it will happen, to acting as if it has happened. This is the power of positive thinking in the Law of Attraction. But it's more effective when you *act as if.*

- Be attentive to the synchronicity of events that are guiding you. Spirit will lead you to the next step. Conscious choice and self-responsibility become a habit. Listen to your breath for the inner guidance of Soul.

- Let go, let go, let go, let go of everything you thought you knew before this point and open your heart to truly living *in* and breathing *in* your life in the moment.

The Fifth Golden Key is next. You may wish to re-read the first four Keys before proceeding to the Fifth. Take your time and do the exercises. Life is a journey to be savored and enjoyed, and so are the Keys.

FIFTH KEY:
THROUGH THE EYES OF SOUL

1. Look through the eyes of Soul.
2. Step back to see the Big Picture. Your everyday life is microscopically in close-up. Many times we are so involved with the circumstances of our own little world that we don't see beyond it. Step outside of yourself and view your life from above. Pretend you are in a hot air balloon looking down at yourself. The result will change your perspective and your life.
3. Detach from ideas, opinions and thoughts. Earthlings get so attached to illusions. Take a step toward compassionate detachment and flexibility. From this expanded vision—Soul's viewpoint—you view the situation unemotionally, and you do not attach to negative influences.
4. Ask: Is what I'm about to do in the best interests of all?
5. Focus by singing a word to help you activate the All-Seeing Eye or Soul's viewpoint. You do not direct the sound at anyone; you use it to gain an understanding or to protect yourself.

(5:1 to 5:5)

S TEP BACK TO SEE THE BIG PICTURE, the world you know is renewing itself and evolving. You, and others like you, are entrusted with special Keys to live in this emerging new world. We are being asked to cross a bridge. By practicing the Fifth Key you will be able to look through the eyes of Soul and see your world from a higher perspective: a universal viewpoint. You will see the world on the other side of the bridge. Can you see what an amazing benefit that would be for you? If you're living in a state of conscious freedom, nothing happens that you don't already intuitively know about.

Through the Eyes of Soul

For a moment, step outside yourself and imagine climbing the tallest mountain. What do you see from the top? The view is so different and everything below so small. You are looking at your world from a new viewpoint. There are those of us who look down from the mountain and see the forest, while others see the individual trees. When you expand your vision, your perspective changes so you see the forest *and* the trees, plus one step further—you see beyond the obvious. Using this example, seeing beyond is the ability to see how the forest and the trees interact with one another, with the inhabitants, the animals and insects. By using the eyes of Soul you focus on what is essential and this is what conscious dream travel is all about. It's about consciously seeing a bigger picture at all times. What if you could have an overall viewpoint of your life and know what's going to happen next; what would it tell you?

The ancient Egyptians used the All-Seeing Eye or Third Eye called the Eye of Horus; also affiliated with the Evil Eye. The Egyptian mysteries involved multi-dimensional, inner travel through the gateway of their Third Eye. If you were to look through your spiritual Eye it would resemble an updatable, multi-dimensional, holographic telescope with a memory.

In point 5:3 of the Fifth Key, it says that by being emotionally detached we will not pick up negative influences. This is a subtle reference to an ancient belief in the Evil Eye. The icon of the Fifth Golden Key is a protection against evil energy exchanges.

For instance, have you ever been in a really good mood, and then suddenly picked up someone's bad mood? That's a form of energy exchange.

The Evil Eye talisman dates back to the third millennium BCE, in Sumerian times. For centuries, no matter what their religion (Orthodox Greek, Catholic, Jewish, or Muslim), many people wore an Evil Eye bead for protection against unfriendly stares and negative influences. The belief is that the eye on the bead, which was often blue, reflects the evil intent back to its source. It can still be purchased in the Mediterranean, Turkey, Iran and the Middle East, Africa, and Asia. In fact, the little blue bead is a common denominator of all these people. Therefore, wearing the Fifth Key's symbol is a reminder that all human beings are similar and to not fear one another; that is your true protection, to protect yourself from fear itself.

360-Degree Viewpoint

Years ago, I realized that one of the reasons I had become a bus driver in this lifetime was to give me two important spiritual tools: How to live in the HERE AND NOW, and how to see from a 360-degree perspective—which is Soul's viewpoint.

Many professional drivers use Soul's perspective. As a bus driver, I learned to use this 360-degree viewpoint and to call on it instantly and intentionally. I learned great lessons on this subject, at times even dangerous ones. I would be driving along the street and then suddenly realize I didn't remember driving that last mile. It's not unusual. In other words, the driver as Soul is out-of-body, on automatic pilot. Usually it is unconscious or unintentional, similar to day-dreaming. When you suddenly come back from daydreaming and wonder, "Oh, where was I?" that is a form of dream travel. Conscious dream traveling is actually remembering where you went and seeing from a spiritual viewpoint. This day-dreaming is the beginning of learning how to intentionally and consciously travel as Soul.

You do not have to be in top physical shape to travel as Soul. In fact, many people in a state of dis-ease can readily dream travel and often spend hours in another dimensional consciousness.

Those who are dying will often drift in and out of the dream traveling state, as do babies and children. The Fifth Key can unlock the Otherworlds for you, and allow you instant access beyond—into Soul's playground.

Develop Your Intuition

When you see the big picture you can also begin to see an expanded viewpoint in order to handle stress, change, and chaos. Developing this ability includes developing your intuition. It is a process anyone can learn and is perfectly safe. Shifting out of consciousness uses one's creative potential and imagination (See the First Key, 1:2).

It has been proven to me that many of us already have well-developed intuitions. We may be called "sensitives," people with finely developed intuitions and extrasensory perceptiveness. I prefer to use the word "sensitive" over clairvoyant to lessen the psychic inference, because it is not the psychic realms that I am interested in visiting. Sensitives seek a new spirituality that embraces intuition, and teaches a new way of looking through the eyes of Soul. When they shift out of consciousness, it's similar to inner dream travel.

Throughout the worlds, both the Otherworlds and our present world on Earth, we will find a Darkside, but it is also a part of the Lightside—there is no separation. They are one and the same. Both hold our karmic freedom. We need to understand and accept both the light and the dark, and the active and passive principle, especially now as millions of us become sensitives, learning to access our intuition and Living Energy field. In the balance between these two poles we experience our wholeness.

I wondered if clairvoyants or psychics use their intuition or Third Eye, and if it is the same as inner dream travel where you access the entire picture. Do they only see sections of the time track? Or do they use their natural intuitive ability? I no longer seek out clairvoyants or those working in the psychic realms, mostly because I prefer to trust my own inner perceptions. But for now I wanted to know if they accessed the Fifth Golden Key. So I asked a person with an active all-seeing-eye how she does it and her answer surprised me. Nancy Shipley Rubin said she didn't know. She said it wasn't unusual not to know. In her workshop *Developing Intuition*, she defines intuition as "the ability to know and understand immediately without reasoning or being taught. It comes into our consciousness as an instant awareness of what is right in the moment."[53]

Reflections of a Child Psychic

 Nancy Shipley Rubin, a small-town girl with a wide smile and a shy worldview, has been psychic since childhood. Growing up in Fort Bragg, California, with a sister, two brothers, a working mother, and a distant father, was difficult enough without having to deal with the sometimes horrific experiences of being a child psychic. At such a young age, she had no idea what was happening to her.[54]

"Shyness is just fear," she told me. "I had a lot of fear that I had to overcome in this lifetime. I was born with it. For as long as I can remember I was scared out of my wits. I had some pretty harsh childhood experiences in being psychic as a kid. I reacted in extreme levels of fear. I've had to work on myself to undo a lot of that stuff. One of the difficulties of being so sensitive is that you experience everything. It's not just the good stuff that happens. You have to find a way of balancing and utilizing the depth of awareness," Rubin said.

Her personal vision involves helping people discover their creative potential: "I feel that a lot of people are depressed now and feel inadequate. We have not been allowed as children to have that full experience of our Spirit soaring in some kind of creative activity. All of us are having to look for new avenues to experience our spirituality. And we're moving through that creative potential door."

Rubin explained her view of creative potential by saying, "The first step in opening up to your creative process is listening to your heart, willing to find out what you love. Give yourself a certain amount of your day; it could be half an hour, to sit with your ideas or the sense of what you want to do."

In school or as kids it is too often the other way because teachers and parents want children to be well-rounded, so they try to be good at everything. But Nancy Shipley Rubin thinks otherwise. "Go with what you're good at, instead of working on your weaknesses. Let's say you have an incredible love of mechanics, and you feel alive and excited whenever you're doing what you love. It's that sense of giving permission for this person to be able to go and say: Okay, let's go out and play in a welding shop where you can do whatever you want to do."

"Life itself is such a miracle and the ability to see it is probably one of the greatest gifts we can ever have," Rubin said. "I've definitely been out on the edge a lot and was saved by the skin of my teeth."

In her thirties when in Hawaii, she and a friend went climbing up a sheer cliff. Hours later her body was on the verge of collapse; she was so frightened, hanging on the edge of the cliff for dear life. Her worried friend couldn't see her over the edge of the cliff. She knew she would be in serious trouble if she fell.

"I prayed for a level of strength and awareness to make it off that mountain. Then I felt this incredible light coming right in through the top of my head. It stabilized me. My whole body changed its awareness and I became totally comfortable and confident. I had strength where I had lost it."

She was able to pull herself up and move off the cliff. "I felt I had been saved by God. God gave me that level of strength to get myself off that mountain."

Trusting Inner Guidance

The Fifth Key will help you discover a higher vantage point from which to view the big picture. It also uses the powerful force of your creative potential by giving you inner strength. I wonder what it would be like to trust so completely in our inner wisdom and follow the guidance that Soul, or Spirit, gives us? Where do you think we'd end up? Would it be any different than if we didn't follow our inner guidance? Why not try it for a day and see?

A famous Canadian musician on tour in Europe was of a mind not to make a movement without first receiving an inner message. She told me she stood on a street corner in Paris for half an hour, waiting for a nudge to tell her where to go next. This is a fun experiment to learn how to access an expanded vantage point.

Another friend, a Reiki Master and Turaya teacher always listened to her inner guides. Once I remember a few friends and myself followed her around Van Dusen Gardens during a festival of lights. At every curve in the pathway, she would stop and listen to which way her inner guides wanted her to go.

I remember the time a friend and I went to Costa Rica. We didn't speak Spanish and we didn't know the lay of the land. We made a pact to only go where Spirit guided. On the entire two week trip we would pause to wait for a sign and then basically follow our feet. There were no rules except to listen to our inner voice. Many times both my friend and I were cued to turn and go down the same street, or to turn the rental car onto a different highway. It was a liberating experience, learning to surrender so explicitly. Try it, it can be very exciting!

You will need this technique of trusting your higher guidance during the changeover, the transition period to the new consciousness. If you can, then you will know what truth is and what is fabricated by those who wish to manipulate us.

Compassionate Detachment

Point 5:3 of the Fifth Key says that Earthlings get so attached to illusions—ideas, opinions and thoughts. Taking a step back is a move toward compassionate detachment and flexibility. From the vantage point of Soul's compassionate detachment you view the situation objectively and unemotionally. Detachment is not a lack of concern for others, but rather the ability to remain centered and balanced in Soul. This is how we can find our own truth in any situation. Once you move into that place of compassionate detachment you are able to surrender and thus, better able to move out of yourself and consciously dream travel to see the bigger picture.

We seem quite able to get attached to our judgments, opinions, and thoughts. They get in our way and block our spiritual sight. Taking a step out from ourselves helps to view the situation objectively and unemotionally, and truly view our world through the eyes of Soul. Imagine taking two steps back from your Self. From there, you can look at yourself and ask: "Is what I'm about to do in the best interests of all?"

Quietly singing your favorite word beforehand also helps you to raise your consciousness and detach from any situation. From this new vantage point you can see forever!

The Night Mom Died

We appear to be born into our present family for a particular reason. The most joyous and the harshest lessons can come from family members. As a youth I had many conflicting emotions and a few arguments with my parents. When I moved away from home, I had to learn detachment from my family—compassion without attachment. Before I became my own person there was a transition period, and I remember it felt as if I was removing old clothes and standing naked until the new clothes arrived.

Years later when my mother lay dying, my angst as a young adult had fallen away. And even though Mom and I still had karmic issues between us, they unraveled without harsh words or drama. Nothing mattered more than staying with her in her last hours. As I sat next to her bed and tended to her needs, as she had done for me when I was a baby, the past hurts mattered little. On the inner, I recalled all the estrangements that had happened between us during my young adult years. Viewing her through the eyes of Soul let me love her unconditionally for who she was. I realized that when she was a young mother with her first child, she was growing spiritually, too. Mistakes and misjudgments were made by both sides. This fast-moving kaleidoscope of scenes showed me that a simple attitude shift changes everything.

While my mother was sleeping in the hospital bed, I closed my eyes and imagined our two Souls sitting on a cloud plane above the bed. We talked and worked through our karma together; and yet, not a word was spoken out loud in the hospital room. We silently moved through the healing energies on the inner planes and overcame the karmic entanglements.

Around midnight, the night my mother died, my middle sister Carol sat bolt upright from her sleep with a deep gasp, feeling like it was Mom's last breath. At the same time, I was at my home in bed, journaling, and moments later saw a radiant light appear at the foot of my bed. There was Mom. She died at age seventy-four, thin and sickly, but now she appeared in her spirit body, young, beautiful, and shimmering. I knew her instantly. She had come to say good-bye.

She said to me, "Always remember to love yourself. You are beautiful just the way you are." It brought me to tears because I knew it was her way of apologizing for the karma that had passed between us in this and other lifetimes; most of our life together was good. She did her best and so did I. I told her how much I loved her, and then she went into the light and slowly faded.

Moments later Anastasia my youngest sister reported seeing Mom walking out the driveway of our family home and into the distance.[55]

You can ask on the inner to quietly heal the problems between yourself and another person. Just ask. Say the words and it will be given, but only if you are open to receiving. We forget to give ourselves permission to ask for help from Divine Source. With my mother, I had asked silently: "Please show me what it is I need to see from this situation, so that we may both move on with grace and love."

One of the most amazing gifts I received during the days before my mother passed was learning to keep my heart open.

Summary of Five Golden Keys

- The First Key says that I am the Key; no one else is responsible for my life but me.
- The Second Key says to follow the Blue Light; I am Soul, an eternal Being of Light.

- The Third Key tells me about Key Guardians and living over and over again, and meeting the same people in a cycle of cause and effect.
- The Fourth Key shows me there is no limitation, and when I use my creative potential, the universe sets up a chain of synchronistic events which leads me to my destination; like the ancient saying, action begets reaction.
- And the Fifth Key teaches me to view life through the eyes of Soul, to look at the Big Picture by standing back and above, and to focus on the inner sound of Soul.

FIFTH KEY STORIES

Here are a few stories that have golden nuggets for the Fifth Key. By staying in the present we are able to see, with the eyes of Soul, the many signs we are shown from moment to moment. When our spiritual eye is open and aware, we can receive waking messages. Here's a story from author Darlene Montgomery about how she looked through the eyes of Soul to experience a miraculous message:

Sign
By Darlene Montgomery

Thomas Drayton was my best friend. We'd met during the breakup of significant relationships in both of our lives. We had both experienced a powerful spiritual experience and been left wandering and wondering about our direction. We found each other in San Francisco at a seminar for our church, Eckankar, and had been friends ever since.

To say that Thomas was an enigma would fall short of the wonders of his character. To describe Thomas, I'll start with his one eye. He was blinded as a teen when someone had thrown a rock up in the air and it landed on his eye. So Thomas often wore a patch. But he saw more with his one eye then most see with two. Thomas was a mystery to all except his closest friends and even we sometimes had trouble penetrating the mystique of his profoundly creative, spiritual character.

Throughout our years together, Thomas and I traveled, spent time on the phone, went to movies, cried, laughed, fought and shared our writing; but, mostly I listened to the reams and reams of poetry written while my friend lay awake night after night. You see, Thomas hardly ever slept more than three or four hours a night. He had several books of poetry published throughout his years, all of a profound and spiritual nature.

Thomas was struck down by cancer suddenly one summer. It came on so quickly and it took him all too fast. Fortunately, I was able to say goodbye. One evening just before he died, I visited him in the hospital. I entered the room to find Thomas looking gaunt and with the signs of death on his body. His spirit, though, filled the room with light and a profound sense of God. Thomas became even more of the person he was as he surrendered his spirit to the divine.

That night, I found myself feeling awkward, as I sat in shock, staring at his emaciated face. The skin on his body had shrunk in the four days since I last saw him. I recognized the signs that he was leaving this earth very soon.

He asked me, "Are you shocked? Do I look like Lily did before she died?" A friend of mine had died just two weeks earlier from a long battle with cancer. The signs were all too clear.

"Yes." I said. I stumbled to ask him, "Will you give me a …"

"Sign?" he filled in. "Yes," he agreed.

I had to leave town for a few days for a conference. I was filled with angst. What if Thomas translated (died) before I returned? I couldn't deal with that. But he managed to hang on another week and left his physical form on October 24, 2007, in the late afternoon, surrounded by family.

I went into a profound shock. It was my first great loss through death. I waited for a "sign" from him. Days passed. A week or more had come and gone. I thought, *I guess I'm not going to get a sign.*

The following morning I awoke and stumbled into the living room of my apartment. Lying on top of the small entrance table was a ticket stub. It had been there since the night Thomas died but I had never bothered to pick it up. I later found out my daughter had attended a play the evening Thomas died and upon her return home had left the ticket on the table. I reached down and started to actually read the words on the ticket.

The ticket was for a play entitled, "Crazy for You." On the left corner was the word "Drayton." *Crazy for you?*

The ticket said the play was produced by Drayton Productions—yes, another Drayton—but the name was the same. The date: October 24, 2007, the evening Thomas left this world to journey to the heavens beyond.

I laughed. So much like Thomas to slip that one by me. I have kept the ticket, of course.

I love you Thomas. I'm crazy for you, too!

∾∾✴∾∾

Here is an example from Mike Dyer of how to use the HU and how to call upon your inner spiritual guide in times of trouble. The Fifth Key says: You do not direct the sound at anyone; you use it to gain an understanding or to protect yourself (5:5).

I Kept on Singing HU
By Mike Dyer

The sun was shining on this Saturday morning in Quito, Ecuador, where I live. I was traveling by taxi to the intersection where I could catch a bus the rest of the way home. When we came to the corner, I paid the cab driver and started to open the door. Two things happened: first, the cab driver yelled, *"Pare!"* (Stop!) and second, a van came whizzing by from behind and munched the door.

Fortunately I was not hurt, but the cab door was a mess, and so was the fender of the brand-new van.

Now I must explain some things about this particular corner and about Ecuador. The corner has some shops and a parking lot, so there was space to "cut the corner" through the parking area. This is what the van did. And because there is no universal auto insurance in Ecuador, the police must be called to decide who is to pay for an accident.

Immediately after the van hit the door, the driver, a young

well-dressed Ecuadorian man, jumped out, ran over to me and yelled in my face, "Gringo! Gringo! *El necessito á pagar todo!*" (He needs to pay for everything!)

I said one thing to him, in a quiet voice, "*Pero, usted corta la esquina.*" (But you cut the corner.) He began yelling some more and I began to sing HU, silently. But I could see this might be a rough time.

Then, a surprising thing happened. The people on the corner, bystanders, maybe eight or ten of them, began arguing with the wealthy Ecuadorian man. They were defending me! How could I be at fault when he cut the corner?

The police came, two of them, and collected everyone's identification, including a copy of my American passport and my Oregon driver's license. Then began a long discussion to try to determine fault, and who should pay.

I simply kept singing HU and silently watched. I think they didn't interview me because they didn't think I could speak Spanish. I told them I was not a tourist, but was a missionary living in Ecuador.

The tide seemed to swing one way and then the other, between me, the driver of the van, and the taxi driver. I was amazed to see that the bystanders kept on defending me to the police. It proved to be such a Gordian knot, that the supervisors were called in. And the wealthy Ecuadorian brought in his lawyer.

I kept on singing HU.

Eventually, after about an hour, the supervisors decided that the taxi driver and the van driver were each at fault and should pay for their own damage. The van driver and his lawyer seemed pleased because he had insurance. But I could see that the taxi driver was devastated. I checked inside and listened carefully to the Mahanta, my inner guide, who said, "Do it!"

So I offered, without admitting fault, to pay for the damage to the taxi. "After all," said the Inner Voice, "you did open the door."

And I continued to sing HU.

Now things began to move. The police ushered me into their car, and, with the taxi driver in the lead, we began looking for car mechanics to obtain estimates for the damaged door. Maybe I'm slow, but at this point I began to get the feeling that I needed help because they wouldn't let me out of the car. I used my cell phone to call my wife Evelyn, but the phone suddenly was out of minutes. Bummer!

In that moment, my singing of HU picked up some intensity—and I asked my inner guide for help.

The police told me to stay in the car, so I did. It was decided that one hundred dollars would fix the door, and amazingly enough, I happened to have just that much with me! When I reached through the window and gave the money to the taxi driver, one of the policemen immediately took it from the taxi driver and gave it back to me. I realized something was strange. Did the police want a $100 bribe? So as the police car drove away, with me still in it, I simply reached out of the window and gave the money back to the taxi driver.

The police began to hassle me as we drove along, saying they were going to take me to immigration because I didn't have my passport with me. (True, but I had a copy. Nobody in their right mind carries their passport around Quito). Things seemed to be getting sticky, when all of a sudden, my cell phone rang. It was my wife!

Evelyn had been in the middle of a session with a client, when she heard a voice inside her say, "Call Mike—now!" So she did.

The policeman talked for about two minutes with Evelyn, who speaks perfect Spanish, during which she had a few choice words to say about the legality of my documents (they are legal) and what they were doing. Among other things, she said, "My husband is not a tourist. He is a missionary and what you are doing is illegal." They immediately let me go.

Suddenly it was all over and I was very grateful to my inner guide and to the protection of the HU.

✥✥✳✥✥

We have an intimate connection to nature and Mother Earth, but most of the time we don't recognize this reverent bond. By seeing through the eyes of Soul, we become skilled at seeing the messages that Spirit sends us. Many messages are given to us through Earth's animals—they are our guides, healers, and friends. Dr. Ingrid Pincott, N.D., tells us a story involving animal signs that came to her after her mother passed away.

Soul Messages from Animals
By Ingrid Pincott

My mother's name was Kristjana Signy Arnason. Everyone knew her as Signy. She was told that "signy" meant swan in Icelandic. During my mother's birth, her mother experienced visions of swans, and the symbol had stuck with her all her life. Ever since Mom passed away, my sister and I have had visions of white trumpeter swans in great numbers flying over head or resting in fields getting ready to migrate north.

In spirit animal medicine, based on ancient Native American wisdom, the symbol of the swan is the most powerful of ancient totems. It is one of the oldest names in the English language and is unchanged since Anglo-Saxon times. The neck of the swan is long and graceful and symbolizes a bridge between the head (higher realms) and the body (lower realms), which is certainly the philosophy that my mother followed. "As above so below," is what she always reminded us. The ability to bridge the outer and inner worlds, and see the beauty within yourself, regardless of your outer appearance is what the swan totem represents. This is also reflected in the story of *The Ugly Duckling*. True to her given name, Mom always tried to awaken in others the realization of their own inner beauty.

The moment we stepped out of the hospital, after Mom died, the first sound we heard was the proclamation of a robin from high in a neighboring tree. But it was pitch black outside! I have never heard a robin sing when it was still dark. For me, the robin symbolizes new growth and a traditional herald of spring. When a robin comes into my life I can expect new growth to occur in a variety of areas in my life. The heart of the robin is the symbol of a strong creative force. Since then, every time I hear a robin sing with strength and conviction, I am reminded of Mom and stop and think a moment of what words of wisdom she might have for me.

A few moments later, while waiting for tea at a local restaurant, a Siberian husky dog in the back of a neighboring pickup truck took that moment to let out a wolf-like howl, transmitting another message from Mom. According to wolf medicine, the wolf can help you to hear the inner and teaches that we are the governors of our lives. We create it and direct it. One of the things Mom would say over and over again was, "We create our own messes so we have to get ourselves out of them!"

My mother's other maiden name, "Arne" in Arnason, means Eagle, a symbol of great power and a totem of accepting a heightened responsibility for your spiritual growth. When I see an eagle it reminds me of my higher self. Recently, I was putting away a few things in an armoire that was completely empty except for one piece of white paper. When I turned it over there was a painting of an eagle on the other side. I felt Mom was telling me through that painting, that even though I was doing mundane things, my work was really of a heavenly nature.

Seeing and hearing all these birds and animals after my mother's passing gave me great comfort. I knew they represented my mother's call to me from the higher worlds of Spirit. They were messages of love and comfort.

I have a sense that Spirit will continue to speak to me through visions and animals, to remind me of what I am supposed to be doing with my life. Each experience with an animal points to a spiritual meaning or life lesson that Mom would have taught me. In the days after her passing, the loon, the sea lion, the eagle, the raven, the wolf-dog, the Great Blue Heron and the robin have spoken to me.

If you hear a robin sing, or a flock of trumpeter swans overhead, or the haunting cry of a loon, stop and listen to what your heart is telling you. At that moment, Soul is speaking directly to you.

ঞ্চ✦ঞ্চ

FIFTH KEY EXERCISE

 ## See the Bigger Picture

Here is a technique for the Fifth Key to connect you with Soul consciousness so you can see the bigger picture and make informed decisions.

1. Choose a comfortable seat and close your eyes. Sing HU or a favorite word to yourself, quietly listening to your breathing, letting the sound shield exterior noises. Gently envision your spiritual Third Eye, and feel it opening like a camera lens.

2. Rise up. Feel yourself stepping out of your physical body and floating up above your head. You may use the image of riding in a hot air balloon. See yourself in the basket as it rises above the ground or floating up at play in a wondrous sea of light and sound.

3. Imagine looking out of Soul's magical all-seeing eye from a 360-degree perspective onto your world; observe what is happening. What is your body doing there on the ground? Are you at work, in a coffee shop, or in bed? Who is nearby? How do they affect you energetically? Are they emanating a positive or a negative charge? Are they withdrawing your energy or sharing energy? Are you in danger? Looking down through Soul's eye, you can instantly see a way out of the situation!

4. People have used this technique in the middle of a war zone, using the art of inner travel to see a way out, keeping them safe. See how you can alter or change your circumstances or conditions for the benefit of all by looking through the eyes of Soul.

Now it's time to take your first step onto the path of the Spiritual Warrior—learning how to help others, help others.

SIXTH KEY:
LIVE TO LIVE IN SPIRIT

1. Live to Live in Spirit! To live in Spirit means to live in the NOW and to be ready for change by living consciously, using the guidance of Living Energy. Living Energy is the true reality. The rest is illusion.
2. Recognize that Soul Energy is a part of Living Energy and exists in all things. No matter what you call it, this universal current of light and sound originated and shaped creation. This is ancient knowledge from our ancestors.
3. Fulfill your obligation as a Being of Light. Your obligation is to spiritualize your consciousness, releasing distractions, and to assist others in their discovery of Soul.
4. Living in Spirit does not mean living in isolation; it does not necessarily mean giving up your comforts; part of it is about giving service and helping others.
5. To Live 2 Live in Spirit is to live with humility in an attempt to live the karmaless life.
6. Spiritual Warriors accept who they are, luminous Beings of Light, and embrace divine service by doing everything in the name of divine love. This is an intentional embrace, living a life of conscious freedom, passion, and purpose.

(6:1 to 6:6)

L IKE A WILD HORSE ON THE OPEN PLAINS, we yearn to be free and to live in conscious freedom, awakening Soul to the reality of living consciously every day. The Third and Sixth Keys introduce you to the realm of the Spiritual Warrior, to the Kids of the New Earth, and how to LIVE TO LIVE®. In this chapter there's also a dare.

We Are Powerful Beings

Do you know how powerful you truly are when you live consciously, knowing you are Soul? Do you remember that you can change the world by changing *your* world? You have the capacity and strength to become a Spiritual Warrior. When you Live to Live you exist in the present moment. You experience the NOW. You add *life* to life. When you are no longer adding to life, you are in a state of dying because you are no longer *giving*. The present moment is perfect because it is as it is, and exists so we can truly live *in* it.

Live as Children of Light

When you live in the NOW, living consciously awake, the present moment becomes life itself and you begin to notice everything. You hear your breathing, the sounds in your inner ear, the birds, and the rush of life. At times you can catch a glimpse of the luminous Soul Energy by squinting your eyes at a living plant, or at your fingertips. A long time ago as a child, I happened upon this technique quite naturally; then years later I was reminded of it when I read *The Celestine Prophecy* by James Redfield.[56]

Here's another technique that I learned from my Qigong Master: Rub your hands together quickly. Now place them together in prayer, and draw them apart about half an inch. Slowly move your palms in and out. Can you feel the energy and warmth radiating between your palms? Can you see the wavering light energy? Practicing this, you will begin to see the living life force more and more. It is all around you. You're swimming in it right now. Humans are evolving into a new species who can see this Soul Energy in all things; it is part of our awakening to a new consciousness.

This universal Living or Soul Energy is known as *Qi* (also spelled *ch'i*) in Chinese and *ki* in Japanese. In Sanskrit and Hindi it is called *shakti* meaning force, power, or energy of the Divine Mother. Buddhists and Taoists believe that *Qi* is a part of everything that exists: a life force, spiritual energy, or energy flow. American filmmaker George Lucas called it "the Force." Many authors have written about how to develop this extraordinary energy I call Living Energy and Soul Energy.

One night my Qigong master showed the class the power of Living Energy. He chose a young, strong and much taller classmate, who had a black belt in Kung Fu. He told him to resist with all his might. The young man stood like a mountain, ready for anything. My Qigong master, a little man about my size, went up to him and placed his hands up to the man's chest level but did *not* touch him. Suddenly, the young man catapulted backward almost hitting the wall. That is powerful energy.

The universal current of light and sound is a powerful force which created all things and exists in all things. The light "lights" the pathway; the sound calls you home. If it is in everything, it is also in the parallel worlds; therefore, you are not separate from these unseen worlds. The Otherworlds are just as much a part of you as the Earth plane world. When entering the inner worlds, you will need to be aware of the matrix of energy all around you. Soul Energy is part of the great river of life that passes through you and resides inside you, making you one with the Living Energy. You are a spark of this living Luminous Energy Field, living as a child of light.

Many belief systems and religions believe that you, as Soul, are a spark of God. The Bible says, "Live as children of light" (Ephesians 5:8). The name Buddha means "the man with a light" and the light is the light of truth. You sense this light when your heart is at peace. You hear the inner sound when you turn off the noise to listen. We are learning how to become *Homo luminous* and to develop our intuitive senses, so that in times of great change and chaos we can instantly center ourselves and "see" or "hear" Soul messages. We are training our Third Eye and stepping into the next level of collective consciousness and a new worldview.

Living in Conscious Freedom

We have forgotten that living in conscious freedom is like swimming in an ocean of magical light and sound at all times. Living with an awakened heart and by the guidance of Soul Energy every moment does not mean living like a monk in isolation, or giving up your comforts. To Live to Live (or, Live 2 Live) means to fulfill your obligation as the wonderful Being of Light that you are. Recognize that Living Energy is in all things and is the source of all things. It will direct your life—if you are flexible. To survive as a planetary community, we need to cultivate unconditional love and accept our powerful beingness, living with humility, compassion, and freedom. By spiritualizing the way you think, act, and feel, you will change your life and, in doing so, receive more contentment and wellness than you could ever have imagined.

When you Live to Live in Spirit, you live life as a conscious, whole being. You are not withdrawing from life and you are respecting the divine rights of all people. If you are asked about your dream travel experiences, sharing your stories will help others on their journey. But you also share your wisdom simply by living your life and showing them the changes you've made for the better. As a Key Guardian and Spiritual Warrior in training, you can assist others in unlocking the secret path by showing them how you Live to Live by right action, as long as you practice non-interference.

Be Open to Change

Life is continual change. Have you noticed how more and more people, especially strangers, want to exchange stories and feelings when dealing with major life changes? As we get older, many of us go in search of our immortality and we choose to express this passage of change in our own individual ways.

On weekends I work as a receptionist at a real estate company.

Usually, the real estate agents I work with are pragmatic and realistic, not given to thoughts of what happens after they die. But lately, many of their parents are dying, part of the World War II "age wave"[57] generation which is leaving the planet in droves because it's their time. These hard-working, career-focused real estate agents are pausing to take a look at their own mortality. They are slowly realizing that there is, indeed, more to life.

Several of the agents who come and go on the weekend stop to chat with me. Some talk about life and death and rebirth. One realtor told me that her mother, who is in a coma, suddenly opened her eyes and started talking to her dead husband. When she had finished speaking, the older woman shut her eyes and went back into the coma. The bedside relatives were astounded. Another realtor told me how his father, moments before he died, saw his wife and their dog at the end of the bed, both long since dead. They were waiting for him, and he could see them as plain as day, he said.

Even though many films try to convince us that the afterlife is scary and horrific, according to most out-of-body reports, it is not. Glimpses into the worlds beyond are quite common, especially for those Souls on their way to join loved ones who have gone before them. Life is a swinging door with Souls traveling in and out. If you practice inner dream travel, you already know how amazing it is.

As I age, I find myself letting go of limiting beliefs. I am actually growing younger, returning to the free mind I once had as a child. Many people become set in their ways as they age, or so we're taught to believe; but for me, that is not the case. The more I age the more I connect with Soul and, thus, to conscious freedom. I love growing older!

Stand Up and Be Heard

We are powerful beings, but how do we use that in our daily life? Let's look at an everyday occurrence in a kid's life. For example, have you ever been bullied?

Kids don't realize the power they have over older kids or adults. Kids are powerful beings with the clout of the law on their side. Bullying or making inappropriate advances toward a child is illegal.

If you accept your situation—I am being bullied—instead of collapsing into it, you gain power over your aggressor. By accepting that what's happening to you is wrong, you can learn to take charge of the situation, to stand up and be heard. But you need to learn that you are allowed to do so: you are allowed to seek help in public; you are allowed to talk back, to yell and make lots of noise; and you are allowed to say "NO!" You are allowed to change into the powerful person you really are! How do you do this? You listen to what your inner voice of Soul is telling you to do in the moment.

Author and speaker Brock Tully [www.kindacts.net] says, "People think something is wrong with them, but there isn't. Something is wrong with the bully." Often bullies harass students out of envy.

Birth of Our New HUmanity

The title *Universal Tides* refers to the *living* body of water that touches every land mass: the action of waves pulling away the old and bringing into shore the new. There is a scene in *Utides* where the heroes are trapped in a subterranean tunnel. They must escape to the other side before the tunnel collapses. The tunnel represents our birth canal to a new life. At the end of the birth canal is an opening into a new humanity, a new age. As our old political structures, greed wars, and aggressive ways cave in, the old way of doing things is cut-off. We can't go back because the way is blocked. And so we struggle toward accepting the changes that recognize our divinity on the new Earth. It involves a revolution of the heart, an uprising of Soul, and becoming a Spiritual Warrior in the divine service—an intentional embrace.

The **outlanders** in *Utides* are fringe-dwellers, living on the edge of society with the purpose of saving the planet. They know there is something more to life than what they're told. They believe in living a life of freedom, passion, and purpose. During the Spiritual (R)evolution they become proficient dream travelers, standing up for Spirit! Our new humanity is centered in living with love, kindness, and compassion, and hopefully something similar to the 12 Golden Keys or the Spiritual Warrior Codes.

From Caterpillar to Butterfly

There is nothing in a caterpillar that tells you it's going to be a butterfly. What the caterpillar sees as the end of the world, the spiritual master sees as the butterfly.

The **Kids of the New Earth (KONE)** are at the forefront of a movement to forge a new planetary awareness.[58] KONE represents the growing number of children, teenagers, and young adults who are forming their own communities, the reasons for which they will soon realize. They already have a spiritual toolbox residing in their DNA; all they have to do is remember their purpose.

No matter what the present date, if you're a child or a youth (from birth to late-20s), you were born with the latest DNA to survive in the present era. This means you are automatically a KONE, a child of this new Age of Consciousness. The Age of Consciousness is a spiritual-survival age during which the KONE and others live in conscious freedom, fully aware of their divinity, knowing they are Soul, divine Beings of Light.

What has taken others decades to cultivate, you were born with in your genetic codes. If you were a computer, you would be running the latest program. Now new energies are lighting up in your ever-reforming cellular makeup, and even though you struggle, all you need to do is *remember* and *focus* on why you've come here to this planet at this particular time. Why believe negative people who pit our own fears against us for their own monetary gain, especially when they tell you it is hopeless? No matter what happens, you have the capacity to live and to change things. YOU are the Key.

We are Beings of Light, beings who are one with Living Energy in a cosmic community. The KONE are at the forefront of this new movement; yet, we *each* have a spiritual toolbox residing in our DNA. Practicing the 12 Golden Keys will help you remember and upload the latest energy matrix in order to take your place in the new world age. It's important to know that no one is meant to be perfect in this physical realm, so forgive yourself as you walk the path. Underneath your man-made armor you are a perfect being, and we are learning to remember to be all we are intended to be.

Be at Home in Your World

As I write, I gaze at a photograph of my niece traveling some-where on holiday with her mother. It doesn't matter to me where

My niece in Angkor Wat, Cambodia. Photo by Carol Milne, 2003.

they are. The point is, she is in a land far removed from her normal surroundings, and yet she looks totally at home—she is a true child of the new world. She arrived on this planet with the tools she would need to survive. What took me a lifetime to acquire, she was born with, fully loaded with all the spiritual survival programs embedded in her DNA. And like those of each young generation, she needs a plug 'n play mechanism to get started, toggling the cursor erratically at first, until the ever-present pinpoint of light opens her Third Eye and she awakens to her own individual truth. It is at this moment that she can light up with a trillion stars lined up behind, guiding her onward.

Kids of the New Earth (KONE)

As the new energies proliferate, changing our very cellular make-up, there is an emerging global culture. The KONE are today's new HUman who, unlike their numbed-down counterparts, have already made the shift to the new planetary consciousness. These new-consciousness children, and many adults as well, have shifted their consciousness to accept the new luminous energies.

From a young reader of *Universal Tides: Barbed Wire Blues*: This young man in his twenties believes, as do thousands of others, in the new world.

> *I am from Ohio in the United States. I hope that* Universal Tides *gets a big following in the US; this country really needs a spiritual revolution. Sometimes you feel helpless here in America. There are a lot of people who just really don't care about Soul. When you talk about it they look at you like you're crazy. Believe me I've been called all the names. But you know what, I don't care, at least they got the chance to encounter the truth. What they do with it is up to them. Tell the Spiritual Warriors not to give up. It's a very tough road and sometimes very lonely. Friends and family will be against you, but you must speak your truth …. This is no longer a game; it's a battle between the Lightside and Darkside. We must prevail.*
>
> – N. F., May 4, 2007

The world youth's sense of community with their own kind is awe-inspiring. The Kids of the New Earth have banded together, becoming a support network for one another; they are the true outlanders of society. Many of them acknowledge they are already fully awake. They have walked through hell and fought their inner demons, cried many tears, realized their fears, struggled to hold on, and are now prepared for a major turning point in their life. They finally get it.

"Children born since around 1982 really are different, like no other generation of record," notes P. M. H. Atwater, part of the movement to get rid of labels describing these children, such as

Indigo Children, Star Kids, and Crystal Children. Atwater goes on to say that many teachers have quit teaching because they can't deal with the supposed lazy, rude, disinterested kids in their classes. It's the worst it's ever been, they say.[59]

I wonder if the teachers realize that many youth work two jobs, sometimes three, and have amazing drive and energy. These youth are survivors, trying to survive the best way they can. I watch my niece and her friends work at two different part-time jobs while going to college. They struggle with monetary survival, but they have banded together, helping one another. They may come from different lands and speak different languages, but they are the same Soul Energy. Know that you are not alone!

What teachers and many parents have missed is the rise of dyslexia in kids today. Christine Gorman, health columnist in *TIME* magazine for 22 years, offers this comment,

> *Dyslexics are over-represented in the top ranks of artists, scientists and business executives.... They talk about the ability to see things in 3-D or as a multidimensional chess game. It may also be that their early struggle with reading better prepared them for dealing with adversity in a volatile, fast-changing world.*[60]

I haven't researched whether the youth of today are either dyslexic, autistic, or Indigo children, so I don't know; but I do know there's much more to the story, and it's about survival. It has to do with seeing through the veil into the Otherworlds and, also, reincarnation.

An example of the latter is the amazingly talented twelve-year-old girl who entered *Britain's Got Talent 2008* contest and blew the judges off their seats. Everyone in the large theater, including the judges, were amazed at the seasoned operatic voice that came out of this thin, small girl. There is no explanation for her well-developed operatic talent other than she is a re-incarnation of a famous opera singer.

Another possible explanation for her well-developed talent is that she is a crossover from a multidimensional realm, similar to another young boy.

Two Advanced Souls

I have heard there is a young boy who lives in the Volgograd area of Russia who has total recall of his past life on Mars and of the times he visited the ancient Earth city of Lemuria. At age four, his knowledge of history and several languages was extraordinary. Today, the boy from Mars believes that children are born with special abilities because of the coming changes to the planet. An eminent professor who conducts research into Indigo Children has studied the boy. The professor now believes that these children are here on this planet for a reason: To help in the development of a future Earth civilization.[61]

What I found most striking about the stories of this boy is the way he so easily talked about the afterlife, of not being afraid of death, and about multidimensional space. The boy is likely a very old Soul, and one of the children who were born for the purpose of assisting us in our planetary transformation. He tells of a pole shift on Earth in 2013. When asked if he is afraid, he answered that he had no fear of death because we live eternally. Living fully in the moment as an eternal being is what matters most.

Here is another example of a Soul already living in full conscious awareness. Eighteen-year-old Violet is bored with insipid adults. In fact, she's more adult than the adults she has to deal with all day. She's a brilliant artist who is out in the world eating up knowledge. She's also not from this world.

According to her homeopath, Violet arrived in full conscious awareness that she is an advanced Soul. Compared to us, she's totally dialed-in. This is because she arrived on the planet long before the new energies were set in place. It's as if she's running on an accelerated time program, waiting for the rest of us to catch up. Daily life has accelerated. Have you noticed your life speeding up? Everything is faster! You have to live your life ten times faster to keep up. Violet is already living in this faster time track.

No wonder her parents can't handle her; they don't understand what's happening. So since childhood, on the advice of a well-intentioned medical doctor, they put her on every nervous system suppression drug they could find. Her homeopath is helping her withdraw from legal prescription drugs.

Violet is trying to figure out what's happening on the planet. She's trying to fit in, but she can't. She sees through inauthentic behavior, but she's vulnerable. She's trying to find others like her so she can enjoy living here while in a higher level of conscious freedom. She is in a position of accelerated spiritual awareness, meaning she can instantly open her mind and Third Eye to access the spiritual knowledge that already resides inside her. If Violet and other KONE kids can do this, then so can you, by practicing the 12 Key exercises herein.

By becoming skilled in this new way of living you can learn to navigate in a new, expanded consciousness. Many people can access spiritual knowledge, but they are unaware of it and/or refuse to believe it, having been taught to disbelieve or distrust Soul messages. Let that go now. Turn off the propaganda blinders. Take charge and be a Christopher Columbus navigating in search of another new world. We don't need to hide anymore. We can shine our luminescent light. It's time to no longer be afraid to speak your truth. You are now safe to be who you are, a Being of Light. Start your own KONE support community in your neighborhood. Invent it. You will amaze yourselves!

GenNEXT Syzygy

After World War II, advertisers tagged the generations with names so they could target them with marketing campaigns: Baby Boomers (born after 1947), Generation X (born between 1964 and 1983), Generation Y (born after 1983), and the Echo Boomers (children of the Baby Boomers, born between the late 1970s and the early 1990s). Eric Greenberg, with Karl Weber, in *Generation WE* (Pachatusan, 2008), says the Echo Boomers, or millennial generation, are the largest generation in American history. Born between 1978 and 2000, they are 95 million strong, compared to the 78 million Baby Boomers.

To confuse the marketers, let's call this newest generation GenNEXT. To me, GenNEXT means those who accept the best and go to the next step, living in the present moment. Today's galactic GenNEXT are at the forefront of this global culture of mixed races. They are becoming a multicultural *syzygy*, which signifies unity-friendship-community.[62] You can build your own syzygy circle and create a new world order of peace and coherence. A Hopi Indian prophecy speaks about this emerging planetary cultural hybrid. It said:

> *When the Earth is sick and the animals have disappeared, there shall come a new tribe formed from all cultures and all races, to heal the earth. This tribe shall be called the Warriors of the Rainbow.*[63]

The Sixth Key asks us to remember that we are Spiritual Warriors in the divine service (6:6). The new tribe of youth are the outlanders that Skip speaks about in *Utides* who bring about a Spiritual (R)evolution, performing a divine service.[64] They become the Thirteenth Tribe, created from the union of the twelve tribes or races in existence on planet Earth. They bring to life the symbiotic syzygy circle or, as the Hopi prophecy of the Rainbow Warriors said, a "unity in diversity." We live in a time of great cultural diversity, witnessing the co-existence of the coming global unification. We can now see what's on the other side of the bridge that we are meant to cross.

Buddhist monk Thich Nhat Hanh says, "The next Buddha may not be an individual, but an enlightened community."[65]

Don't Die Before You Die

I watch today's youth struggle with their reconnection to Soul, not to mention worrying about work, money, and finding a loving relationship. I know of many young adults who feel lost because they lack the connection to themselves, to Soul. Many youth try to survive in abusive family situations, while others are learning to survive on the streets. Some troubled young adults indulge in chemical drugs such as *meth* (crystal methamphetamine), drugs created for the purpose of keeping the youth of the world numb. They trade their freedom to connect to Soul Energy for enslavement.

> ### Inner Message to the World Youth:
> *Don't let them enslave you. Retain your freedom.*
> *Why be so willing to be controlled or to control others?*
> *Find a way to get free and live your own life, and help others.*
> *LIVE TO LIVE!*
> *(See the First Key: You Are the Key)*

The Sixth Key says to Live to Live by fulfilling our obligation to help others in their discovery of Soul Energy (6:3). In today's world of media hype and negative influences, the sleeping members of the present generation must raise their consciousness or they will remain numb, asleep at the wheel. How can we spiritualize our consciousness if we continually bombard ourselves with distractions? After all, it is our choice.

I'm convinced that modern drugs were invented for the sole purpose of keeping the youth numb and silent, as were the opium dens in the late 1800s. For those who want to control us, drugs serve a specific purpose. Today's controlled media would have you believe that *all* the young celebrities go to drug and alcohol rehab. But realistically, there are only a few who risk ruining their careers, preferring to live a clean and healthy lifestyle because they want to live longer. This is part of the new world consciousness.

Suicide among young adults can be linked to self-isolation, to long periods alone at the computer, or to negatively-based activities such as playing violent video games in an isolated environment. Cocooning, as Fay Popcorn called it in the 1990s, can create a sense of hopelessness because of alienation from society, feeling alone. When love of one's self is hidden, hopelessness takes over, breaking down mind and body.

There is a flip side to cocooning. When you are isolated from the world because you are creating a piece of art, or working, or corresponding and connecting with people around the world via the Internet, or text messaging, etc., you are still cocooning. However, if it gives you contentment, instead of hopelessness, then it does not manifest a negative result.

Cocooning and alienation can be complicated by the use of alcohol, anti-depressants, and chemically-addictive drugs. The false power that crystal meth (ice) and other chemical drugs give the user wears down the body and eventually kills. You can save yourself years of difficult disentanglement simply by not trying it. Why die before you die, when you can Live to Live? Help one another steer clear of drugs. Help raise one another up into the new world consciousness.

Inner Message to the World Youth:
If you let yourself become negative, you close the door
to the love that we give you and it can't come in.

When we are trying to escape something, what we need is to be loved. Instead of relying on outer dependencies, rely on your inner connection and spiritual guides (Third Key). You can go on a natural high simply by inner traveling! And what a trip it is. But it cannot work when you're on drugs.

The 12 Golden Keys can assist those on the road to higher consciousness, but it is known that using drugs delays your spiritual development and keeps the gateway to enlightenment locked shut. To use drugs for spirituality is like strapping rocks on to one wing so you can only fly in one direction, if you get off the ground at all. Addictive drugs or any addiction of any kind is not recommended for your spiritual evolution. I dare you to get high on divine love. Rise up and move on!

Inner Message to the World Youth:
To Live is to Give. To Give is to Live.
Proverb: If you want happiness for a lifetime,
help the next generation.

When helping your friends, one kind word can change someone's life. Divine love is an energy and it's contagious. Remember, you are a powerful being, and when you steer unconditional love toward another human being, that loving energy boomerangs back to you as well. To Live to Live means fulfilling your obligation as a Being of Light by assisting others in their discovery of conscious freedom. It means to recognize that Living Energy is in all things. Consider using it for your own benefit and for the benefit of others. When you help to improve the world, it benefits you, too!

> *Rise Up! You are the New Human!*
> *Helping Others Help Themselves.*
> *Helping Others Help Others.*
> *Helping One Another.*

Spiritual Warrior Code:

If you live to serve life,
you will have lived a life of purpose.

Stop the Neg!

Here's an exercise to help you filter negativity, raising your consciousness. Consider placing the image of the Blue Star or your Key Guardian (inner guide) in front of you at all times. Or perhaps envision that she or he always walks beside you. Imagine all your actions have to pass through your guide first. So that you put nothing out into the world that can boomerang back to you with a negative charge. And everything that comes to you must also be filtered for your protection. You can also carry a memento in your pocket or wear a ring on your finger or an elastic band on your wrist. Whatever you choose, its purpose is to remind you to filter negativity. Stop the neg!

The Live-2-Live-In-Spirit-Nation

Let us aspire to inspire others to Live to Live and not merely survive in places that hold no light. Seek the highest! When you learn how to enjoy your life, respect yourself, and create your life, you will truly Live to Live rather than just exist. Let us dare to get inspired ourselves, and then go out and inspire others. In order to help the world, we need to practice using our gifts of intuition, inspiration, and spiritual illumination.

What would happen if each one of us inspired one person a day to make one small change in their world? We would become a planet of *inspiration,* an *In-Spirit Nation,* if you will—a nation of people who live in Spirit, consciously living in the spirit of divine love (Living Energy). When you inspire someone to Live to Live you give them hope, and we become a *Live-2-Live-In-Spirit Nation.*

Simple Acts of Inspiration to Share Daily

- Lend a helping hand—friends helping friends
- Listen to someone's story, problem, or situation
- Inspire someone to find something positive in their life
- Inspire change or seeing from a positive viewpoint
- Inspire someone to step up to the plate and take part in the game of life.

> **Help Others Help Others**
> **LIVE to LIVE**
> *as an In-Spirit Nation*
> *inspiring ourselves and others to do*
> *one positive change for the world every day.*
> *Let's start a movement and share a little love!*

Helping Your Friends Help Themselves

Live to Live means fulfilling your obligation as a Being of Light. Your obligation is to spiritualize your consciousness and to assist others in their discovery of Soul. Live to Live in the present moment is key to accessing a new emerging spirituality.

Young people today are coming together in community and helping one another. They are questioning who to include in their gang—I prefer the word *pod,* similar to the social group and lovingly close relationship of whales, porpoises and dolphins.

Movies sometimes try to convince us of our separateness. I watched a film recently that is a sociological satire and psychological commentary on how people react while in a state of fear.

The question it asks is: In a survival situation, would we kill one another to keep food and water, or would we pull together and help one another survive? The film says we don't help one another. However, reality has shown us over and over again that in major traumatic experiences such as the tsunami in Indonesia, the earthquakes in Haiti and elsewhere, the bombing of the World Trade Center, and the flooding of New Orleans, that PEOPLE DO HELP ONE ANOTHER.

The film also tries to make us fear going through the portal into the Otherworlds, supporting a possible agenda to keep us afraid of the dark. Perhaps the people who think they are in control want us to fear what they don't understand, because they can't figure out how to use it against us. Ha! But they do know how to use it as disinformation and confuse us.

When you come upon such things, remember to replace fear with love, and the entire world will shift for you. Ask yourself: "How do I see myself in relation to this?" If it supports the negative, then shift your energy. See yourself in little shifts of energy, moving toward unconditional love. Then bring it HERE in the present, back home to yourself and Soul.

Just as important is helping a friend in need. If someone in your pod community needs help, the other members rush to lend a hand. My twenty-year-old niece and three of her friends decided to help the fifth member of their pod. Their friend had developed a serious bleeding ulcer from drinking too much alcohol and clearly could not stop on her own. My niece and her friends went through a period of partying and drinking until the wee hours, but all five of them took an oath to quit drinking for one month in order to help their friend stop cold turkey. It worked. By forming a small community that had a common cause, they saved her life. If you were to take that idea and build it on a grander scale, it could save the planet.

Michael Harrington who recorded talks with John Redstone, a wise Elder, told me, "The Chief used to say, I wouldn't walk across the street to help anyone ... but I'd go to the other side of the world to help someone who asked for my help."[66]

This brings us back to Robert the waiter in the Fourth Key. We're always taught not to talk to strangers. Robert and I were strangers. But after a few sentences, we were two people sharing our wisdom. Our exchange in the restaurant, however brief, helped build community. The time has come to start talking our truth about life-changing, challenging moments, and sharing our experiences and knowledge. In this way we inspire one another. In order to walk out of our self-imposed isolationism to arrive at a global village mindset, we need to realize that each of us has wisdom worth sharing. The heart of Kabbalah wisdom, a branch of Jewish Mysticism, is to achieve oneness with the Creator, the Source of all joy and fulfillment, but the only way to do this is by sharing.

Live to Live and Travel

I remember when my middle sister, Carol Milne, left for her two-year-round-the-world trip. She took with her only a small packsack. She traveled on her own for most of the two years, but would meet up with friends and people along the way in far off, distant lands. Her trip through Africa was her most memorable, she said. Here is a photograph of her helping a group of African women that is especially telling. It was taken in 1985 in Mali, on the horn of West Africa next to upper Volta, Togo, Senegal.

My sister, Carol Milne, in Mali, Dogon country, 1985.

On the photograph is written *Hiking 3 days to this village. Mali, Dogon country.* The Dogon were an isolated tribe. And yet, Carol looks right at home performing a chore amongst the village women. The only division between them is our own perception.

To become community members of the global world shift, we are meant to connect, travel, and experience each other. The KONE are unafraid to travel. From the streets of New York City to the beaches of Borneo, the world they know has become their small global village. Everyone is connected digitally through technological highways. There is a new multicultural mix happening, a mass migration of people. Isolationism has ended. We are coming together.

This planet is beautiful. Enjoy it responsibly while you can. Be at play in this wondrous sea of light and sound—the twin aspects of Living Energy. Live to Live! And travel. Get to know your planet—it is your community.

A revolution is underway because people are realizing that our needs can be met without destroying our world. We have the technical knowledge, the communication tools, and material resources to grow enough food, ensure clean air and water, and meet rational energy needs. Future generations, if there is a livable world for them, will look back at the epochal transition we are making to a life-sustaining society. And they may well call this the time of the Great Turning. It is happening now.
—Joanna Macy[67]

Halfway across the Gap

Life is sometimes like trying to get across an abyss. You can suddenly find yourself halfway along a rope that hangs across a deep valley gorge. You are strapped into the hanging gear and then pushed off, sliding along the rope on a wonderful downhill ride. Now you have stopped in the middle, halfway, the weight of your body pulls the rope downward into a deep V. You hang upside-down, scared out of your wits, looking down at the gorge below, and wondering how am I going to pull myself across? There is no one who can help you. Yelling from across the gorge are those who have already made it. They encourage you to keep going, "You can do it!" they yell. But it's all uphill from now on. Do you have the strength to keep going? The answer is a resounding YES. Find that strength inside yourself! You are halfway through the 12 Golden Keys. Keep going! Keep growing!

❧❧★❧❧

SIXTH KEY STORIES

To help illustrate the Sixth Key, I interviewed Squamish Elder Mazie Baker who had sage advice for the Kids of the New Earth.

Be Proud of Who You Are
By Mazie Baker, as told to M. J. Milne[68]

Mazie Baker is a seventy-nine-year-old Indian, a mother, grandmother, an Elder of the Squamish Nation, and a political activist. The Squamish Nation is an amalgamation of Coast Salish bands from Greater Vancouver, Burrard Inlet, and Howe Sound on the west coast of British Columbia, composed of approximately 3500 members. Mazie Baker is concerned about a lot of things, especially political, but she's very worried about the youth of her nation and also of the world. She has nine children by birth, seventeen grandchildren, and twenty-one great grandchildren— that's forty-seven children! All of them seek out her advice in times of trouble.

When I asked Mazie Baker what she thought of today's youth, this is what she said:

The kids of today are so lost. Kids are getting lost with alcohol and drugs, and no education. If you have a chance to get some education, do it. It will see you through your entire life.

I teach the kids that, no matter what you do, you have the right to say yes or no. "No" is the hardest word to say. You *do* have the mind to say "No." So say "No, I don't want that drink." Say no.

The parents are not home for the kids, the young

people. Money comes first, not the family. The parents aren't there to deal with the problem right then and there. Or else they shove the kids off to a movie or to daycare. They're missing all the days together.

To be an Elder is about being a teacher. We need to use some of the band money for the education of our youth. Our youth need money for education. The Elders of the Squamish are not teaching our young people. They say they're training Junior Elders—that's what they call them—but I don't agree with it. As soon as you turn fifty-five-years old you automatically become a Junior Elder, even if you don't have any people skills or know anything about the council meetings.

In the 1950s, I was about age twenty-one when I began attending the meetings and listening to Chief Moses Joseph and the counselors. The old-timers only allowed status card holders into the meetings. Not today. Today they let in outsiders like lawyers to come and listen. It's wrong.

But the Chiefs won't let the young people speak at the meetings. Why? We need our youth to listen to the meetings and to speak up. To learn the old ways. To learn from the Elders, and then they will know if they have it in them to become Elders. They either are an Elder or they're not, it comes naturally. We need young people who walk the talk.

I teach young people to stand up for their rights. You can't change the color of your skin. Be proud, look toward your culture. I want to tell them that to be an Elder, learn the ways of the old-timers, and listen to them. In the days to come you will need to know these things.

❧❧✶❧❧

"Poem to a Teenager"
by Jane Siberry[69]

the hardest thing I've ever done
is to stand back when I wanted to run
after your tiny, unprotected back
as you walk out into the world
steadfast, trusting
...
know that we are waiting on the other side
praying, urging you on towards safety
in this particularly perfectly difficult part
of your private journey
between you and the largesse of your soul
...
get safely through, little friend
we are nearby, waiting for you

in the end, we are all one

❧✦❧

Opportunities to do one positive thing for the world every day, like lending a helping hand to someone in need, can arise when we're least expecting it. The simple act of listening to someone's story can inspire and give hope when needed. Here, Carol Milne shares a story of how a stranger reminded her of the many homeless people.

Angels on the Eastside
By Carol Milne

Around 5:00 p.m. I emerged from a business meeting and walked through the rough Downtown Eastside area of Vancouver to my car. The car's interior and the black leather seats were hot when I climbed in, so I rolled down the windows. Out of nowhere, a woman ran up to the window, looking panicked. She had a black eye, and blood dripped onto her clothes from her bloodied nose.

"My boyfriend just beat me up!" she cried. "Can you take me to the hospital? I have no money and no way of getting there." She looked like a homeless person and was very pregnant.

Without thinking about it, I told her to get in.

As I started to drive to the hospital, she said, "Could you please just stop by my place? I have to pay the rest of my rent or the landlord will kick me out. And when I come back from the hospital I won't have any place to go." She also said she was short on cash for the rent.

"How much more do you need to pay the bill?" I want to believe in the honesty of people, but I was suspicious.

"I just need twenty dollars."

I gave her a twenty-dollar bill. She seemed surprised, but took it, of course. If someone is in trouble and I feel I can help them, then I will. Perhaps it comes from my being a global traveler, where I've had to count on the kindness of strangers for many things, especially when I've traveled alone. I also have to count on my intuition to keep me out of trouble.

Minutes later, we pulled up at a locked-down tenement building, with bars on the doors and windows. She buzzed. I thought to myself: Okay, what's going on here? Why doesn't she have a key or a code? Finally someone let her in.

Waiting, I made a few phone calls, a bit nervous in this run-down area at Hastings and Main. Then I noticed her coming out of a grocery store, carrying two cans of pop and some chips. She ducked into the alley, out of sight. After several minutes, she reappeared and got into my car.

"You didn't pay your rent, did you?" I asked.

"No, I'm so sorry," she said.

"You bought drugs with the twenty dollars?"

"Yeah, I know, I can't help myself," she said. "Here you are, such an angel for letting me in your car an' driving me around, an' I didn't think really anybody would do that. An' I feel really bad that I've lied to you, but I'm addicted."

This led to a long conversation about her drug addiction, her HIV status, her life with a violent boyfriend, and how she shouldn't be taking drugs during her pregnancy.

"Your nose is still bleeding, we should go to the hospital."

"No, let's just drive and I'll show you where I really live."

She lived in a room for pregnant HIV-positive women, in a wing of Vancouver General Hospital. As we drove there, she told me her story: she'd had another child and had given it up for adoption; her old boyfriend got her addicted to heroin and she hasn't been able to stop; she lives mostly on the streets and turns tricks for money.

When we pulled up to the front entrance of the ward, she pointed to her bloodied face and said, "I'm feeling better. I can go get checked out, but as you can see, it's not really that bad. It just looks bad." Then she asked me to come upstairs for some tea, "I really want you to see my place and meet my roommates."

"No, no," I said, having spent almost two hours with her. "I have to go home now."

"Well, you've been very kind to me. I never in my wildest dreams thought someone in a fancy BMW would stop and help me. An' take the time to drive me around, an' care about me a little bit," she said.

I saw the glimmer of hope in her eyes—maybe she was thinking that not all people would treat her badly and there are still good people out there willing to help others.

"You're my little angel," she smiled, and we parted for the last time.

On the drive home, I thought to myself that I was meant to be there for her. All I had planned to do after my meeting was go home and putter around the house. I thought about what's happening in the world, how people like me who work a lot and just collect things don't actually get to touch the world every day. I realized that she was brought to me so I could remember the desperate situations life has given to some and to bring my focus back to the important things, like how to help out and pay some kindness forward. I discovered how a little bit of kindness to "pay it forward" can make all the difference in someone's life, including my own.

❧❧✱❧❧

SIXTH KEY EXERCISE

Live in the Flow

The Sixth Key exercise teaches you to live in the universal energy flow at all times. Throughout your day, envision the Living Energy and practice focusing on your breath. Use these spiritual tools for your healing, protection, and safety. You can also teach others how to do the same. In times of great trouble, these Keys to self-responsibility and self-protection are at your fingertips.

1. Get comfortable, close your eyes, and begin to sing your favorite word, focusing on your breathing in and breathing out. Behind your closed eyes, look for a pinpoint of light. Gently float toward it and through the portal of the Blue Star, leaving your physical body.
2. Envision yourself standing in the middle of a bustling city sidewalk, everyone whooshing past. Your spiritual guide or Guardian joins you and stands beside you. She or he shimmers in a light body that is composed of pure luminous Soul Energy.
3. Now look down at your hands. They are filled with healing light. Then this flow of energetic light travels up your arms and turns your entire body into glowing *Qi* or healing light energy. This is your light body. You are composed of healing Soul Energy.
4. Practice using the energy to protect yourself by slowing the flow of pedestrians on the sidewalk. Witness everything is now in slow motion and you are able to walk between the people to safety. You are invisible to them.
5. Allow your Spiritual Key Guardian to either take you somewhere, or give you a gift, either a little box that you open, or a secret word to sing, or perhaps the sword of divine protection. Pay attention. Where you go and what gift you're given is for a purpose. If you're given a word, repeat it slowly. If it's the sword of divine power, similar to the legendary Excalibur, use it wisely for your own protection to bounce

back danger with healing energy. Each gift is a powerful spiritual tool, and each must never be directed at anyone. They are meant for you alone.

6. Upon waking, write the experience in your dream journal. Try to be specific, if you can, by recalling where you went, or what you were given. Whatever you received, know you are meant to use it to Live to Live in a new world, to help you embrace a new state of lucid beingness, that state of being consciously present.

You are now in the realm of the Spiritual Warrior, and the adventure continues with the Seventh Key.

SEVENTH KEY:
LIGHTEN UP TO LIGHT UP

1. Lighten up to light up! The worlds are full of diversions to keep you from truth.
2. Mental: Detoxify your mind. Cut away the mind clutter in your path. Empty yourself of rigid thoughts, opinions, beliefs, judgments, expectations, and controlling emotions in order to be open to hear Soul. Break free by emptying the mind vessel even one day a week, so divine guidance can lead you. Place a gate keeper at the mind's entrance.
3. Physical: De-clutter your space. Get rid of the "junk" to see clearly. De-mess your life of unnecessary physical possessions and distractions for a clear focus. If you fill your life with needless things they become a burden, cosmic dust collectors.
4. Spiritual: Find your authentic self—Soul. In order to see your way clearly and get to the prize of inner truth, you have to continually let go of attachments that keep you from your true path of authenticity and a Soul-connected life. Your goal is conscious freedom—living the sacred path of the awakened heart, consciously aware.
5. Clearing Mind-Body-Spirit attachments to the old ways involves releasing the energetics and vibrations which have entered your being. To freely travel along life's journey, light your pathway with new energy by lightening up!

(7:1 to 7:5)

EFORE YOU PASS THROUGH THE SECRET GATEWAY of Soul, you need to first detoxify your mind-body-spirit of its unessential baggage. As my sister says on her website at www.lifecleanse.ca, DE-STRESS, DE-MESS, DE-TOXIFY! In this chapter we will talk about how to clear away the stress of mind overload, the mess of physical distractions, and detoxify your spirit to find balance and contentment in your life. To light up with Spirit, lighten your life.

The Mind Minotaur Matrix Game

Just for fun, think of life as a game known as The Mind Minotaur Matrix in the land of non-authenticity. Our Earth world is a labyrinth or maze. If you choose to play the game, the objective is to negotiate through the three-dimensional (3D) maze to reach your goal: conscious freedom—living the sacred path of the awakened heart, consciously aware. Usually, to walk the 3D maze, society or someone gives you a set of blinders; thus, your view is usually that which is at your feet. Or you could call it *maya*, illusion, or a veil that covers your spiritual portal or Third Eye and prevents you from seeing the truth of your origin. The veil ensures that you live encapsulated. As you journey through the labyrinth called life, you accumulate stuff to distract you from your true direction, taking you on countless side roads away from truth.

We're so brilliant at inventing distractions, disruption, and disturbance to discombobulate ourselves. The modern digital information age has created diversions designed to keep you from your true purpose. To be a true Spiritual Warrior you must learn to embrace the hungry and demanding *Mind Minotaur* and all its distractions, such as personal weaknesses, laziness, and fear. By embracing the Mind creature, you displace the garbage and fill it up with the energy of love. This is to dispel fear, and fear cannot exist in the presence of love. It's impossible because fear is the absence of love.

The labyrinth is thoroughly known. We have only to follow the thread of the hero path, and where we had thought to find an abomination, we shall find a god ... Where we had thought to travel outward, we will

come to the center of our own existence. And where we had thought to
be alone, we will be with all the world.

—Joseph Campbell, *The Power of Myth*[70]

Game Instructions for Earthlings

In order to get out of the Minotaur's maze, you have to let go of the attachments of negative influence (mind), non-nurturing things (body), and negative people (spirit). How can you do this? *De-toxify, de-clutter,* and *de-identify.*

1) De-Toxify Mind Attachments

Your first move is to frag (game-speak for "get rid of") everything from your personal space that energetically brings you down and allows the Mind Minotaur to control you. This is a bigger task than you may first imagine. In the mental-emotional realm, anything that tries to sway you, persuade you, or invade you with a negative charge needs to go. That means certain music, video games, movies, television, and peer pressure. The good news is it's within your power to get rid of them. Turn them OFF.

Choose, instead, influences that are non-controlling, those with a positive charge. As you lighten up and grow into becoming a warrior of the light, you will find yourself listening to music with a positive message, choosing television shows about hope, and reading books that help you grow.

When the Mind Minotaur is in control, we attract the negative. If you let yourself live in the negative, you close the door to love. For instance, if you worry too much, if you gossip, or if you say awful things about yourself or others, these negative frequencies will harm you. Words are magic. Be careful what you say. You can cast spells of negative magic with your words and like a boomerang the effect comes back to you. One of your core missions in life could be to give up your judgments about yourself and no longer hold yourself in contempt.

There is also power in not accepting what *others* say about you. Have you heard this saying? "What others think of you is none of your business." How freeing is that! Meeting don

Miguel Ruiz, I sensed his sincerity and found his talks and book, *The Four Agreements: A Practical Guide to Personal Freedom*,[71] very helpful in freeing myself. In one of his videos he explains how symbols in our environment create our knowledge. We are born with no symbols in our mind, but as soon as our eyes open, information floods in and our mind begins capturing other people's judgments and opinions. When we begin to unlearn all the lies we've been told, the new consciousness can enter.[72]

So doesn't it figure, that you become whatever you have around you? The energetics and vibrations of things in your immediate surroundings enter your being and hold you back from embracing the new. To spiritualize yourself in order to hear and see the inner nudges of Soul, your mind must be clear. To light your own pathway through life, lighten up!

Guardian at the Gate

Spirit dwells in the present moment. When you live in the present, you no longer judge the past actions of people. To stop negative thoughts from coming into your mind, place a gatekeeper or a Key Guardian at the mind's entrance. Imagine that your inner guide stands at a gateway of light that leads out of the maze. Across the threshold is the prize of Truth and pure Soul. The Mind Minotaur can't chase you past your Guardian, no matter how hard it tries. And neither can negative thoughts. If necessary, every time you hear someone gossip or bully you, envision yourself alongside your Guardian, using the shield of protection against such psychic attacks. Singing your favorite word also works to dissolve the negative vibration.

2) De-Clutter Your Physical Space

A second game move is to get rid of *dead attachments*, the material possessions that no longer hold a nurturing energy for you. So you're standing in front of the gateway to "heaven" and you've carried seven suitcases of cultural baggage and pushed a full shopping cart up the steep "yellow brick road." But as you go to enter the wonderful new world, you realize the gate is locked.

The Key Guardian says, "Pick one thing to take with you."

You look over everything, picking things up in the cart, opening the suitcases, but then you stop to ask, "Why? It's too hard to choose one thing."

The Key Guardian, half smiling, says, "Then take nothing."

"Nothing!?" you balk. "That's not fair, you said one thing." Still not getting it, you add, "Can I bring one suitcase?"

The Key Guardian points back down the hill and you follow the direction of his finger, until you see the Mind Minotaur hoofing it up the hill toward you.

"You'd better hurry and make a choice," the Guardian advises. You frantically toss things out of the shopping cart, one thing after another shoots out. Throwing even more out, you are finally down to one item. You hold it up, feeling the pure love it gives to you. "That one can stay," the Guardian tells you. "Now off you go!"

And the high gate opens and you walk through easily into the Otherworlds, waving to the Mind Minotaur below.

Moral of story: We can live with much less than we think, so keep those things that nurture you. The rest you don't need. They are usually things you only *think* you need.

Owning possessions is a gift of this planet. There's nothing wrong with having beautiful things, except when your attachment to these possessions becomes more important than your spiritual development. Our striving for possessions is really a desire for connection with the love of Spirit. We search for this divine love everywhere, feeling the connection but not knowing where to find it. Some people turn to religion, others to drugs, or emotionless sex, or become shopaholics. The search is the same. As a result, we are discontented, the game of life still in play, everyone searching for their connection to Soul, most unaware of what drives them.

As you grow you will discover the unimportance of inanimate objects, and instead, you will nurture the divine love of friends, family, and self. Soul needs clear focus. You may want to lighten your heavy load by keeping those things that hold loving, nurturing energy. To see how this felt, I did an experiment.

Lighten Up to Rise Up!

Once, between moves, I put all my possessions into a storage unit and lived with very little, including a bed and a desk. "Between moves" turned into two years. I never once needed to go to the storage unit for anything. In fact, I was quite happy not to have all my belongings around me. I had what was truly important to me and what I needed for my body to be comfortable.

When I moved into a larger space, the wonderful empty space was suddenly filled with all this stuff that I hadn't needed for two years. I discovered that these things, made of fluid atoms in an ocean of motion, were now heavy solid masses and blocked my breathing space, becoming dust collectors. It was an interesting experiment. As a result, I found a happy medium. Now I have only those things around me that make me feel energetically clear, elegant, and nurtured. After all, love of stuff breeds more stuff, not love.

My Chinese friends have a wonderful tradition. Every winter, usually around Chinese New Year in February, they buy a new winter coat. But, they have to give away last year's winter coat.

The Heart-Shaped Rock

 My friend Karla Joy from Washington, USA, told me this wonderful little tale: Walking along the beach in contemplation one day, she found five heart-shaped rocks. Not having room for all of them, she started giving them away. Later on, she was amazed that one of her friends had only one rock in her whole house—the heart-shaped rock—displayed prominently in the center of a beautiful, round, glass table, all alone. "It was compelling!"

Purging Junk 'n Stuff Is Fun

Now it's your turn! Look around your personal space, and ask, "Is there enough space for me to grow, or have I filled up my world with so much stuff there's no room for the new?" Then ask, "What can I let go of? What am I not currently using?"

Living in the present is using what you need now. Storage is clutter that you probably never use—junk 'n stuff hidden in boxes under our beds, in closets, storage rooms, the garage, the car's trunk. Ask yourself, Do I really need this?

Does It Nurture Me?

You might like to try a favorite Seventh Key exercise, originally suggested to me by Dejai, an intuitive. Completely empty your clothes closet onto the bed; everything, including shoes. Dump it all on top of the bed. Then wash your closet down with rose water so it's fresh and clean. Light a candle, position a mirror beside the bed, and take off all your clothes. While standing naked, take each item of clothing and hold it up to you in front of the mirror, then ask: "Does this nurture me and make me feel good about myself?"

You're looking for the first impulse. Notice if you are trying to convince yourself, saying things like, "But I just bought this, I can't give it away!" Or, "I'll wear it again when I lose weight!" If you decide it doesn't nurture you, toss it into the giveaway or for sale bin and go on to the next item. I did my entire living quarters with this technique once, it taught me a lot about why we become so possessive and unconsciously develop an emotional bondage to stuff. I related it to core issues of fear and abandonment.

This exercise becomes easier when you realize that we only wear 20% of our clothes, the other 80% just hangs in our closets for years! Let's give them away for others to enjoy!

> *You will receive everything you need when you stop asking for what you do not need.*
>
> —Nisargadatta Maharaj[73]

3) De-Identify from Inauthenticity

The third game move is to recognize and then de-identify from karmic attachments to pessimistic, inauthentic people who do not support your spiritual well-being. These are people who zap your energy. They literally feed on your energy and when they leave, you feel drained. Up front, they could be the nicest of people, but if they only take and not give, let them know or let them go! We can become so attached to certain people that we stay, even when we know the relationship is unhealthy for us. Sometimes the only way to escape is to run. *Hejira*: an Arabic word for running away honorably. Karmic attachments are strong spiritual clutter.

The opposite of this is non-attachment or detachment. It is a vital step to becoming your authentic self, as we learned in the Fifth Key (5:3). Your authentic self is who you were created to be: an ever-evolving Being of Light known as Soul. The process of reclaiming your authentic self or Soul can begin by doing the exercises at the end of each chapter. The exercises can help you see your way clearly and to recognize yourself as Soul. Once you step on the path of conscious freedom you will de-identify from the old you.

The Golden Light

Spiritual insights happen on the outer all the time and, sometimes, if we're paying attention, we hear them loud and clear. Here is an example of a waking experience that initiated a major turning point in my life, allowing me to let go of an attachment to a negative relationship, to learn how to break free and Live to Live, and to practice releasing judgments and expectations. It also allowed me to understand how energy plays a part in emotional attachment and showed me that Beings of Light come in all shapes and sizes. (This story also illustrates Key points 1:5 and 6:1, and of course, 7:2 and 7:5.)

I stood in my kitchen facing the turmoil, anxiety, and sorrow of a ten year relationship in the process of dissolution. I wasn't living. I was dead inside. And to make matters worse, I had consented to totally isolating myself from the world. We lived on a remote parcel of land overlooking the sparkling inland waterway of Indian Arm, BC. It was accessible only by boat, and if the boat wasn't working, we couldn't go anywhere. We were an isolated community of eighteen small cottages, but only half were permanent residents. I thought we were close, but found it was just talk after all.

My neighbor bludgeoned an incredibly massive 500-year old maple tree that was on communal property. He said the ancient tree was in the way of his satellite dish and disturbed his television reception. So when no one was around, he had it cut down. Another one of the beautiful ancients had been massacred. I had a spiritual connection to that maple tree. When I came home that afternoon and saw what he had done, my whole being started to quake.

While standing in my kitchen and gazing out the window at the dismembered tree, I went into a state of numbness. I had been unhappy for a long time within an emotionally abusive relationship. I knew my relationship was at an end, although I hadn't voiced it yet. The last vestiges of my relationship fell with the death of that tree. And I felt utterly crushed and destroyed. The killing of the tree tore open my heart and my world came crashing down.

I was crying and looking out my kitchen window at the fallen tree and the next thing I saw was a large glowing ball of golden light. It was about the size of a basketball, and it shone so brightly the light filled the space in front of me, and I reached out for it. It levitated about five or six feet off the ground and several feet away from my outstretched arm. Within seconds, it came at me with great speed, hit my chest right in the heart center and knocked me against the kitchen cupboards. I ended up in a squat position on the floor, absolutely amazed at what had happened.

A few seconds passed while I caught my breath, totally conscious. Then my voice said out loud over and over, "Everything's going to be all right now. Everything's going to be all right now." My life changed from that moment on.

When you are ready, the secret path will appear. I was ready. Immediately, my heart opened. I noticed the forest, heard the birds, stood at the window to watch the sunset, listened to my heartbeat, and listened to my inner voice with a new clarity. I had changed, shifted. There was a new understanding and an acceptance. I had surrendered to Spirit.

It wasn't long after that I was given an opportunity and the courage to leave and begin a new life, knowing I was going to be all right on my new journey. I learned that we must continually remember to keep our heart open and to trust in the journey. Every day, we have the choice to follow our inner nudges and guidance, and to wake up smiling, no matter what. That one physical act of smiling can rearrange the energetic structure of our life.

Summary: Re-Pattern Emotional Habits

What does the Seventh Key tell us about the story above?
- Finding your authenticity might involve getting free from energy vampires.
- When you become emotional over something, it attaches to you.
- Emotional habits are also junk to get rid of.
- Emotional addictions may have carried over from a past life.
- Anything you are addicted to needs to be blessed and thrown away.
- To break an old habit or addiction you must first bring in new awareness and then establish a new pattern of spiritual well-being.
- Opening your heart to change changes the way you handle change.

SEVENTH KEY STORIES

Discovering how to travel in different worlds involves learning how to maneuver around your cultural baggage as well. Sasha Jordan, a singer and Reiki practitioner, traveled to India and learned about non-attachment to possessions through living amongst the locals. She also received many other spiritual life lessons. One of the most important to her was about trust.

Trusting In God
By Sasha Jordan

Trusting has never come easy to me. During my trips to India I have been graced with the opportunity to change my way of perceiving and to learn how to trust in the Divine. Over the past eight years I have been back five times, staying three to six months each visit. It has been an intense period of spiritual growth with many challenges, but I wouldn't change a thing.

India is the MahaGuru (great teacher) stripping us of our masks, as we stand naked, our unresolved issues bared for all to see. If you are open and willing, Mother India will guide you along your path of awareness.

In Puttaparthi, the village where I lived, I became friends with a group of boys who survived by begging. They loved to go swimming. So I would hire rickshaws, squeeze everyone into them and head out to the "lakes." After one fun-filled day of swimming with several boys, we passed through a neighboring village. Noticing there was a market, Rakesh, one of the boys about thirteen years old, asked us to stop. Then he took off with a couple other boys. We told them to be back in twenty minutes.

After cruising around the market we came back to our meeting place, but no boys. It was close to an hour before they showed up with big smiles. In the meantime, my mind was full of distrust, imagining they were up to no good, maybe finding drugs or doing something they shouldn't. As they got closer, I noticed Rakesh had a bag overflowing with fresh vegetables. He had chosen to use some rupees from begging to buy food for his mother and family. I had jumped to conclusions, judging from past experiences. I had assumed he was doing something bad.

One of my friends had managed to enroll the street boys in school, but after a couple of weeks they were back on the streets begging. I continued to attempt to coerce Rakesh into school for the next couple of years. He kept refusing. One day while we were having a heart to heart conversation I asked Rakesh why he hadn't taken my offer. He replied, "If I go to school, who will take care of my mother and little brother?" The miniscule amount of rupees he made by begging was their only income. I had to come to terms with the realization that it was my desire, not his, and I stopped trying to convert him.

A couple of years later, I saw Rakesh and the boys riding bicycles with huge jugs strapped on their backs. They smiled and told me they'd started their own business collecting slop (kitchen waste) from the hotel restaurants. They were raising pigs, selling them, and providing for their families. They were resourceful and had found their own way, happily. I no longer saw any of them begging.

So I had to ask myself, "How do I know what is best for another on their journey?"

Things are not always as they seem to be. Obviously trusting is a big part of my journey as I have been faced with it on numerous occasions. Another lesson in trusting taught me that God always takes care of us when we ask for help and then step out of the way.

Over the years I have experienced a lot of illness while in India, spending days in local hospitals and emergency care. The first occasion happened very late one evening. It was my first day in my new home in the village. We had had a birthday party for a friend, and there had been lots of food and celebrating. I awoke at 2:00 a.m. with excruciating pain in my solar plexus. I felt like I was going to die, and I was alone. I had no phone to call an ambulance. I had to get to the hospital, but how?

The pain increased as I waited for daylight. About 4:30 a.m. I looked out the window and noticed a cooking fire. I got myself ready to go to the hospital, about a twenty minute walk away. I set off, doubled over in pain—there was no other way. The village was silent and dark. I was scared but had no choice but to keep going. Stumbling down the dark alley, I noticed a couple of stray dogs. They began growling at me. I was frightened and looked for a place to run, to escape, but more dogs joined in. Now there were eight ferocious dogs.

I called out, in my mind, to my teacher, Sai Baba, "God, help me, I need a rickshaw!"

I prayed with all my heart. The dogs were baring their teeth and circling me, ready to close in. Then out of the darkness a rickshaw came around the corner. I quickly jumped in. Once again my prayers had been answered. I was overwhelmed with gratitude, feeling truly blessed.

Living in the village, I experienced true community, sharing food, resources, the care of the children, every need is accommodated. I feel the breath of India calling me to return. I trust that one day I will move to Kerala where it is green and lush and build a wholistic retreat center and a self-sustainable community with eco-friendly housing, an organic garden, a raw food kitchen, and meaningful service work with the children of India.

> *All the beings in the universe are the creation of God. There is nothing in this world that is not divine. People observe differences between one another. This is a great mistake. All are one.*
>
> —Sai Baba[74]

❧✦❧

Cathy Stevenson has been a nurse in Canada for over twenty years. She wanted to do something special to mark her 50th birthday. One of the things she loved about being a world traveler and visiting distant lands such as Borneo, Vietnam, and Peru, was connecting with the local people, especially the children. This is her story about learning life's lessons through children.

Simply Giving Love
By Cathy Stevenson

I originally went into nursing, wanting to help in a third-world country, but I never fulfilled my dream. I knew that being with the local people was what excited me most when I traveled. They always touched my heart. I wanted to go somewhere, not as a tourist, but where I could help and be with the people. And connect with the children, too. I had no idea where or what I would be doing, but after the Indonesian tsunami and Katrina in New Orleans happened, I knew it was time for me to find my way.

I began by sharing my quest with others. And finally, I heard about an orphanage in southern India and the possibility of working there. After applying and being accepted, I took my vacation from work and flew to Tamil Nadu province, in the village of Podanur, India, to volunteer at an orphanage. I was a little apprehensive about going, unsure of what I was going to do, but once I arrived I felt overwhelmed with happiness.

I sat on the step of the orphanage and said, "I finally made it, and it just feels right!" I did not feel sad surrounded by orphaned children. It felt uplifting.

There were approximately 450 children, many handicapped with special needs. They were orphaned for varied reasons: death of parents, poverty, lack of education, or the support to care for them. The local people knew that the orphanage could provide a better life. This orphanage was founded twenty-seven years ago, so had children from birth to twenty-seven years old. They lived together in different houses and were separated into age groups, attended by staff who loved and respected them. Many of the healthy babies were adopted by Indian families and some were adopted abroad.

When traveling to India I had to leave my North American mind at home or I would have had to battle with the "why's" wondering, "Why is it done this way?" I didn't go there with the understanding that I was going to change anything. I learned quickly that the way I thought was not necessarily the way they thought, due to environment, upbringing, and culture.

I worked with twenty-two babies in one room, rocking, walking, singing, and hugging all of them. Their faces bright with light, I could see that even a warm touch could mean so much. There was endless love to be given and received, goat milk to be fed, diapers to be changed, and cradles to be rocked. The individual attention given filled an entire day. We'd always end up sitting around with music and dance. When you don't have the language, communication is usually done through body movements and music. That carries you through with all ages and cultures.

In the evening I would visit the older girls, ranging in age from fifteen to twenty-three. After working full time all day, they would cook for each other. Each one took turns being responsible for the night's meal. Praying before the meal, sitting on the floor, eating with our hands was the nightly routine. After clean up, the girls would naturally split into their groups and have their own time. One night one of the girls expressed how her hands were so dry and I asked her if she would like some cream for her skin. I brought out a bottle of lotion I had brought from home and all the girls gathered. It became a nightly ritual with someone requesting "cream time." I would provide the cream and they would line up, hands open to put lotion on their arms and legs, laughing and connecting with each other. It was my way of bringing the group together. I looked forward to it as much as they did and, through this, communication and bonding with each other deepened.

They were grateful for whatever they received and never asked for anything. Each child owned a metal suitcase to store their clothes and a few valued possessions. They opened it every night and were eager to share their pictures, a card, or a toy that they had received over time. They even kept the wrappers from the chocolate bars I gave them, folding them neatly into the suitcase.

I found that my greatest gift was not my nursing skills, but my playfulness, giving them permission to laugh, sing, joke, and dance. When you live so close together, it is difficult to be in tune with your emotions because you lack the space to feel. These children were not in touch with their emotions. They learned very quickly, through abandonment, not to feel. The minute they'd shed a tear, they'd stop. They didn't allow themselves to cry. My playfulness gave them permission to be playful. That was my gift to them. I played. When listening to their music, I'd start to dance. Many of the girls watched me, smiling, and then one by one they would begin to dance. Watching them release a fun side of themselves was a gift to me, too.

As a result, I was called "joker sister." I would walk around and children that I hadn't yet connected with, would scream "Joker sister, sing and dance for us!" and then we would all laugh. The mere touch of a hand, or an ear to listen, were the simple pleasures of our connectedness.

"Simply, simply, it is the very simple things that matter the most," I thought.

These children have limited life experiences due to their environment. As a volunteer I was able to add new life to a routine with these simple gestures.

Whatever I gave them was little in comparison to what they gave to me. My only regret was in not discovering this wonderful place sooner. I have been back once, and plan to return again.

Behind this world-show, behind these physical phenomena, behind these names and forms, behind the feelings, thoughts, emotions and sentiments, there dwells the silent witness, thy immortal friend and real well-wisher... the indivisible Power of consciousness or hidden sage. That is the only permanent Reality and the living Truth .... The goal of human life is to realise the Reality behind the changing phenomena.
—Swami Sivananda, Hindu spiritual teacher, from Tamil Nadu.[75]

❧❧✹❧❧

Rick Steves' Europe Through the Back Door, *the title of his guidebook, TV series, and radio program, is well-known in the USA. He has spent one third of his life living out of a suitcase, being a world traveler. Rick believes in developing a global perspective through travel because travel helps us celebrate differences and overcome misunderstandings. In 2008, Rick visited Iran in the Middle East. At the time of writing, Iran is a presumed enemy of the US, but he was led to let go of his attachment to preconceived judgments. Here are a few of his reflections from his blog.[76]*

Dear Traveler
By Rick Steves

Arriving in Iran:

Buckling my seatbelt, it occurred to me that someone could come on the plane's loudspeaker and say, "We're taking this plane to Tehran" and no one would be alarmed. The plane was filled with Iranian people—their features were different from mine, but they dressed and acted just like me.

These people were well off—well dressed, healthy. It was horrible to think of fighting them in a war. Then I wondered if it is easier to bomb a society ground down by years of sanctions.

Are scruffy, poor looking people easier to shock and awe? As we all settled into the wide-body jet, I wished the big decision-makers of our world weren't shielded from an opportunity to share an economy cabin with people like this.

As the pilot began the descent, rich and elegant Persian women put on their scarves. With all that hair suddenly covered, I noticed how striking long hair can be, how it really does grab a man's attention. Looking out the window at the lights of Tehran, the sight reminded me of flying into Mexico City at night. Tehran, with 14 million people, is more populous than all of Greece (where I was just traveling).

I'm starting this trip a little bit afraid. I don't know what's in store for us. We are anticipating a challenging and extremely productive ten days here.

Visiting:

The Islamic Revolution is a "revolution of values." People here tell me they support it because they want to raise their children without cheap sex, disrespectful clothing, drug abuse and materialism, believing it erodes character and threatens their traditional values. Sometimes you don't see an excess in your own world until you find a different world without that excess. Traveling in Iran, it's clear to me that in the US our religion is freedom and materialism. Just about everywhere we look, we are inundated by advertising encouraging us to consume. Airports are paid to drone ads on loud TVs. Magazines are beefy with slick ads. Sports stars wear corporate logos. Our media is driven by corporate marketing. In Iran the religion is Islam. And—at the expense of the economy—billboards, Muzak, TV program-ming, and young peoples' education preaches the teaching of great Shiite holy men.

Departing:

Walking down the jet way to my Air France plane at Tehran's Ayatollah Khomeini Airport, I saw two blonde flight atten-dants—hair flowing freely—at the plane's door. It was as if they were pulling people symbolically back into the Western world. The plane was like a life boat, and passengers boarded with a sigh of relief. Women whipped off their head scarves. Suddenly, we were all free to be what (to us) is normal.

For ten days I'd been out of my comfort zone in a land where people lived under a theocracy—a land which found different truths to be god-given and self-evident. I tasted not a drop of alcohol (Islam is dry). I never encountered a urinal (Islamic men sit). Women were not to show their hair or shape of their bodies (they were beautiful never-the-less). And people took photos of me, as if I was the cultural spectacle.

On my first day back in Europe (in Italy), I noticed hair, necklines, and tight pants like never before. I sipped wine as if it was heaven-sent. And every time I peed standing up I was thankful to be a Westerner.

But I gained a respect for people who are living what they call a "values revolution"—a respect that I could only gain from actually traveling there. And I overcame some of the fears that plague many who have yet to visit Iran.

This experience has reminded me of a fundamental value of traveling. When we travel— whether to a land our president (George W. Bush) has declared part of an Axis of Evil or just to a place where people yodel when they're happy—we enrich our lives and better understand our place on this planet.

SEVENTH KEY EXERCISE

Light Up! You Are a Star of God!

You can have so much fun with this exercise. Enjoy the process! Clearing the clutter in your mind and your world is all about loving yourself so you can benefit from receiving the new healing energies full strength with no blockages. As you read over the words below, let them inspire you to start clearing and making a space for the new you!

1. Envision a tabletop cluttered with stuff. It's so full that you can't find what you're looking for. See yourself pushing things out of the way, searching for YOU—the new you

that you already are underneath all that junk. Things fall off the table as you search. You finally find yourself, hidden behind something that was blocking you. Clearing everything away, you start to shine brightly; you are a star of God.

2. Now open your eyes and look around your immediate environment, wherever you call home. Is it so full that you have no room for the new you? Does it represent your new life, or does it vibrate with old energy?

3. Clutter is anything that does not directly relate to your goal, including people, things, habits, judgments, opinions, and possessions.

4. Slowly, day by day, or all at once, clear your clutter, while keeping your focus on the new you. Keep the best and release the rest! Toss it, sell it, or give it away!

5. Anything that does not nurture you or make you feel lighter, must go. That means anything that no longer fits with your new life in the new world shift.

6. Give everything away except that which you truly need and love. Toss stuff that no longer holds healthy, vibrant energy. Only keep what is energetically positive and nourishing.

7. If you're unable, at this time, to do a full sweep of the things that no longer nurture you, then find one small thing to let go of each day. You will surprise yourself how easy it will become to love and nurture yourself. Live-2-Live your best life!

When you're ready, your personal spiritual journey continues to the Eighth Key which is all about love.

EIGHTH KEY:
LOVE AND GRATITUDE ARE KEY

1. Love and gratitude are keys to conscious living. To know love, love gratitude!
2. This is the relationship Key. The word "love" is meant in the highest form of divine love. You are here to learn how to give unconditional love and be of service to others. Unconditional love means to understand. In understanding others, you learn to have compassion with an awakened heart.
3. Gratitude is an attitude; it is also energy. By adjusting your attitude with little shifts of energy and by reversing your patterns, you change your vibrational frequency, and it changes your state of consciousness, aligning with Source.
4. Focus on gratitude and it instantly lights up your heart, becoming an awakened heart, opening your entire being to an embrace with infinite Source—the infinite embrace.
5. Accept responsibility for your intention and interaction with others. You connect with a particular person for a reason, both teaching and learning. When you view them as Soul, as equal, you nourish them, and move through life disentangled. A true made in heaven relationship!
6. Life and relationship are choices.

(8:1 to 8:6)

LIVE IN LOVE WITH LIFE! LOVE IS THE KEY! We are here to learn love and gratitude, anything else is distraction. Love is the universal language of our world and the worlds beyond. If we don't know the language of divine love it's difficult to live in this world. Love has everything to do with conscious freedom. When we live in the heart of Soul we learn about unconditional love of self, love of others, love for the planet, and love for the universal spiritual laws. It takes less effort to love than to hate, even in unconditionally loving someone who has been unkind to you. In this chapter you learn about love as an eternal river, the new way to be in relationship, and the *infinite embrace*.

The River of Love

I'm sitting in an outdoor restaurant while I write this. Across from me is a table of five women. They converse with lunchtime chatter. I watch them in their individual isolation. They speak but they do not talk with one another. They laugh but they do not connect. They are interested in ego-relating, rather than heart-relating. But I am hopeful. On the inner I ask the group of Souls why they do not connect with one another through their heart center. They say they don't know how; they've forgotten.

Spirit replies to them, "It's time to be authentic with one another, to go into your heart and speak your truth. You will remember how to do this once you begin."

I see an instant change at their table. Each person now looks at the other person, instead of talking over them without seeing them. One person even places her hand over her opening heart, and their entire intention shifts. Two people leave separately. They are not ready to open. It is as it is.

We need to find a way to connect authentically every day. The simple fact is, to receive love you must give love. But, "What is love?"

I always thought finding the answer to that question would be easy. What a surprise to discover that we can go through an entire lifetime without knowing what love is. I know what being in relationship means, and sharing one's life with someone you care for, and giving with no thought of reward, but knowing why our entire universe depends on love is rather elusive.

Love as the divine current runs through us like the water in a river. This river is a divine current that runs out from Source, the Living Energy, and is the energy force that passes through everything, including our body electric. Putting our attention onto this very real river of divine love, we tap into the field of limitless possibilities. The way to tap into it is by keeping your heart open. An awakened heart is needed to practice a Soul-connected life, living consciously—often easier said than done. The awakened heart is a state of consciousness that connects you to divine love. How open you are is how much love you get. Once you have the awakened heart, you will sense it in everyone. You can also hold the world in your heart to help heal it. I once did a drawing exercise and what I envisioned, and then drew, was the planet Earth inside a big red heart—the global heart. We are all important to one another.

The problem arises in the physical plane when the energy current gets interrupted and we can no longer freely conduct Living Energy. Something dams up the river. The blockage occurs when we define ourselves by our physical bodies, instead of as Soul, that which is a part of the infinite Source of all life. Soul resides in a physical manifestation temporarily. Practicing the exercises of the 12 Keys helps us plug in to Source, diving into the river. We are learning how to swim again.

For me, the story in the Old Testament of Adam and Eve is a prohibitive act to keep us from knowing we are Soul. When Adam takes the apple from the Tree of Life, he's actually taking from the Source of all life. In hundreds of ancient mythological stories the snake is also a symbol for the life force. So banishing Adam and Eve from knowing about the life force is a form of spiritual enslavement. The banishment was akin to ripping an electrical power cord out of the wall socket and then wondering why the appliance doesn't work. This story represents the suppression of the great secret that has been hidden from us.

To fill the human heart with compassion, mercy and universal love, which should radiate to all countries, nations and peoples of the world. To make a true religion of the heart as the ruling factor in one's life. To enable each one to love God, love all, serve all, and have respect for all, as God is immanent in all forms. My goal is that of oneness. I spread the message of oneness in life and living. This is the way to peace on earth.

—Kirpal Singh[77]

To Know Love, Love Gratitude

Love and gratitude are keys to conscious living. To know love, love gratitude. If you're in search of a loving relationship, know that there is enough love in all the worlds for everyone. Love is the abundant element. Love is infinite. Elevate your expectations and love will find you. Say "Yes!" to a "made in heaven" relationship. But first, many of us have to relearn how to love because often Earth-world love hurts, and so we close the door to our heart, spending the rest of our life trying to reopen it. By giving a helping hand to another, or by loving a pet, we relearn how to love ourselves again and reclaim an awakened heart.

Intention and expectation of outcome guide your reality here. If your intention is to be open for love, love will find you; but if you put conditional expectations on love, there will be obstacles. Surprisingly, whoever is meant to be your next lover is none of your business! It's in the realm of Divine Spirit.

The Eighth Key, the relationship Key, teaches us that we are here to learn how to give love with an awakened heart and then to give service to others. Love is a state of consciousness, an energy that needs to be accepted into our heart before we can truly serve. The way to serve is to have an awakened heart in order to practice gratitude and compassionate awareness. In this instance, the compassion is for yourself, along with all your relations. Compassion for self means giving up judgmental self-criticism. The message here is to offer yourself gentleness. The XIVth Dalai Lama, Tenzin Gyatso, is said to have been born under the ray of compassion, and the Tibetans believe it is also our homework. He describes his message as the practice of compassion, love, and kindness.[78]

Opening to Infinite Embrace

What can you do right now to turn your life around? Open your heart to the river of divine love! If your life is not serving you, you can start by feeling thankful for little things. Gratitude, along with kindheartedness, is a powerful force, and it's time to give them more accolades. Focusing on gratitude can instantly light up your golden heart, opening your whole being to an embrace with infinite Source—the *infinite embrace*.

When you're ready to change an aspect of your life, such as your job, your relationship, your health, first move yourself off the negative frequency of hating it (reversing your patterns), knowing that nothing can change as long as you stay in the negative energy. It's important to feel grateful for living. You are experiencing the situation for a reason. You do not have to love the situation. Instead, feel love for yourself *in* the situation.

Count Your Gratitude Seeds

Gratitude, or thankfulness, is a seedling that keeps growing. Being thankful is the easiest way to start the gratitude seedlings to grow, and then watch as your world begins to change for the better. Count your gratitude seeds by asking yourself: "For what am I grateful?" Then count them out either verbally or write them down on paper. Writing is a direct experience of living in the present moment.

Try the following daily exercise: Write down five things in your dream journal for which you are grateful. Find something to be grateful for, even the fact you're breathing. At first it might be difficult to think of five things, but keep writing. Be grateful for the small things such as walking, having clothes to wear, having something to eat today, for food in the fridge, or to have a fridge!

Find those gratitude seedlings and nurture them, watching them grow. Gratitude is an energy force. When you focus on it, it changes your vibrational frequency and this energy aligns with Source. It's hard to change unless your frequency changes, so you've got to be willing to try something different. You're the only one who can start these changes in your life. When you are thankful, your world will improve.

Practice the Attitude of Gratitude

The Eighth Key (8:3) is also about attitude and how reversing or "flipping" your attitude and emotional patterns can serve you. In this way, shifting your energy changes your state of consciousness, co-creating your life.

Practicing kindheartedness and gratitude aligns us with our awakened heart and is a powerful tool, known to heal lives. If you have an illness, whether physical, mental or emotional, find something to be grateful for and *live to love.*

Another effective exercise to practice kindness toward yourself and others is to watch what you say for one week. If you catch a negative thought, or critical self-talk, flip it and change it into a positive affirmation. Your attitude toward life changes by restating it in a positive way.

Throughout your day, you might even ask your family and friends: "Has something happened today for which you can be grateful?" Start with small things like, "I'm grateful I caught the bus today. I'm grateful we have food on the table." Soon everyone will be counting gratitude seeds, planting them throughout the day, and watching them grow.

It's fun to keep a section in your dream journal for your gratitude list. On those days when you feel depressed, you can glance at it and remember all the things for which you are grateful.

Live to Love

My neighbor, who was a full-on, 24/7 executive at the top of the corporate ladder, has pancreatic cancer and it has changed her life. But what really changed was her attitude toward living, taking time to be kind, being grateful for moments. The unwell state renewed her Spirit, connecting her with family and friends on a spiritual level. Her illness was a flower that opened the hearts of everyone around her. Between bouts of anger and depression, she would balance her emotions through inspiring others to live and be grateful, giving herself a reason to live. Her remarkable innate wisdom is shifting her world and her illness. Life is a choice. Gratitude is a choice.

Keeping Our Hearts Open

By practicing gratitude we keep the heart open to receive and give love. When you ask this simple question from the Fifth Key (5:4): "Is what I'm about to do in the best interests of all?" you can always be assured that your actions are for the benefit of everyone, and it will assist you to live your life with an open heart. With a compassionate heart, love and gratitude just naturally keep flowing. But how do we keep our hearts open? Many times all we see is the negativity in the world. We forget to find the balance by looking for the lighter side of life. To rise up, think up! Here's an excellent tool to "flip" your emotional patterns.

Pollyanna's Glad Game

Pollyanna—both the book and the movie[79]—had a major influence on my life. Looking back I have no doubt that I have always played Pollyanna's "Glad Game." Researching it on the Internet I discovered that I am not alone. There are blogs, websites and forums dedicated to this little story; along with a board game and paperback reprints. It doesn't surprise me in the least.

The basic storyline is as follows: The young girl Pollyanna, whose missionary parents die, is dropped off into the clutches of an unloving and cold-hearted maiden aunt in a town inhabited by embittered, unfriendly townsfolk. To survive, Pollyanna uses the Glad Game that her father taught her to see the good side of even the worst situations. By the time she leaves, the community and her aunt are transformed for the betterment of all.

The Glad Game is an easy game to play. Simply find something to be glad about in everything. When someone tells you a negative, react with a positive. Other similar beliefs include:

"When life gives you lemons, make lemonade," "Give thanks in all circumstances," and "Always look on the bright side of life." And one more: "Every cloud has a silver lining, and yet, there doesn't have to be a cloud to have a silver lining."

These words by Abraham Lincoln are inscribed on Pollyanna's brooch, a gift from her father: "When you look for the bad in mankind expecting to find it, you surely will."

Playing the Glad Game doesn't mean we ignore tragedy and sadness, but that we practice the Law of Attraction and focus on what we want in our lives.

Play the Glad Game

When you play the Glad Game, you are choosing to live on the positive side of life. It does not mean hiding your head in the sand. You can be based in reality, seeing beyond the illusion, and still choose to see life from a higher viewpoint. Soul is a happy being. To help you remember to play the Glad Game, create a sacred healing space, a place in your home or at work that makes you feel good to be there. Your sacred space can have a few items such as photographs of family and children, people who inspire you, a row of favorite books, Post-it Notes with inspirational quotes, and other symbols of grace and hope; or nothing at all. It doesn't matter what you use as long as it instantly brings you to a place of love. Your sacred healing corner is not meant for worshipping anyone or anything. It's not about adulation. It's about reminding yourself that the positive side of life is all around you, and you are loved.

The Evolution of Relationship

In the evolving new Earth affected by the new energies, relationships are evolving, too. We are co-creating a new way of being together in a relationship bond, with partners supporting one another in their spiritual evolution, embracing a celebratory freedom. We give each other the choice to no longer fall into interdependence with one another. The Winds of Heaven are free to dance between us. We are redefining what it means to be in relationship.

I'm not advocating jumping from partner to partner in an addictive sense, nor am I advocating polygamy, or any of the other excuses we use to possess other human beings. A loving relationship is a bond that honors our partner's spiritual journey.

In redefining relationship, we give to each other the space to discover our individual creative potential and celebrate who we are evolving into. Each partner honors this newfound spaciousness and nurtures the newness of our individual becoming. The old way will no longer serve us as there is much karma to understand and cast off. We can't do this tied to the shore. Possessiveness will only create struggle. Once we find the balance of assisting one another in co-creation, we will move through the changes more effortlessly.

> Love one another but make not a bond of love:
> Let it rather be a moving sea between the shores of your souls.
> Fill each other's cup but drink not from one cup.
> Give one another of your bread but eat not from the same loaf.
> Sing and dance together and be joyous, but let each one of you
>   be alone,
> Even as the strings of a lute are alone though they quiver with
>   the same music.
> —Kahlil Gibran[80]

What is Sacred Sex?

The Kiss by Gustav Klimt (1907) portrays a couple in an intense embrace on the edge of forever, where nothing else exists except for their kiss. It is an erotic heaven, which begs the question: Is sexuality a part of a new world consciousness?

Sacred sex is about uniting with divine love in an intimate loving relationship. It can unite heart and mind, body and spirit. The links between sensual pleasures and religious rapture are universal and innocent. Through the art of intimacy with a loving partner, you can connect to the infinite embrace, opening your entire being to an embrace with infinite Source (8:4).

Sensual love can be a spiritual experience that draws you

closer to your partner. Each relationship involvement has a karmic reason behind it which draws people together. The path to love is a spiritual path, because love comes from Source; and ecstasy comes from a connection with infinite Source.

The Eighth Key (8:5) tells us to accept responsibility for our intention and interaction with others by viewing them as Soul, an equal. You are in a relationship with a particular person for a reason, for teaching and learning. By seeing your mate as an equal, you are nourishing their Soul and it bounces back to you in a hundred positive ways. Also, if you take responsibility and treat others the way you want to be treated, and if you treat yourself the way you want to be treated by others, you and your partner will have a healthy respect for one another. And this builds trust and respect for a "made in heaven" match.

We can't love everyone, but we can give unconditional divine love to all who honor it. With those who do not honor our love and, instead, abuse us, we can use the law of discrimination while still keeping open the channel of compassion. In cutting off all contact with them, we are careful not to withhold our love for purely selfish reasons.

When you become responsible for your actions and intentions, you no longer play the blame game. (First Key: You Are the Key) Instead, you move through life disentangled from another's control over you, and you don't buy into their game. You know when someone isn't honoring you. If you realize this, then you have realized your karma together.

In the quest for control, some people will experiment with violent sexual aberrations, thinking it will lead them to gratification and personal power. It doesn't. Why stay with someone who does not honor you and nourish you? Learn the lesson and say, "I bless and release you" while packing your suitcase! Enter the new energies without negative attachments.

Is It Love?

To ascertain the quality of a relationship with anyone—family, friend, lover, spouse, or co-worker—ask yourself the following question. It is helpful to look at the person, or a photograph of them, while asking on the inner: "Does she or he nourish me? Do I feel nourished in this relationship?" If the answer is no, then it is not love, it is something masquerading as love.

Seriously, I had a relationship once where my dog nourished me more than my partner did! We are part of the divine current, but there are times when we are swept to shore and must learn, like the salmon swimming upstream, how to make our way back to our true reality as a powerful Being of Light. We spend most of our life flopping around outside of the river, wondering what we're doing! Jump back in and swim toward your true path, living a life of conscious freedom. Life is for the living and for giving.

Create a Master List to Unlock Your Dreams

A successful businessman once said to me, "Live for today, save for tomorrow." He paused as if frozen, and then asked, "Is there something more to life? I need more time! After I've fulfilled my obligation to my children, driving them to sport's games, here an' there, and visits with family and friends, and time spent working, there's not enough time left over to be with my partner, or time for myself. It's crazy! There's got to be something more to life!"

In this fast-paced world, most people would agree: "There's not enough time for me. I'm on a treadmill 24/7. One leg runs one way, and the other leg is going the other way. And there's no hope of catching up with myself." That's when you need to jump off the treadmill. It's an old metaphor, but still relevant today, in fact, the treadmill is spinning out of control. Or is it? Actually it's always been an illusion. You can always stop the treadmill and ask for a slowdown. No matter what, it is still your choice. There is always a way. What you do is create new choices. Make each day your choice, bringing your new reality one step closer.

Sit down with your partner and talk about making a master list of what you want your life to look like. If you have no partner, you can ask Soul, "What is it I need out of life?"

Each partner writes down their list on a separate piece of paper. For example, less time working, less stress, time to yourself, a holiday, more time to get physically fit, anything that you need in your life. Spend one week compiling your list. After a short while, come together and go over each other's list. You will find similarities.

Now create a Master List together, one that will stand the test of time. Write down your similar goals, your individual dreams, plus things you wish to accomplish together. Put this list on one piece of paper and intend for everything on the list to be a part of your new reality. Notice I didn't say for the list to come true. "Spirit moves in mysterious ways" is not just an old adage. It is true. Therefore, leave room for the universe to co-create with you an even better life.

Now that both of you know what is on each other's mind, and what you both desire, store the master list in a safe place. One year later, review and, perhaps, revise the list together. And each year afterward, set aside a master list anniversary. As you go through your daily life, you will move closer together, knowing you have goals, and these goals will move you into position, so the universe will assist you in ways you haven't even considered.

EIGHTH KEY STORIES

The Eighth Key says: You are here to learn how to give unconditional love and be of service to others. Many of us have no idea how a kind act, a good deed, or a warm smile can send ribbons of positive energy out into the world; or how dedication to helping others to help themselves sets up a synchronistic series of events. Even those who organize fundraisers for worthy causes might not understand how Living Energy works through them to change lives, including their own. Life and relationship are choices.

Karethe Linaae had a major turning point in her life that most certainly changed her life's purpose.

I Am Grateful
By Karethe Linaae

Having spent time in and out of hospitals as a young woman, I learned early what gratitude meant. When I finally came back home after a life-saving surgery at fifteen, I promised myself that I would be grateful every day I was granted on this earth, every second of each day, every breath I could take and every meal I could eat without pain. I would cherish each moment as if it was the last.

However, as most humans, I am quick to forget. Time passed and I would start to move easier, breathe freer, and eat quicker. Gradually, I would take my life for granted. I had lost the mindful awareness and sense of sacredness of every single moment.

A few years back, I was provoked to do something to spread thankfulness. I decided to organize an art exhibit in the name of gratitude. I had no experience as an art curator, no connections in the art community, nor did I have any idea where this event would take place, but I had a name for the exhibit. The name would be in first person singular: "I Am Grateful." Everyone would leave the exhibit having been reminded to express their gratitude. That is all I knew and all I needed to know.

Goethe inspired Scottish mountaineer W. H. Murray when his dream of climbing the Himalayas seemed doomed, helping him to see the power of divine providence once one decides to act on an idea:

> Until one is committed, there is hesitancy ... the moment one definitely commits oneself, then Providence moves too. All sorts of things occur to help one that would never otherwise have occurred. A whole stream of events issues from the decision, raising in one's favor all manner of unforeseen incidents and meetings and material assistance, which no man could have dreamed would have come his way. I have learned a deep respect for one of Goethe's couplets:
> Whatever you can do, or dream you can, begin it.
> Boldness has genius, power and magic in it. Begin it now.[81]

The "I Am Grateful" exhibit was a true example of divine providence at work. Starting with a simple idea, it unfolded quite like magic. I spoke to friends, who knew other friends. I met an artist, who knew other artists. I went to an art show and heard of someone who eventually ended up donating the space for our exhibit. Of course, all was not rolled out on a red carpet. Providence will test you, to see if you truly believe. The first exhibit venue went bankrupt and we were left on the street.

Making an exhibit on gratitude was truly a crash course in going with the flow. I reminded myself that obstacles are only obstacles if one sees them as such, instead of as an opportunity to explore other avenues. It was my goal that we would not pay for anything. All would have to be offered in gratitude. Nothing would be sold; nobody would be charged. Who can put a price on someone's gratitude? At the end of the exhibit, the art works would be returned to the artists. The event was not to raise funds, but to raise awareness and celebrate the potential of gratitude.

Our venue also came to me "by accident." I went to an exhibit of young Canadian designers. The venue was an in-the-raw warehouse space in Vancouver's Gastown which belonged to a local developer. I set up a meeting, expecting to defend the art of gratitude over a boardroom table. Instead the owner met me in a café, arriving on his bicycle. I knew "gratitude" had a home!

The space was in dire need of a cleanup. There were parts of walls missing, loose electrical wires hanging down everywhere, truckloads of rubble and layers of smelly carpet. We wanted people of all ages to attend, so we needed a safe venue. I put out a call for help, contacting every carpenter, painter and electrician I knew in the film industry. And help came. We had a full crew working all hours of the day and night, and within a month our space was ready for the city inspector. I was so touched by all the people who offered their help. Friends, neighbors and workmates all joined in, as Goethe had predicted. Everything—from the printed invitations to the bottled water we served at the opening—was donated. The latter was given to us by an author who later became world renowned—not for speaking of the power of gratitude, but for the power of Now.

The press got curious. Who were these people working like bees in a hive, transforming a dark downtown warehouse into a light and lively space of thankfulness? I spoke to newspaper, radio, and television reporters, explaining why we all should be grateful and why it is worth celebrating. Without a cent spent on publicity, over a thousand people attended the opening to celebrate gratitude.

On the morning of the art opening, I got scared, knowing I had to make the opening speech. So I prayed. I asked that my words be guided, not for my sake, but for the sake of spreading the notion of gratitude. I had no time to think about it for the rest of the day, running to a live radio broadcast, picking up last minute supplies, and making sure my young son, who helped all the way through, had something to eat. Suddenly the lights were on me; I repeated my prayer: Please guide my words. I opened my mouth, starting my speech without a quiver: "I am grateful."

When someone asks me what I am most grateful for in this life, the answer is adversity. Without adversity, how will we grow? Without problems, how will we learn how to cope and how to recognize harmony? Without needs, how would we know what gratitude is?

Now, ask yourself: what are you grateful for?

❧❧★❧❧

Lyvia L. Smith is seventy and suffers from severe health issues, and yet in public she's always smiling and sharing love with everyone she meets. She is a testimony to one woman's strength of positive doing. "There are a lot of lonely people in the world," she said. "I try to inspire them to live life by positive thinking."

Look for the Silver Lining
By Lyvia L. Smith

Eventually, there has to be something good to come out of every situation, no matter how bleak it may be at the time. You may have to dig quite deeply to discover the silver lining in a very dark and depressing cloud. Sometimes we have to wait for life to evolve and then it might be easier to see that one small positive outcome.

My dear husband of forty-four years of marriage passed away after a courageous battle with pancreatic cancer. It seemed that one moment he was a very healthy and youthful sixty-eight-year old man and suddenly he was told to go home and wait for this excruciating death. My father and mother had also suffered similar fates not that long ago. Losing loved ones is always a devastating experience. So how could I find the silver lining hidden behind this very dark cloud? What good could possibly have come out of these tragic events? I imagined that if I concentrated hard enough, there must be a silver lining that would come to me in time.

I am a senior with many disabilities and have spent eleven years confined to my bed or wheelchair, so I must know something about how hard it is sometimes to find the silver lining! I felt that my predicament was even more pronounced because, out of my illnesses, I had written a book on the subject of positive thinking and also specialized in motivational speaking. My talks try to help others find the sun behind every cloud.

Psoriatic and rheumatoid arthritis, fibromyalgia, diabetes II, asthma and countless other medical problems kept my life limited in so many ways. I required help with even the most simple of life's daily rituals. I had not organized any plan to have someone other than my husband take care of me. I had been so very sure that he would outlive me by at least 10 or 15 years and never stopped to consider that a terrible accident or deadly disease would befall him.

All of a sudden, many months later, it came to me. The silver lining had been all around me for so long—literally! I realized that the amazing people that I had hired to take care of my mother and my husband were people who had helped them above and beyond the call of duty. And now, these same people were also caring for me. They became wonderful and loyal friends. In fact, I remain very close to almost all of these wonderful people to this day. Millie came into my life about seventeen years ago and she's now in her 60s, still a very dear friend. Then when she could no longer come, I met a friend of hers who I've now known for 14 years. I see them socially and our relationships have evolved into close friendships. I shall always be very grateful for the efficient and loving care they provided each and every day to make our lives as pleasant as possible under the circumstances.

Of course we also enjoyed such comforting love from our two beautiful daughters, Sheryl and Jodi. Their love is constant and so very special always.

I suppose that my point is to continue to look for that silver lining, no matter how elusive it may seem to be. And when you discover it, embrace this discovery as it will fill your life full of comforting compassion and love. Things turn out the best for those who make the best of the way things turn out.

❧❧✴❧❧

The love and gratitude from, and for, a pet is a special bond between Souls. Here is a story about how my sister Anastasia was given the gift of love and protection from her loyal dog.

How Love Saved My Life
By Anastasia Milne Parkes

My dog Ia, pronounced "ee-ya," was carried in her Czechoslovakian German Shepherd mother's stomach to Canada. At six-weeks-old, she found *me*, and since that time we have been connected at the hip, learning everything together.

Raised in the mountains of North Vancouver, Ia and I would go for daily hikes in the forest. One such day, we were in an area where there had been reports of people living in the woods and warnings not to walk there alone. Ia and I went anyway as it was a truly beautiful part of the forest valley. We were late coming back and it was getting dark. I didn't see him coming. She did. From out of the forest and with great speed came a man with a large club-like stick in his hand. I would have been a goner if not for Ia. She jumped up on him, and grabbing the weapon arm in her mouth, pulled him down. She lunged on top of him, her teeth bared, saliva dripping, a very serious threat. The man was scared to death.

I was somewhat in shock and didn't really know what to do. I backed off about thirty yards and called Ia off. She ran to me, as the man ran away in the opposite direction as fast as his legs could carry him. Back home I called the police, but of course he was long gone. Ia had not been taught to do this, it was simply part of who she was. This unquestioning loyalty, devotion, and love that she was simply born with, teaches me every day to be a better person in my own life.

The second time Ia came to my rescue occurred when I went berry picking with some friends. The best berry bushes were close to a cliff, and below was a rushing river with lots of big rocks. There is an unwritten law here that you never drop berries, and if you do, you must tell the person next to you and so on down the line. Well, my friend did not know this. She dropped some berries by mistake and just kept on picking while she walked along the path. Coming up behind her I slipped on the berries and went sliding down the side of the cliff grasping for anything I could as I fell. I managed to grab onto a large tree root. There I hung with everyone above me shouting and no one knowing what to do! No one had a rope, nothing.

Out of nowhere, Ia came running down the side of this cliff like a mountain goat, pushed her body up against mine and gave me her tail to hold onto. I grabbed onto her tail and she pulled me about ten feet to where I could get a foothold on the cliff. I reached for her collar and together we clambered up the rest of the cliffside.

No one knew what to say, they had never seen anything like it before. I was in tears, but not out of fear. This beautiful creature, unthinking and without hesitation, was giving her life to me.

Years later, when I was moving out to eastern Canada, I was confused as to what to do with Ia. She was a mountain and forest dog, born and bred. What would she do in the suburbs of Montreal? How could I do best by her, this amazing being who had taught me so much and given her heart to me? So I asked the universe for a sign.

Then one day, with only one week before leaving for my new life, I came home to what I can only call a true message. That morning I had put my big leather suitcase out to pack. Open, full of clothes, it lay in the hallway. When I walked into the house I saw that Ia had crawled into the suitcase and the lid had now fallen down on top of her. There she lay with just her head sticking out of one end. I came to tears and thought, now if THAT isn't a sign, I truly don't know what is! From that moment on I have been an avid listener to all of life's waking dreams.

Ia now lives with my partner and I on our hundred-acre organic farm in Ontario. She is the ripe "young" age of seventeen, and in her opinion, far from retired. She's a tad wobbly now and has lost much of her hearing, but she loves to lie longingly on the front porch watching over us and her two older pups who now do the prancing and protecting. She will never give up on us, and we will never give up on her. She has given me more than I can ever say, including my life, and a loyalty and love that breaks all boundaries, and will stay with me all my days.

EIGHTH KEY EXERCISE

Relax and Open Your Heart

This is a spiritual exercise designed to relax and open the heart center. On the *Utides* logo (below), the heart center is represented by the universal spiral symbol of the ancient Goddess religion that lasted for tens of thousands of years beginning around 30,000 BCE. The spiral represents the nourishing energy of the divine sacred feminine. This design symbolizes the spiral movement toward the heart center and, also, the spiraling journey into the Otherworlds. The bars below the spiral design symbolize the infinite universal ocean of Living Energy which nurtures us and replenishes our loving heart limitlessly. This exercise uses a visualization technique to create an image, because thoughts are things in our present physical reality.

1. Look into the spiral design for a few moments and sing the word: *"c o n t e n t m e n t"* in a long drawn out voice.
2. Slowly visualize holding a newborn baby in your arms.

3. Look down into the baby's smiling face, rock it gently, hear the little gurgling sounds, and smell the baby's forehead.
4. Now, look at the baby and see *your* face. Feel the love you have for yourself as the little baby and let it wash over you.
5. Hand the baby to a loving Soul—your Guardian, mother, mentor, a spiritual master[82]; a shaman, elder, yogi, or guru—someone who nourishes and nurtures you.
6. Feel the warmth and the love from this person as you are being held. Feel the spiral of loving energy in your heart area opening and expanding.
7. Open your eyes, and then ask, "How much love was I able to accept from this person? Would it fill a glass? Half a glass? One-quarter of a glass?"
8. Then visualize the glass spilling over with divine love and gratitude.

NINTH KEY:
GO WITH THE FLOW

1. Go with the Flow! Ride the current and surrender to the flow of life.
2. Surrender and ride the wave of outflows and inflows of currents in the ever-present vibrational matrix, whether composed of light or the harmonics of sound, to give you full access to all Otherworlds and infinite choice.
3. Visualize the living earth below your feet for the purpose of grounding. Then merge consciously with the living matrix field beyond your physical body for the purpose of "seeing" (i.e. visiting) what's *out* there in parallel dimensions and what's *in* there in your own energy field. Use your inner spiritual eye to see that which is constantly changing.
4. Discover your Soul's purpose by being a clear channel between your world and the worlds of infinite Living Energy. When Soul's purpose and mission is in alignment with your outer life, then you are in the flow, and the door to the creative force is wide open.
5. A spiritual healing uses the flow of Living Energy. Due to the flux of incoming and outgoing energy currents, for spiritual healing to be effective your spiritual body must also be healed, not just the physical. No matter what you call it, simply stated, it's all about *energy,* and also, dialoguing with Soul.
6. Know that the inner worlds are not outside of Soul, they *are* Soul.

(9:1 to 9:6)

HEN YOU'RE IN THE FLOW YOU'LL KNOW because the universe stands aside to let you pass. The Ninth Key lights up the pineal gland so we may consciously dream travel, leaving the dense and lower physical body behind. Here we bask in a new lightness of being and higher vibratory existence. In this chapter you will learn how to ride the wave of energy currents and see your life from a higher perspective. Remember to open up to any spiritual experience, letting no one tell you your experience is wrong. Truth is the individual's experience. Living in the flow of life can manifest in many of the following ways:

- You will experience more harmony than you have ever known.
- Your life will flow smoothly, effortlessly, without struggle.
- You will begin to vibrate at a higher frequency.
- You will be reborn, fully accepting the spiritual renaissance of a new world.

Ride the Wave!

Life is a continual process of discovery, re-discovery, and re-generation. The word "process" means progression, route, and course of action. As I grow older, I process who I am, noticing how my body changes, how my thoughts change through ex-perience, how my emotions have settled into my body and relaxed, and how not to take life so seriously. We are works in progress. All life dramas dissolve into the realization that keeping the heart open is the most important aspect of life.

The Eighth Golden Key tells us about the river of love. The Ninth Golden Key (9:2) explains how to tap into this river and ride the current. We travel along with the river's flow easily at times, and other times we are cast about in rapids or momentarily beached onshore. But as we re-enter, the current takes us along in its loving embrace upon the river of divine love, and once again we are in the flow. As you evolve into the higher vibrations, it's important to stay liquid. Where you are at present is where you're supposed to be. Of course, you don't want to get stuck in one particular state of consciousness—keep moving forward like an ever-flowing river.

The universal flow of the life current is strong in us. It allows us to ride this divine river, floating through an ocean of motion. It runs from a point below your feet to the top of your head, and continues out into the vast ocean of luminous Living Energy. You can visit the Moon and the planets in galaxies far away in the blink of an eye, or travel into a parallel dimension through your Third Eye portal. Once in the flow of life energy, this river of divine love, your entire life shifts into the higher vibratory energies—on a natural high!

Living in Higher Vibrations

How do we live in the higher vibrations? Many authors talk about the different dimensions, and call them by many names. When we strip away the labels, we are left with what is: energy.

It is all a question of energy within a vast ocean of motion, Living Energy. A different vibrating energy equals a different world. For example, we can travel from the heavy and coarse physical energy to the lighter, non-physical, higher vibrating energies. Infinite Soul in the physical body feels coarse and heavy on Earth, but when you leave the physical realm, Soul becomes a pure wave of energy.

When you are ready to live in the higher dimensions, or connect with an inner guide or Being of Light, you need to spiritualize your frequency to match theirs, if possible. Therefore, if you want to join a spiritual traveler from another dimension for an extended period of time, either they lower their frequency vibration or you raise yours.

Arrivederci, Roma!

 On a recent trip to Rome, I had an experience that showed me how I could remain balanced—living in higher vibration—even when everything around me was in utter chaos. On my last night in Rome a friend and I were sitting at *Quattro Fiumi* restaurant in the Piazza Navona. We were celebrating and saying *"Arrivederci,*

Roma!" while clinking glasses. Then I heard shouting. I looked across the plaza to see where the loud voices were coming from. The university students were having a *"manifestation"* as the Italian waiter called it, meaning a demonstration. The riot was swimming in lower vibrating energy as evidenced by a wall of *Carabinieri* military police wielding machine guns. Even though we were close to the riot, my friend and I were celebratory, living in higher vibration and, thus, untouched by what was happening around us. This is meant as a small example.

When the sky is falling, with riots in the streets, war, terrorist attacks, earthquakes—or whatever is happening in your corner of the world—if you are living in an expanded vibratory state, the fallout of anger and violence will miss you. It might be by inches, but it will miss you. There is always a boundary of calm beyond the violence, a curtain or wall of protection to give you space to safely depart, but only if you remain calm, listen to the signs, and then, take proactive measures.

One example happened before the devastating Indonesian tsunami hit the beaches. Some islanders were alerted by the elephants. The usually passive animals suddenly broke free and stampeded to higher ground. The Elders of the local village knew this was a sign and got everyone to follow the elephants to safety. No one in the small community died.

These are the greatest times in which to be living, because we are heralding in a new world age. Time is of the essence now. Go higher. Close your eyes and focus on the inner Blue Star and listen for the inner sound, doing this can take you to a higher perspective, to see through the eyes of Soul, to rest and relax your mind, or to even help you survive in a dangerous situation. When we are in balance, in the flow, we are better able to choose and co-create our direction. Miracles happen when you are in the flow. You create the miracles!

Surrender to Change Your Life

If you want to change your life, you must first surrender to the flow. The Ninth Golden Key reminds us to go with the current, not against it. Surrender and see with your inner spiritual eye that which is constantly changing. Surrendering to the flow of life gives you infinite choices. In order to surrender, listen to your heart and follow the inner guidance that comes to you. It sounds so simple, doesn't it? And it can be. But most of the time we don't listen. We're usually too busy doing whatever it is we think we're supposed to be doing. What are we supposed to be doing? Listening.

Go to the Next Step

Here's an experiment you can try. Take notice of what's around you. Listen to the sounds. Each one is speaking to you, asking you to listen to it. Do you hear? You are now in the present moment. Surrender. Close your eyes if it helps you.

Now listen to what you want to do RIGHT NOW, in this moment. And then do it. When you've done that, stop and listen again to the sounds around you and within you. What is Soul asking you to do next? Go to the next step. Keep going to the next step throughout your day and see where it leads you.

We need to become skilled at listening to our heart if we want to accept and surrender to change. This is important if we want the Ninth Key to work for us. Be accepting of change by staying in the present moment. Life is an energy force. It is as it is. We need to learn to let change reshape our lives without fear. We are in the Great Turning or the Changing Times, heralding in a new age, and staying in the flow of Living Energy's universal consciousness is of great importance for our survival.

When we stop resisting and surrender to our situation, exactly as it is in the present moment, this acceptance brings change—*we* change. It represents the moment when we merge our personal energy field with the universal field, allowing the life force (Spirit) to step in. Surrender allows us to gain a clear channel to know our Soul's purpose. And when Soul's purpose or mission is in alignment with your outer life, then you are in the flow.

Ken Hancherow noted in his Fourth Key story: "The trick is that your goals and your outer life must be in alignment with your purpose and your inner life. Then you are in flow!"

Let's study this for a moment.

The trick is that your goals (let's say you want to make lots of money) and your outer life (the ability to make lots of money, like a good-paying job) must be in alignment with your purpose (let's say your Soul's purpose is to teach others about divine love) and your inner life (learning about divine love on the inner to unravel some karma). Therefore, what you need to do is find a lucrative way of teaching others about divine love. Perhaps write an award-winning film on the subject, or start a dating service for spiritually inclined people, or ... the possibilities are unlimited.

So, ask yourself three questions:

1. What is my inner purpose?
2. What are my outer goals?
3. What do I need to be doing to bring both in alignment and be in FLOW?

Surrender to Change

 In my twelfth year as a city bus driver something happened that was a major turning point in my life. A turning point is something that happens to spin you around in a different direction. I witnessed the aftermath of a terrible accident where a woman died under the rear wheels of a co-worker's bus. As a professional driver, the experience deeply affected me and made me take a closer look at my life. It forced me to re-evaluate my job and go with the flow of what the universe wanted for me. I had to learn to surrender to change, that what I witnessed was for a reason. Once I realized this, I was able to allow Source (Spirit) to drive my life. I asked for a waking dream to show me which direction to take. I started by listening.

In my twenties and thirties I had been a creative artist. But time and life interfered with my true direction. Soul, my true self, started to show me the way back. I started to write and re-entered the creative flow. I wrote several stories called "Tales of a Bus Driver" and realized this was my true path, Soul's purpose. I was following my bliss as Joseph Campbell called it. I call it "following the loving guidance of Soul." Soul had plucked me from one state of consciousness, that of a tense bus driver in the middle of traffic war zones, to place me into the state of consciousness of a creative artist, one more befitting of my true nature. I quit work, having worked as a bus driver for twelve years, and entered a new twelve-year cycle of life.

Chart Your Turning Points

What was a turning point for you, one where you surrendered to change? Chart your life in twelve-year cycles, starting at birth. Write down the most memorable turning point in your life, and then see what happened twelve years before and after. By doing this you will know when the next life change will happen in cycles of twelve.

Throughout history, the number twelve has been venerated for its powerful influence. There are twelve months in the Gregorian calendar, our day is divided into two twelve-hour periods, the lunar cycle is twelve years, the twelve-year cycle of animals appears in the Chinese zodiac, the Jews had twelve tribes, Jesus had twelve apostles, in Islam Muhammad was born and died on the twelfth day of the month, Buddhism has twelve principles, the ancient Greeks and Romans had twelve gods, and so on. What happened in your twelve-year cycles and when does the next one begin?

What Is Spiritual Healing?

[Disclaimer: None of the information herein is intended to diagnose, treat, or prescribe; it is for information purposes only. Always seek potentially curative conventional care from a healthcare practitioner. Any person making the decision to act upon this information is responsible for investigating and understanding the effects of their actions.[83]]

When my mother got sick my world collapsed. That can happen when a loved one is critically ill. You stop thinking about your own life and start giving to someone else, dropping everything to help them heal. For the person who is unwell, their entire life comes to a standstill and nothing is more important than getting well. It's a wake-up call. Major life changes take place that they hadn't even considered.

They start thinking about their life—who they need to make amends to, why they didn't take that vacation, or why they haven't opened their heart to enjoy life more, or gotten a pet, not been so stingy, and a thousand other things; but especially, "Why did this happen to me?" Many people feel the reason why illness exists is to learn selflessness and how to consciously give and receive love. Many people who become unwell talk about how it forces them to surrender. It gets their attention and alters the course of their life's direction.

As an author of ten books, one of Mary Carroll Moore's primary themes, after struggling with two bouts of cancer, is "deserved happiness," which she defines as "a fascination with the choices we make after personal disaster or suffering." Mary says, "Cancer forces you to re-evaluate your life. I began to make choices, weeding out what was not sustaining, making room for creative work. I can't say my cancer was a blessing, but it was certainly a wake-up call."[84]

Illness is as much a part of God's plan as anything else is. It's almost as if it's Soul's choice whether to accept a healing or to continue the illness experience. Disease is *not* the reason you drop your body and move on. Souls usually leave because their mission is complete. Doctors are often amazed that a critically diagnosed patient goes on to live for years; or that another with a hopeful prognosis succumbs so quickly. I read somewhere that one third of all reported healings come from believing you will get well; actually, the number is probably a lot higher.

This Ninth Key (especially 9:5) can be used to learn about spiritual healing. It says that for spiritual healing to be effective, your spiritual body must also be healed, not just the physical body. You've probably heard the phrase: heal the body, mind, spirit. For me it means, learn how to be in tune with your body, to access the power of your mind, and to dialogue with Spirit and, thus, the hyperdimensional energy field that surrounds us, in order to heal all parts of the whole. In other words, "your spiritual body" refers to your highly advanced light body (Soul) which you use for inner dream travel. And your light body is composed of the field of Living Energy. Therefore, to heal, you need to *dialogue* with Spirit and Soul.

I was taught that we have different light bodies for travel in different planes and through various chakras, and this one does this, and that one does something else. Now I understand it differently. Soul is one spiritual body throughout the vast energetic ocean of Living Energy, and by using little shifts of energy, we learn to adjust to where we are. That explains why you can be in two places at once. Thus, spiritual healings occur on all levels—physical, emotional, and mental, as well as in your spiritual body. Receiving a spiritual healing aligns your inner light body to Source so it becomes a clear channel for the Living Energy, the field of informational light and sound. It's as if the Living Energy re-sets a state of energetic imbalance or dis-ease when you dialogue with it.

The Living Energy field known as divine love heals. Our role is to surrender and consciously awaken the capacity to co-create the healing. Follow your inner guidance and nudges when they lead you to solutions, changes you need to make, karma you need to consider, and personal research into what it is that YOU need—such as better nutrition, exercise, kinesiology, meditation, holistic dentistry, alternative medicine, swimming in water, connecting with Nature, working in the dream state, and anything else to which you are guided, but especially to accessing Living Energy. Surround yourself with loving, positive influences for regeneration, taking responsibility for your healing and making healthy changes. The body is an amazing vehicle for Soul and is capable of overcoming any illness when you consciously assist in the healing. Get involved in the healing process. You are the Key! You are the healer within.

Our Healer Is Within

The ability to access the "healer within" has been lost to many over the last centuries through our dependence on outside sources, mostly pharmaceutical drugs which suppress our immune systems. We need to ask Soul to lead us to the healing modalities that we need. We have the capacity to heal ourselves and assist others (with permission) and to perform miracles from a place of love and surrender, using the informational fields of the Living Energy—*if it's karmic right action.* But I had to ask myself whether I believed that *we* do the healing, or if, through love, acceptance, and surrender, we open our hearts and become pathways for Living Energy, the source of divine love, to align with our karma in agreement with Soul. Then I realized it is one and the same. In my experience, having an open dialogue with Soul is the difference between a long-lasting healing and a short-term psychic healing.

In the near future the new quantum medical sciences, including informational and energy medicines, will blow our present minds and will be the next frontier of medicine. The medical profession is now aware that they do not know everything. Medical scientists are realizing, once again, that our healer is within. In fact, it's all around us! Whether from our immune system, light balance, repairing our strands of DNA, or from divine guidance, spiritual healings are finally being acknowledged. Author Abraham-Hicks believes the secret is that you and everybody in the world is Source energy in physical bodies.[85] And it is also a healing energy.

The advances in energy medicine are truly miraculous and well-timed for our present new world age. We are meant to relearn how to heal ourselves. Living Energy or Source or whatever you want to call it, also has the power to create a universal wave of healing energy to transform our planet. Dr. Richard Gerber M.D., in his now classic book, *Vibrational Medicine: New Choices for Healing Ourselves*, explains it this way:

> ... *science has actually begun to confirm that love is indeed a healing energy and that it can produce measurable, healing effects, both within ourselves and in those around us. If we can produce a ripple effect of healing energy upon the waters of humanity's collective consciousness, it will be carried by the flowing stream of Earth's magnetic field and grid work systems .... An energetic tidal wave of healing energy, fueled by the power of unconditional love, might transform our planet in a way that could only have been dreamt about in past times.*[86]

The Healing Power of Love

 This story illustrates how love is a healing energy, and how the healer is within. Helen's twenty-three-year-old son had leukemia, a form of terminal cancer. Unlike other types of cancer, leukemia isn't a solid tumor that can be surgically removed, because it's in the bone marrow. Helen and her son lived in the USA and had no medical insurance. It was going to cost thousands of dollars for his medical treatments. The oncologist said he would need chemotherapy and/or radiation therapy.

At the time, Helen was going through a painful divorce from her second husband. Her emotional state was very tenuous when her son called. He lived in another part of the country and they had lost touch—their mother-son bond no longer close. But when he told her about his cancer, she dropped everything, including her own emotional/mental pain, and moved lock, stock, and barrel to her son's bedside. For two years she tended him through the worst time of his young life. He went through horrific cycles of pain, and she felt every bit of it. After various painful treatments, exhausting every avenue, the doctors finally gave up. But Helen didn't.

During this time she and her son would sing HU together. They realized how much they loved one another, Soul-to-Soul, and recalled many past lives they had experienced. Singing HU started to unravel the karma between them.

When they went in for the quarterly cancer check-up, they were told the test results did not find any cancer in his cells! The doctor was amazed that the boy had been cured of the usually fatal disease. Helen and her son felt that the power of their love and the healing of their karma together had a major impact that helped engage the cure. They had been brought together under the auspices of cancer, and a spiritual healing had taken place for both of them. Love is a powerful energy field, as is the HU. The power of love is real and absolute! There are thousands of stories that demonstrate how love can heal in ways both mysterious and miraculous, just as love helped heal Helen's son.

Is Healing a Choice?

 A friend of mine is a single mother who raised three sons while she recuperated from debilitating back pain. For ten long years the pain was so excruciating that all she could do was lie down. So while lying on her stomach she studied and then wrote her Naturopathic Doctor's exams! Because she learned whatever it was she needed to while incapacitated, her inner guidance led her to someone who corrected the problem with her back. Through a simple procedure, the pain was suddenly gone. Soul was ready to move on to the next experience.

From that day forward, she promised herself never to waste another day. As a result, her life now moves like a speeding bullet, and it's hard to keep up as she makes up for lost time. But time is never lost.

During a divorce, a friend was going through an emotional ringer, on a roller coaster of positive and negative emotional charges. He became very ill. When an emotional disturbance such as this affects one's health, we tend to blame the event or those people who we feel caused our emotional upset. But once we understand that whatever we see in the other person is precisely that which we are supposed to be looking at within ourselves, the experience shifts. The basic key to solving this dilemma is to accept the emotional disturbance, as is, and give one's self the love to let go of that which no longer serves us. My friend was able to accept the responsibility for his part in the scenario, which completely neutralized the emotions, and allowed him to solve his problems rationally. His health improved immediately.

Another friend, "John," had a major health crisis. He'd recently lost his job and was having family problems. Already overweight, the extra burden and stress led him to overindulge in junk food, mostly sugar and fatty foods. He was a sugar-holic. When he was diagnosed as having diabetes, he was given two choices: change his diet or die. John did more than start to eat nutritious food; he and his wife started walking, and also bicycling, getting lots of exercise, which resulted in his losing forty pounds. His lifestyle change saved his life.

The husband of a friend rolls his own cigarettes with strong tobacco, smokes like a chimney all day long, drinks tons of beer, and his idea of recreation is lying on the couch watching television every night and all weekend. He can hardly breathe his lungs are so clogged, and he coughs even as he lights a cigarette! In his mid-sixties, he's already had two mild heart attacks, has an extended belly, and refuses to change his sedentary lifestyle. Is he a happy man? Is it a death wish? Is he living out his karma? Regardless of the answers, it's his decision whether to change or not. An old saying comes into play here: If you keep walking down the same path, you will always end up in the same place. He's not interested in getting well. Life is choice.

Why would anyone *not* want to be well? Some Souls come into the physical plane for the primary purpose of living a life of physical and emotional pain, believing they will evolve spiritually by overcoming or enduring illness. Or, perhaps they come here to learn how to love themselves, first learning compassion for themselves and then for others. Or, perhaps they performed heinous acts against another in a past life and they choose to experience their present life in a certain way. Anything is possible; it's not for me to say. There are many facets to a spiritual healing, including the use of healers and practitioners who assist us in our healing.

Keepers of Energy

Many healers are teaching us about the new healing paradigm of energy and informational field medicine. Adam Dreamhealer from Canada's west coast is a young man who has the ability to heal using what I believe is Living Energy. Although he doesn't call it that, he is certainly aware that an energy force or field exists, referring to it as a "light-emitter." A witness at one of his workshops explained to me that he goes into a trance and sees the tumor or the ailment that is creating an unwell state in someone. Next, I believe he creates an intention for their immune system to heal the issue involved—something he believes anyone can be taught to do. He may even do it visually, setting up an inner vision to see it happening. And even though Adam says he doesn't understand how it works, sometimes the person gradually regenerates into a state of wellness. Adam feels that everyone has the ability to heal themselves. He believes that our intentions and thoughts influence our health. He tries to teach people to use their focused intention and positive thoughts for healing. It's not the only tool you can use, but it is one thing you can do for yourself.[87]

We do what we're guided to do, and if so guided, there is no reason why we can't develop these healing skills and access the flow of energy. However, I believe that we can develop skills to direct the flow of energy *without* establishing the intention. In other words, to give permission or open the door to allow the field interaction with Soul, and to let the field decide what is best for us. To heal, you need to dialogue with Soul. By dialoguing with Soul and the field of Living Energy, we influence our health. This is not difficult to do; but it is difficult to understand because we're so conditioned to rely on an outside physical source, and some need more outside help than others. Humans are waking up to the fact that we are keepers of energy. Living Energy and the purity of divine love regenerate the body every day, every moment, in our dream matrix. By believing we take action. By taking action we help ourselves. By taking charge of our own life we make a difference in the world around us. Divine love as a force of energy is real and is free for everyone.

Free the Energy!

Although I was not unwell, I had the opportunity to allow two different energy healers to work on me free of charge in the same month. They came from different teachings and different parts of the world, but the energy was the same. One was a famous light energy teacher; the other was a student doing a practicum. Before I said yes, I went on the inner to ask what Soul wanted. The answer I received was truly unexpected.

The inner voice of Soul laughed at me. It said, "Why? You're already doing it yourself."

I went to the first session. Healers from all over the world had gathered to take part in a one week intensive with the famous energy healer. They needed guinea pigs. I was lying on the table with four healers working on me, when I suddenly saw many inner masters arrive. They wanted to watch.

They huddled around and said things like, "Now why would she want to do that? Doesn't she know she can do it herself? She doesn't need anyone to do it on her."

I interrupted them, saying, "Excuse me, but it's sometimes nice to allow other people to do the work. I get to lie back and take it all in for a change." I knew how stupid I sounded as soon as I said it. I mean, of course it's not work, it's the energy, and it's always there!

One spiritual traveler chuckled, and then whispered an aside, saying, "She likes the idea of freebies, even though light energy is always free!"

That's when I learned what many healers already know, or at least I hope they do. Many healers realize that they do not do the actual healing; they perhaps act as a canal lock, opening the flow, dialoguing with our own healing energy field. It's up to us (Soul) and Spirit, how much we let the energy flow through us, and then, interact with it; for instance, asking to see the next step, or asking for what we need to know.

Ask for What You Need

The next time you practice a Key exercise (for example, singing a favorite word and looking at the Blue Star or Third Eye portal), pause for a moment. Ask to be shown what your illness has come to offer you. What is Spirit trying to show you?

Then ask, "What is my next step?" Ask to be shown the best possible present that Spirit can give you. Desire it in a healthy way, meaning "for the benefit of all relations." And state that you are willing to make the necessary changes.

End by saying, "May the blessings be."

Some may even want to write a letter to God, asking for a spiritual healing. If you do, then place the letter under your pillow for a month. Each night before you fall asleep, read the letter, and then go to sleep. Take the words with you into the dream state, and detach yourself from the outcome.

Writing the above section "What is Spiritual Healing?" was difficult. I did not want to interfere with the perfection and wisdom of Divine Source in any way. No one person, outside yourself, knows what you need or what's best for your spiritual unfoldment. When your ever-expanding experience—including energetic imbalances (dis-ease)—brings you meaning and value through living from that greater center in your heart, then your life and purpose are fulfilled. And when you accept what is, in the present moment, then you can listen for what you need to do, including a spiritual healing. To paraphrase an old saying: There is not much you can do about an approaching storm, but you can prepare for it, and then go out and dance in the rain!

Becoming Galactic Beings

Is it our spiritual purpose and destiny to become galactic beings? Perhaps the Ninth Key (9:3) is telling us we are becoming galactic beings, able to travel as Soul, out and beyond, past our galaxy for the purpose of seeing (i.e., visiting) what's out there in the physical universe and on parallel non-physical dimensions, and what's *in* there, in our own energy field. Our journeys *en masse* to the Photon Belt and the galactic core have caused waves of energy to enter Earth and affect our external environment. They also affect us internally in our body electric. We need to accept these new flows of energies which can help us travel beyond.

Recently I went for a dentist's appointment. When the dentist froze my mouth by using a needle, I received a strong electrical charge, reminding me that our bodies are composed of electricity. The Sun's charged particles on Earth's magnetic field and other natural disturbances, including earthquakes, changes in underground rivers, volcanoes and electrical storms, can cause us physical discomfort if we're unaware what to do.

Two friends of mine have become so sensitive to EMFs and changes in frequencies that they can't sleep at night because of a constant vibration that disturbs them. This could be the infamous "Hum" which is heard by many around the world. Humans are in transition, and the energies are only going to get stronger, therefore it's important to honor yourself, your reactions, and your sensitivities. The same applies to manmade energy fields, including cell phone towers, TV satellite dishes, or satellite waves hitting Earth.

Can we use the EMFs to help heal us? Does it matter if the waves are from manmade machines, even ominous ones such as HAARP in Alaska? Remember, there is no limitation (Fourth Key). Everything material has been created by us, through God. Evil and darkness do not exist, except in our minds. So there is a not-so-obvious reason why we've invented these unhealthy energy exchangers. Therefore, why can't we choose to allow the EMFs to heal us as they pass through our body? Is that the hidden purpose? Who knows? Maybe these manmade instruments were unintentionally invented to help us! Our responsibility lies in how we use them. I believe we can use these new, stronger energies, both celestial and manmade, to heal us and our planet. Anything is possible. Are we meant to relax into the energetics of a new world, accepting them as loving vibrations, in gratitude for who we are becoming: galactic beings? Go with the flow could mean to let the flow pass through you, unhindered.

Open to the Energy Flow

Be aware of how you're holding onto these energies in your body with fear, worry, or anger. Learn to let these waves pass through you, instead of tightening your solar plexus and blocking the flow. See yourself as an electrical cord and unknot the blockage to let it conduct its passage through you, flowing away from you. It's also important to remain positive. Accept the energy that's passing through as a wonderful opportunity to drink in the Luminous Energy Field, the river of divine love. That's why in the Fifth Key (5:3), Sixth Key (6:3), and the Seventh Key (7:2 & 7:3), we ask you to stop the distractions, especially negative ones, because they also block energy in your body.

Bless the Water

This Key Tip is for you to do as either an inner con-templation, or a physical exercise: you can go to a beach, lake, or river and stand in the water, lie in the bathtub, or hold a glass of water. Either way, you are standing in front of water. Feel the water, it's liquid essence. Look around at the amazing scenery, the colors, the sights and sounds. Slowly edge your way into the loving waters of luminous Living Energy. Feel the water's live energy currents surround you in a loving way. Breathe in the energy, its pureness. Bless the water. Water is the giver of life. Without it humans would not exist. At this moment in time, water needs your love. Release loving energy into the water. Watch the light energy flow from your fingertips or around your feet as it dazzles the water with sparkling phos-phorescence. You are exchanging healing energy. Then say "May the blessings be."

Summary of Ninth Golden Key

When you decide it is your time to contribute to the emerging new world, you will naturally aspire to a better, fairer, and more peaceful way of living, paving new pathways toward social equality. Let the lessons of the Ninth Key show you how to maneuver in this new world. When activating the Ninth Key your lesson is to learn:

- To realize we have infinite choice and the ability to manifest what we want, including a spiritual healing
- To listen to your heart and reshape your life without fear
- To practice flexibility and have the ability to shift gears at a moment's notice
- To take action, knowing instantly it's the right choice for that moment
- To handle change and chaos, knowing we must all learn this skill
- To surrender to the flow of life, trusting the changes

❧❧★❧❧

NINTH KEY STORIES

The Ninth Key helps you discover and clarify your Soul's purpose. By living your life as a clear channel you gain a direct connection to Soul's purpose and guidance. Marjorie Haynes, R.M.T., describes her experience of realizing her healing abilities and trusting the gift.

Trusting Our Gifts—Brownie's Gift to Me
By Marjorie Haynes

There is a sweetness of being so easily lost in this complicated world. And sometimes the simplest event can become a lifelong lesson we can always draw upon. Brownie was just that sweet, special event in my life. Brownie was a vibrant chocolate brown lab who taught me, more than any human teacher, to accept the fact I am a healer.

Trust is essential before healing can occur. Not only do the sick and injured need trust, but the healer also needs trust, most of all to allow the opportunity for miracles to happen. So it was with young Brownie who was running and jumping on the beach, leaping with joy into the air, carefree—until she slipped on a log and twisted her back. Her plaintive yelp sent her owner running to help her. For days after, she moved with a painful limp and slow swagger.

Her owner, a childhood friend, asked me, "Do you ever work on animals?"

As a newly licensed massage therapist I answered, "No, I have very little knowledge of animal anatomy."

With more than a little coaxing I agreed to see Brownie, if only to pet and soothe her. When Brownie walked toward me with such trust in her eyes, I thought, maybe I will just touch her like I do my clients and see what happens.

The moment I touched Brownie she dropped to the ground, limp and in a trance. I was shocked. "Is that what happens to people on my massage table?"

I began to understand why people were booking so quickly for sessions. It certainly was not to see me, but to experience what was working through me. As I ran my hand along Brownie's spine, her vertebrae rippled, and I clearly saw pressure on the discs in her back and the twist in her hips. I spoke out loud to her owner about what my impression was, and that I thought she should definitely see the Vet. Then Brownie's body began to stir, and she slowly got up, looked at me with a peaceful eye, and walked easily to her bed where she slept for hours.

A few days later, Brownie's owner came to see me at the clinic where I worked and entered the staff room with the biggest grin, and an arm filled with X-Rays. She pulled one out and said, "I want you to see this. It's a picture of exactly what you said you saw in your mind."

I will never forget that moment, seeing Brownie's spine in black and white, validating my inner impressions which, up to then, I had discounted as my imagination. What my mind's eye was seeing was REAL!

Forever, my work was changed, because I recognized the healing gift I was given, and I realized it could now be given to others without hesitation. Thank you, Brownie, for teaching me so much and for reflecting back to me a most important aspect of myself, which I could only see through you—trusting in my gift. Through your eyes I found a new trust in small miracles, and that changed me forever.

❧❧★❧❧

Reverend Sharon Richlark has a personal recollection of Hanna Kroeger that relays many spiritual principles: following your inner guidance (Second Key), learning how to help one another (Third and Sixth Key), using the dream state, going with the flow, and discovering your life's purpose (Ninth Key).

Discovering My Life's Purpose
By Sharon Richlark

In 1987, while I was advising people on how to get in touch with their spiritual guides and their higher selves, I was given a message to start an angel store in Vancouver. There were no angel stores in Canada at that time. Through my research I discovered that the only angel store in all of North America was in Denver, Colorado.

My three women business partners and I decided to drive to Denver to visit this angel store and see what it was like. After visiting the store, we were leaving Denver to return home when I mentioned a story that had been told to me by two people who didn't know one another.

Years earlier, my bio-kinesiologist advised me that there was a woman in Boulder with whom I would come to have a very strong connection relating to my work and life's purpose. Later, one of my students who had an accurate talent in accessing the spiritual dominions and information flows, told me I would meet a woman who was to be my life teacher, and that this woman would be like a mother to me. It would change my life and I would carry on her work, adapting it in such a way as to be the "messenger" of her work. I would study with her, sitting at her feet, taking in every word, handwriting everything that she said and did.

In the car, my friends asked, "Well, have you met her yet?"

"No! I'm not interested in meeting her. My life is too busy."

But, within half an hour, we were heading to Boulder where this woman lived. I had been given her name by the kinesiologist, and so, when I told my partners her name, they wanted to meet her. But I didn't have any interest in pursuing it.

On the outskirts of Boulder we saw the long dirt road that led to a country residence. There was a large iron blue cross in the middle of the field with a sign that said, Peaceful Meadow Retreat. I sensed that Spirit was very much present on the property. We drove up to the residence, went to the screen door and knocked.

Out came a very tiny and angry woman. She was angry at *me*, no one else. She wore black stockings, a navy blue German-style dress with a white bib apron, a little white frilly cap on her head, and she held a wooden spoon, which she shook at me. I had never met her before in my life! She was Reverend Hanna Kroeger.

She proceeded to bawl me out because I had taken so long to come to her. She was so angry she couldn't speak to me. She took the three ladies into a common room and left them there with their mouths open! Then she pushed me into another room and told me to sit and not disturb her. She was going to talk with the other ladies but not with me.

I sat in the other room, looking at pictures and statues of Jesus and Mother Mary, and beautiful plants that were growing wild. I saw a map of the United States of America and on this map Hanna had placed string, sand, copper wire, pieces of fabric, crosses, and various crystals in order to help purify and heal North America. The energy of Mother Mary and the presence of angels were very strong in the room. I realized I was supposed to be there and became comfortable.

Hanna would come in and check on me every so often. She became less angry because she realized I was doing what she wanted. She reminded me of my mother.

An hour later, Hanna led me out of the room. She had made one of the women write down strict instructions, things to do about my health. We were to go to her herb shop in Boulder and purchase the list of items that had been written down. She said she was not going to contact me again until I did exactly what was written there. My friends were upset, concerned about my welfare. They'd never experienced anything like this before.

And so, on the way home we stopped at one of the nation's first health food stores, the now famous Hanna's Herb Shop on Pearl Street in Boulder. Opened in 1957, Hanna's Herb Shop became recognized around the world for helping people. Many people in the area said that Hanna had saved their life and they called her the "Grandmother of Health." She was a Master Herbalist and she understood the dynamics of natural laws, working with old and ancient methods from the obscure Aramaic texts of Jesus which had come into her possession years before in Europe. We purchased everything that was on the list.

Upon returning home, I proceeded to follow Hanna's protocol and my health improved dramatically. Within two months I returned to Boulder to train with Hanna, knowing I was meant to master her techniques and become one of her people. Hanna recognized our direct connection and told me I was to know my life's purpose by knowing her.

I remember that on Sundays for church services in the Chapel of Miracles, cars would arrive starting from early morning and park everywhere on the property. People came to receive her sermons and dissertations for health and spiritual healing. Students and facilitators would also sit and pray, working with the vibration of healing through the chanting of prayers and traditional hymns. After church, there would be a seemingly mile-long line up of people waiting to see Hanna. Well-known individuals of all walks of life came to greet Hanna for healing, inspiration, and understanding. I witnessed miracles on numerous occasions.

Hanna passed away in May 1998 at the age of eighty-five. That following Sunday they held a commemorative service—on Mother's Day.

NINTH KEY EXERCISE

Go With the Flow

Here is a two-part exercise that will clear energy blocks in your outer environment and find a safe inner place.

Part One: Clear Energy Blocks

1. Find a place in your home that you feel has an energy blockage or is uncomfortable—for example, a telephone pole outside your window that has transformers or transmitters on it, or a thick black cable running from pole to pole or from a pole to your home, or a cell phone tower. Does the energy bother you? Can you get to sleep?
2. If your calls to the telephone or electric company fall on deaf ears, there are a few things you can do. Feng Shui consultants suggest hanging a crystal in the window between the intrusive energy and your home. Or you can do this...
3. Envision the manmade frequencies as a flowing current of light energy entering your body through your feet, up your spine, and exiting freely through the top of your head. It is accompanied by a sound frequency which purifies your

physical body.

4. Listen to your breathing, and then slowly listen for a sound either in your inner ear, or outside yourself, like the planetary hum underneath all manmade sounds. Keep listening, it will come. Now boomerang this healing energy back to the manmade transformer or cell phone tower. And witness how its energy shifts for your betterment.

Part Two: Find a Safe Environment on the Inner

1. Imagine the inflow and outflow of this river of divine love as an energy always flowing through you, always filling you up with its essence. You are awash in Living Energy as you step into the flow of the divine current, healing and purifying you. There is never any depletion of energy except in our own limitation.

2. Now see yourself following the channel of divine energy into the universe and go wherever it leads. Go out of yourself.

3. Find a special place in the universes, whether in another dimension or in an inner room in a golden temple, a cloud plane, a meditative garden, a tree house, a location on the Moon, another planet, anywhere you are led. Imagine it as real as anything in your home world. The energy in your safe environment has a pure healing effect to renew your Soul essence.

4. Start to sing your favorite word. Let it roll off your tongue and into space as you ride this sound current. Then quietly ask, "Show me that which I need to know, either now or after I awaken." You can put a time limit on it, in 24 to 72 hours.

5. After making the request, your inner guide may appear and take you somewhere. Go with the experience for however long it takes. You are about to receive a gift.

6. Open your eyes, remembering everything. Write it down in your special journal. And expect a major realization—a miracle—within your specified time period.

∾∾★∾∾

TENTH KEY:
LET GO AND DREAM TRAVEL

1. Let go and dream travel, living in the present moment.
2. Picture yourself in a boat on the ocean of Living Energy. You untie the rope and the boat drifts away from the dock, free to go wherever the current of divine love takes you. Surrender, let go in order to experience daily miracles, or that which Spirit wishes to show you in the inner worlds. Soul and Spirit know best.
3. Raise your state of consciousness above the physical or material worlds. There are many states of consciousness, and many worlds to explore while dream traveling.
4. When you consciously soul travel you shift your attention from the here-and-now to another here-and-now based in the spiritual worlds. Like sailing from one point to another, you are always in the here-and-now, consciously aware, even though the location has changed. You can control when to shift awareness and, thus, can choose when to dream travel.
5. Let go of preconceived Earthly beliefs that no longer serve you, and immerse yourself in the Spiritual (R)evolution of the heart. You are a caterpillar becoming a butterfly, discovering the path of the awakened heart, living consciously.

(10:1 to 10:5)

WHEN YOU CAN LET GO AND DREAM TRAVEL, you begin to believe in miracles and live in the present moment. Thus, the Tenth Key may change your life dramatically, because you will start to see miracles all around you. This chapter reminds you that through conscious dream travel you gain the ability to shift your attention from the material world to the worlds of Soul, by letting go of preconceived Earthly beliefs that no longer serve you.

Letting Go = Rebirth

When you let go and learn to shift gears it's like being reborn! In the First and Fourth Keys you learned about the creative imagination and how to use it to do the inner dream travel exercises. When we use the creative power within, we begin to live a creative life, which allows us to Live to Live! Once rediscovered and embraced, it is a powerful tool to reclaim more gratitude, health, joy, success, hope, abundance, and love. Fear and guilt have stopped us from living our potential, but now we can choose to live life abundantly, as Spirit intended. We can use our creative power and imagination to let go and tap into Soul's guidance.

...And the Caterpillar Becomes a Butterfly

Our one purpose in living on the Earth plane is to learn how to give and receive love. The Tenth Key (10:2) describes letting go as untying a boat's rope from the dock and letting the waves and the breeze carry it along in the flow, as the Ninth Key said. However most of us try to steer our own boats, giving full reign to the Mind Minotaur. What would happen if we took our hands off the steering wheel? Think for a moment, what would your life be like if you let go of trying to control your reality, or for that matter, anyone else's? How would it be different?

You will soon discover that Soul and Divine Spirit will do a better job of driving your life. How wonderful to let someone else do the driving for a change and all you have to do is rest and relax into the arms of Source. The veiled haze across your

Third Eye is suddenly taken away and the illusions you've been living under disappear. When reality is finally revealed, what is underneath is divine love. You awaken from your cocoon to be reborn as a butterfly, rebirthing passion in your life and learning to Live to Live (Sixth Key). As we let go and evolve from fear and guilt to unconditional love and innocence, we find ourselves effortlessly judging less and loving more. Only in a state of non-judgmental and non-analytical mind do you become detached and disentangled enough to surrender to unconditional love, and that is when miracles happen!

Basically, there are two ways we can walk through life:

- Walk the path of ego/will, which leads you to fear, guilt, and anxiety.
- Walk the path of the heart, which leads you to content-ment, passion, and purpose.

Most of us fluctuate between these, but as a child of Spirit you are divine love—a child of innocence, not guilt. To embrace the new consciousness, I needed to let go of beliefs based in guilt. When you feel guilty, you are controllable. But, of what are we guilty?

The Electric Blue Butterfly

 From a young age I took myself to Sunday school, to either the Baptist or United Church, whichever one I decided to go to on Sunday morning. I read the Bible and loved the stories of Jesus and the little children. But I knew there was more.

Having been a monk, a priest, a nun, and other religious devotees in past lives, my interest in all religions in this lifetime was a past-life carry-over. Thankfully, the Sages remind us that we can reconnect with Source through dream travel. While dream traveling our terrestrial form (the physical caterpillar) is set free to wander in spiritual flight (the ethereal butterfly).

The Tenth Key asked me to let go of my past church-influenced, one-sided knowledge in order to raise my state of consciousness above the laws of the Earth plane, that is, to evolve from a social consciousness to a Soul consciousness. I had to let go of my traditional religious guilt, too, in order to move toward an inner spiritual path, one based on love, not fear. As an emerging butterfly I had to intentionally embrace what I was becoming and remind myself that I am only here temporarily, to learn to give and receive divine love.

One night I was in the dream state and saw a blue butterfly. The wings were an incredible electric blue. It flew by me, wanting me to follow. When I started to run after it, I felt my feet lift off the ground and my body embrace the air, floating. Following the butterfly over fields, rivers, and farmhouses, the delightful experience lasted minutes, but seemed like an hour. When I woke up, the morning sunshine filtered through the window. There was a butterfly on the glass, drying its wings with a flutter, and asking me to follow it again. I realized that the two states of consciousness, the inner dream state reality and our outer reality, are connected; and we notice it when we're alert to the subtle nuances of Spirit. Now, whenever I see a butterfly, I know Soul wants my attention.

How to stay present in this world shift in consciousness is the challenge, and whether to love or to fear. (Actually, keep a little fear, it keeps us alert.) The answer lies in the ability to shift your attention from your present reality to another consciousness based in the spiritual worlds of Living Energy. Find the balance between having an authentic spiritual experience as Soul and multi-tasking here in your present life. You can be in two places at one time, and both are in the here and now. (10:4)

My over-zealous seeking was the result of mistrusting my inner experiences. I used to spiritual travel all the time, but because no one told me my experiences were real, I kept seeking for something on the physical Earth plane. As I learned to stay in the present, I was able to remember being in the Otherworlds and to value my experiences. I would pop back into my body and wonder, "Where was I? Where did I go just then?" I wasn't just daydreaming; I was having a fabulous, simultaneous, multi-dimensional, out-of-consciousness experience! If we were to live consciously in the present moment at all times, we would do that all the time. Together let's momentarily let go, resting our weary minds as we try this next exercise.

He came to make the human heart a temple, and the soul an altar, and the mind a priest. These were the missions of Jesus the Nazarene, and these are the teachings for which He was crucified.

—*Kahlil Gibran*[88]

Let Go to Become a Butterfly

When I was a child I innocently caught a butterfly and held it up to my cheek, feeling the soft flutter of its wing. The butterfly's gentle caress was tenderness personified. And then I released the butterfly and it would fly away in a gentle whisper. We are learning to let go in order to be reborn into conscious freedom, living our life with passion and purpose.

It is possible to raise our consciousness above the material planes. But can we let go of the dogma and opinions that others have taught us? Yes, by simply listening to our own breath. If you are unable to, or choose not to, that's okay, too. But for now, try it. Let go of your outside environment and listen to your breathing. I knew a construction worker who used this technique while walking the steel beams of tall buildings. It helped him focus, he said.

Breathing in and out deeply, listen to the breath. Then go deeper with each breath, listening deeper, too. Listen to what the breathwork does to your inner core, your belly, your gut; feel the releasing of your intestines, the straightening of your spine, the loosening of your shoulders; sense yourself aligning with your breath.

Finally, listen for a sound that enters your Third Eye, flooding it with light. It is the sound of Living Energy rushing in through your breathing and is as gentle as the fluttering wings of a butterfly.

Let go of all of it, except your own breathing. The Persian poet Rumi wrote, *Fahi ma Fahi* or *It Is What It Is* in the present moment.[89] From that place, focus on what's best for you and see yourself going to what's next. Spread your wings and fly out of the cocoon, becoming a butterfly. Waiting for you on the other side of illusion is a brand new world. Whenever life beats you down come back to this exercise; find a quiet spot, anywhere you can, and breathe.

Stay in the Present

One way to practice staying in the present moment, accepting your new state of consciousness, is to write what you're seeing and hearing, smelling and tasting, from moment to moment. By practicing this daily exercise, you will soon learn how to let go and focus on the present moment.

Sit quietly and listen. With a pencil and pad, make note of all the sounds you hear: the sights, the feelings, the smell in the air, the breeze on your skin. Keep writing, keep sensing, and keep the present moments coming off the tip of your pencil. The more you practice this exercise, the easier it becomes. You can even write a letter in your dream travel journal to your spiritual guide.

Live 2 Live in the present moment is key to accessing the new spirituality (Sixth Key). Because you live in the present, you no longer worry about the future. The future will, after all, unfold without your worrying about it. Therefore, you no longer fear the future. Your life is full because everything you need to know is in the present. And more importantly, you trust your inner experiences. Being fully in the present also prepares you for the future through the guidance of Soul.

Awaken to the New Reality—"God's Creative Freedom"

It's time to awaken to the new reality of conscious freedom. The Spiritual (R)evolution is awakening more and more people every day, and at an accelerated rate. Once you realize that spiritual travel exists and is real, you will never look at the world in the same way. Your inner life is real and always has been.

The foundation of this book is that we are composed of Source—Living Energy—and our physical bodies are vehicles in which Soul resides temporarily. Soul is ever-changing and growing, supported and loved by God. We are not our bodies, we are Soul, and so is every other person, animal, or reptile that lives on this planet, including extraterrestrial beings who visit us. Intergalactic beings are also Soul, like you and I.

We actually meet one another on parallel planes to exchange information energetically. The fact is, seventy-percent of our communication is through exchanging energy; and only thirty-percent is through words and gestures. Energy exchanges can happen unconsciously, such as while talking to one another at a social event, or consciously while meeting one another in the dream state.

Many of us have conscious dream travel experiences involving spaceships and meeting strange beings from other planets. No physical UFO sightings have been scientifically proven unequivocally. But then neither has the existence of God been proven by science. It is reported that some US astronauts on the Apollo missions had UFO sightings, but I cannot verify them. Unlike the movies, all were positive encounters with no invasive action from either side. What is true, is that space is a frontier for all beings and is meant to be shared peacefully.

Even the Vatican has commented on UFOs: "The extra-terrestrial is my brother," affirms the Vatican's chief astronomer, Father Jose Gabriel Funes. "How can we rule out that life may have developed elsewhere? ... Just as there is a multitude of creatures on Earth, there could be other beings, even intelligent ones, created by God. This does not contradict our faith, because we cannot put limits on God's creative freedom," Funes said.[90]

I know an Australian couple who witnessed six flying objects. The large flying objects hovered above them for several minutes. Another friend told me she saw flying objects hovering over San Jose, Costa Rica, in the mid-1990s. Apparently, it was not an unusual event. She said the mayor always requested the electricity be turned off so that everyone could have a better view of the UFOs.

What would it mean to you if the existence of UFOs was confirmed or you witnessed them for yourself like thousands of other people have claimed? How would it affect your life?

Would it surprise you to discover that Extraterrestrials, beings of another origin besides Earth, are similar to you because they also have feelings, social lives, and loving relationships? Would you react in fear, or would you be curiously compassionate? Would you like to find out? First, let go of preconceived Earthly beliefs. Make your intention, and then, let go and dream travel!

What Are the Benefits?

What are the benefits of learning the 12 Golden Keys? As Soul, our higher being, we are learning the 12 Keys in order to achieve ascension of consciousness while living in a physical body. Knowing the Keys allows us to remove the veil between worlds and view everything through the eyes of Soul. This allows us to learn about divine love and take a giant evolutionary step forward in communion with other inter-dimensional beings. The Keys also help us live in present reality on Earth as a member of society. By using the inner guidance of Soul we can plan ahead, envisioning and manifesting our future, creating wealth, wellness, and happiness.

Summary of Ten Golden Keys

1. You are the Key, live with self-responsibility.
2. Follow the Blue Light into the keyhole of Soul.
3. You are becoming a Key Guardian.
4. There is no limitation, everything is possible.
5. See truth through the eyes of immortal Soul.
6. Live to Live passionately in Spirit, with purpose.
7. Lighten up to light up, getting rid of distractions.
8. Live from love and gratitude.
9. Ride the inflow and outflows of energy.
10. Let go and be HERE/NOW in order to dream travel.

❧❧✦❧❧

TENTH KEY STORIES

Experiencing other states of consciousness includes meeting other Beings of Light within those different realities and promoting a bridge for the emergence of a planetary consciousness. Marie Eklund believes it is time for our First Contact with extraterrestrials, if Earth's humans can just get into the galactic game.

Our Once and Future World
By Marie Eklund

We may have arrived at one of the greatest moments in human history, yet few can see it. I see our approach to 2012 as a celebrated universal playoff between forces of darkness and light. Let's pay attention—this could be the greatest game in history, when teams for the Light can score the winning point. Right now the game is in the closing ten minutes of the fourth quarter for Earth and the galaxy beyond. Watching from the skyboxes, advanced beings and agents of God are cheering us on! From their viewpoint, humans have been living on a kindergarten planet, learning by experience to know ourselves as Soul, not just as physical beings.

I, for one, am celebrating this moment in history. There is very good news: Mankind's spiritual evolution has been moving upward from kindergarten, advancing rapidly through the grades. Spiritual masters, angels and guides of peace, along with extraterrestrials and non-terrestrials of benevolence have been coaching us, assisting us in every way. If you have ever believed in them, been aware of their presence, now is the time to call on them. We have free will to decide when and where to invite greater beings into our lives, to ask them for assistance. They will never interfere and quietly wait for us to ask. But, will we ask? Will we allow them into our lives?

The dark forces are just one of the tools our creator uses to test us and make us stronger. They use fear to control our lives until we find another way beyond it, and divine love is the only way. Which will we choose, fear or love? This is the final test which stretches our understanding: To find the meaning of divine love and to overcome fear.

For a time, the forces of darkness appeared to be winning. Predictions of great upheavals around 2012 reached me early in 2008. Rather than become alarmed, I contemplated, asking my present spiritual guide and inner master to help me understand these coming changes. Within 24 hours I was led to a forgotten, out-of-print prophecy, written by his predecessor, my former spiritual teacher, in 1964. He had brought transformation into my life, decades ago, by healing my heart at a time when it was broken and cynical. It was a miracle to experience my heart filling with divine love and gratitude.

My teacher had a great love for the world, teaching me that even the darkest, most despairing, moments can turn around and change when my heart opens up to divine love and gratitude in a practice which lets God's light and sound flow in. This healing brought with it a new way for me to look at everything— through the eyes of Soul. Finding his prophecy this year was like discovering a buried time capsule which I was meant to uncover over thirty-five years later.

My teacher had the spiritual ability to look at the world's probable futures, depending on mankind's choices. One great approaching danger came to his attention back in 1964: a dark galactic force from beyond our planet which could gradually take control over Earth. Its greatest force would be that of mind control. As a spiritual teacher, his role was not to change the future, but only to awaken and prepare those moving into it. I believe this is one reason he devoted his life to the spiritual evolution of humanity, teaching the control of your own imagination through spiritual practice, dream study, self-responsibility, and self-discipline. These teachings were meant to counteract the mind control methods.

More and more evidence is coming forth indicating that in 1964 Earth *was* in a secret, galactic war in which Earth's moon and Mars eventually became staging grounds for the dark side.[91] And looking through the eyes of Soul, I can see the silver lining: Mankind's spiritual evolution upward since 1964 has affected the course of history positively, allowing benevolent extraterrestrials to bring an end to the long, galactic war and to enforce a peace treaty in 1995.[92] They are Earth's defenders and we are surrounded by these forces of light as we approach 2012—the ending of one cycle of evolution and the beginning of a new one, uplifting all of humanity and our entire galaxy. I believe we are now looking toward a remarkable future, leading to a Golden Age.[93] We now have the possibility of understanding the universe beyond us and will sometime soon become citizens within the Galactic Federation of Light, those benevolent, star-faring races.[94]

How do we meet the fear-based powers of the mind? Love and awareness do what confrontation cannot. Life is not about winning or losing. Life is a test of how we handle ourselves in difficult situations. Agents of God are watching our team with great optimism. They're the referees of this amazing game, and the winning play has divine love written all over it. Or, as I used to hear my inner master say, "The only kind of true revolution is a spiritual revolution."

❧❧★❧❧

When we ask Spirit to show us certain things, we are learning to surrender to whatever Spirit wishes us to know, either in the dream state, or in the inner worlds. The Tenth Key asks us to surrender, to let go in order to experience daily miracles. Denise Kellahan writes about her husband who died suddenly and then helped her from the other side.

Messages from the Other Side
By Denise Kellahan

We left on vacation anticipating a time to relax, rejuvenate, and spend time letting each other know how much we mean to one another. The lake, sunset, a dock, the dive, and the dance ended; then numbing shock settled in with terror and no understanding of the pain to come. And the search for his spirit, the driving obsession to know he is somewhere, that his energy continues, that my beautiful husband Richard is soaring and safe.

It has been two months since his tragic death and I have cried for days. I feel hopeless and somewhat helpless. I am supposed to be helping with a new grandchild. I feel as if I am not a good mother, not helping my daughter, that I should be more together. I am in my sunroom and leave to get showered. Returning, I notice a small white card face down on the carpet— the card from my Mother's Day flowers! It's long past Mother's Day. He'd written simply "Love R." How did it get there? It was never in this room and I haven't seen it since Mother's Day. His message, assuring me I am a good mother.

I go to bed one night and long for him to come. He visits me in the dream state. Feeling the physical weight of him on my body, I marvel that I can feel every muscle in his arms, his back, and I touch his hair. I say, "You really are here." He smiles. I ask Richard to please stay, I have so many questions. I get to ask one. I ask "Did it hurt?" He answers, "Not a bit." The message is clear to me: he is still loving me, and we are only separated by a dimension, and the reassurance that he did not suffer.

It has now been three years since Richard passed and it is time to sell the big house on the Island. I am stuck in my grief, living in the past. I walk the beach and speak out loud to him. I ask him to help me make the decision. Hours later, I see his reflection in the window, and hear him in my head. He asks, "What are you hanging on to it for?"

The house sells. I move to my new home on the mainland, and wait for another message.

It comes through my daughter's dream. She was walking her dog and it was raining and dark. A statue of an angel appeared and was illuminated in many colors. There was another statue behind, and it glowed brightly and, then, turned into Richard. My daughter says she experienced a joy that is hard to describe. It is the first time she has experienced contact with him from the other side. He was smiling and in that instant, she was pulled from her body, flying through the air to him.

She said, "It is you," and he smiled and hugged her. She had so many questions and knew somehow her time with him was very limited. She asked one question, wanting to know whether he was taken before his time. She did not remember his exact answer, but his message was very clear: "Your Mama is finally back home. And so am I."

❧❧ ✦ ❧❧

TENTH KEY EXERCISE

Dream Travel Using Sound

A spiritual exercise on how to dream travel by using sound:

1. Let go and dream travel by focusing your attention on the present moment. To do this, lightly focus on the sound in your inner ear, on your breathing, or whatever you're comfortable with. The different outer sounds such as an electrical hum, or an electromagnetic buzzing sound, or using the singing word technique, are all useful focusing tools. The universal sound current holds messages from the higher levels of your own consciousness.

2. Imagine you're sitting in a boat and it's tied to the wharf. Surrounding you is the sparkling ocean of luminous energy. There is a bank of fog hiding the horizon.

3. Now listen carefully for the gentle sound of a bell in the foggy distance.

4. You untie the rope and the boat moves away from the wharf. Paddle in hand, you balance the boat, moving toward the horizon, taking firm but gentle control, and paddling to the eddies of the current. Once in the current, you move with the motion toward the gentle sound of a bell in the mist, and you let Spirit guide the boat.

5. Approaching you out of the fog is another boat. It has a small bell that echoes over the water. You say, "Ahoy!" And the boatman steers the boat toward you. The boatman is a spiritual guide, or a Key Guardian.

6. If you choose, see yourself leave on an adventurous journey. Where do you travel? What experiences do you have? Know that the universe waits for you.

And so does the Eleventh Key.

Eleventh Key:
Share the Magic

1. Share the magic of Living Energy, the breath of Soul!
2. Live to give, helping others help others. Hold more Living Energy to give more, and you become a channel through which the energy reaches the world. The more energy you embody, the greater your ability to share and communicate the magic, while remaining in the Here/Now, anchored in reasonable reality.
3. Sharing the magic of kindness changes people instantly, helping the world move toward a new sustainable humanity based on a realistic and expanded viewpoint.
4. Share the wisdom of Soul by spiritual traveling, meeting others on the inner or by going out into the world and *doing*, living your daily life.
5. Challenge yourself to remain in the higher frequencies while sharing the magic, not letting the heavier and coarser energies of your world affect you. Keep your mind, body, and spirit running smoothly with the Living Energy.
6. Attune to the shifting vibrations of the universal energy, the divine consciousness, and enter the new age of conscious living, aware of your intentions.

(11:1 to 11:6)

WHEN YOU BELIEVE IN LIVING ENERGY, you can begin to share the magic. The Eleventh Key can help us discover our purpose for being here, and what we are meant to share with others for the benefit of all. Everything you can dream or imagine exists right now, waiting for you to manifest it in the present moment. Contentment is now. Allow the life force to work its magic through you to act as a channel to prepare for change. In this chapter we will learn how to be better channels for Living Energy in order to do service and share the magic, and how conscious freedom co-creates a safe haven for you and your family, allowing you to live with an expanded viewpoint.

How to Share the Magic

It is time for each of us to share what we've learned, like the indigenous people have done with their ancient knowledge. The Mayans shared with us their prophecy of a coming shift so we could prepare for change, but not in the normal way. Instead of telling us to store food and water, they prepared us by explaining that to survive we need to do a consciousness shift from our head to our heart. Whatever happens in this great temporary and changeable sphere is all meant to be. Disasters, whether economic or physical, are gateways through which spiritual enlightenment can be gained. Whatever form the great balancer takes, we will survive. For example, in the fall of the world economy, we regain the rise of our spirit. Fear can force us to discover our safe haven or community, which then blossoms into helping others help others.

Sharing a New Community Spirit

What interests me is world community and the aspiration of giving and receiving to forge a new humanity based on helping others help others. The Eleventh Key is all about sharing. We were always meant to become co-workers with Living Energy and to establish social relationships in global cooperation based upon helping one another—friends helping friends. And this is not socialism, or neo-liberalism, or any manmade ideology.

A new dawn of civilization is just beyond reach. The world is our community. You and I on this planet together can come together as neighbors in a world community, a global village. There is room enough for all of us. But there is no room for fear. Where is the Belonging? We've been alienated from one another far too long, sequestered in our cubicles, in our cocoons, in our causes. There is only one cause: Aspiring to love and be loved, to give and receive. We are messengers of the divine energy. We are angels of light. Each and every one of us has the ability to tap into divinity and become one.

—*Utides,* Chapter 36, p. 276

Eileen Caddy, author and co-founder of Findhorn, says: "Set your sights high, the higher the better. Expect the most wonderful things to happen, not in the future but right now. Realize that nothing is too good. Allow absolutely nothing to hamper you or hold you up in any way."[95] These are wonderful words of advice.

The Keeper

While visiting Honolulu, in 1972 I met a young man in a nightclub who described himself as a "Keeper." In today's language, he would mean Earthkeeper.

Chris was a gorgeous blonde surfer-type, not yet twenty years old, who walked the streets of Waikiki barefoot. No doubt, what he wore on his back was all he possessed. It was the height of the Hippie movement; the influences of free love and flower power were everywhere. But he was different.

I spent less than four hours with "Chris the Philosopher" as I came to call him, then I never saw him again. The entire experience was for the purpose of meeting a spiritual traveler, long before I knew what that even meant, and to open my Third Eye. I needed to meet him at that precise moment in my life to remember who I really was behind my adopted veil of illusions perpetuated by society. I needed someone to turn on my light.

Chris said to me, "It doesn't matter whether I believe in the devil, the spirit world, reincarnation, Jesus, or not, only that I believe and live what I was *given* to believe in. Here and now is where we are, all the rest shouldn't matter."

He looked around the nightclub and then said, "What's important is to communicate with one another in brotherhood and to love one another spiritually, Soul to Soul. And let's hope that it comes to pass, for I say unto you that if humanity continues to not communicate with their brothers and sisters, the world will become a stone tomb of buildings, a place of no vegetation, no growth, no food, and no clean breathing air." Remember, this was 1972. He continued, "It will become a world of pill tablet food and of evil in not knowing one another. Therefore, we will experience disastrous cruelty toward each other because of our cold souls."

Chris spoke a long time before giving me the following four points. They are very straightforward and show us how we can share the magic. Briefly, they were:

1. Do not honor any God that is not within you; Soul is within you.
2. You are your children's children; therefore, spread the word of ecology, of love for this earth that it may be a beautiful place, instead of the world becoming a corporate metropolis where the future is leading us.
3. Communication between one another is the most important thing to humanity.
4. You are a Keeper, be a Keeper.

Like the Native American Elders who are the Earthkeepers, Chris the Philosopher embodied a mastership all his own. I was young when I met him, and it was a major turning point in my life. It was the day I woke up.

Be an Earthkeeper

Be an Earthkeeper but don't *keep* the Earth and try to control it. I am too much of a realist to plan on walking barefoot around the world teaching and sharing the magic. I might secretly admire those who can afford to do this, but it's not my mission. I also admire the innocent concepts of ecovillages and living in community with others, but as far as I know it rarely works. And I am not interested in living in a community that is disorganized, has no financial business plan, hides in a bubble, and doesn't know why it exists. This is spiritual la-la-land. If you join a spiritually-based community that is not interested in facing reality and has no business sense, walk away with your money in your pocket. Living communally to meditate all day is unrealistic. Personally, I think a bit of fear wakes us up to the reality behind the propaganda façade, and we look behind the curtain for the real wizard of Oz.

The greater your ability to share, communicate, and elevate the new reality, while keeping anchored in reality Here/Now, the safer and wiser you will be (11:2).

However, there are ecovillages and communities, sometimes called "intentional communities" which *do* work, such as Findhorn in Scotland, Damanhur in Italy, Keuruun Ekokylä in Finland, and a few others.[96] They work because they demonstrate sustainable development in environmental, social, and economic terms. They are attempting to get away from waste, pollution, and violence, but they are economically sustainable. They are for-profit communities, business oriented, and yet, they are in the business to serve others, something Susan Standfield talks about in the Third Key.

Briefly, a social and political example is the "constellation model" of collaborative social change conceived by Tonya and Mark Surman of Toronto's Centre for Social Innovation.[97] It consists of social change activities that are handled by "constellations" or small, self-organizing teams who are connected by a similar mission statement. It is one example of the many options we need to share if we are to have a collaborative future.

Share Your New Spirituality

The best way to share the magic is to simply live your life; living your daily life by going to work, meeting people, connecting and exchanging energies, and listening to the needs of others. It is also the best way to expand your own heart. It can be as simple as doing a kind act for someone. Some of you will be introducing your newfound spirituality, or consciousness shift, to those who still live in the old belief systems. So it's important to remember that you are only a messenger. Stay in your own personal power without judgment toward others and yourself. In other words, don't go to their vibration, instead, have them meet you. At the core of your being, you are love itself, so remember the magic and pass it on!

Recycling the Heart for Kindness

 Sharing the magic of kindness can change people instantly. It's incredible when you realize that your one kind act can lead to one kind step forward for humanity. One man is giving his life for kindness. Vancouverite Brock Tully—author, speaker, fundraiser, and concert producer—began a bicycle ride in 1970 long before bicycle touring became a sport.[98]

"People of all ages, color, and race want a kinder world; the ripple effect from just one warm smile can be so far reaching." So began a six-month bicycle journey across Canada, the United States and Mexico to spread kindness. The first tour was a journey to find himself. Thirty years later he jumped on a bicycle once again and pedaled out to share simple acts of kindness. Brock and his support team inaugurated his Cycling for Kindness Tour in February 2000 and rode 11,000 miles around the USA and Canada. In 2008 he rode out again.

"I set out on the journey to raise awareness about the importance of kindness and inspire people everywhere to take positive action in their lives, in their homes, communities, schools and workplaces," Brock said.

Brock Tully's message is simple: Living to the fullest by giving to the fullest.

His 2000 ride for kindness drew media attention everywhere across North America, and he found himself being invited to do presentations at schools and community centers which further raised awareness. After 205 days of pedaling through freezing temperatures and blistering heat, battling fierce wind in his face, changing numerous flat tires, being almost sideswiped by semi-trucks, and having close calls with snakes and even an alligator, Brock and his team arrived back home in Vancouver to a motorcycle parade and cheering supporters.

During his journey through hundreds of towns, meeting thousands of people, Brock saw how much alike we are and realized how he could inspire people to view the world from their heart instead of their head.

Brock writes in one of his series of *Reflections* books: "...when we communicate, we see that our likenesses are greater than our differences ... when we don't communicate, we're more likely to 'only' see our differences."

Brock created the KindActs Network of BC to inspire children and adults to do acts of kindness through various programs. Members feel that, by focusing totally on the solution, they will create a culture of kindness and this will lead to less bullying and violence in schools.

"When you do preventative things it is very challenging, but most important is to get to the 'cause' and solution," Brock says.

Through the Coin-spiracy program, schools take part in circulating special coins. Youth groups and schools in over forty-five countries have now taken part in the program. If you receive the coin you must do three acts of kindness: one for yourself, one for the environment, and one for another person or animal, and then the coin is passed on.

An eight-year old student once told Brock, "If every school did Coin-spiracy, then what would happen is hardly any of the world would have cruelty to animals; the environment would be nice; there would be lots of kind things going on; lots of poor people would have blankets, clothes, toys and food. I hope the coin gets passed on all around the world forever and others learn to be kinder."

A school principal told Brock: "What is really important for us is the whole idea of kindness to self, kindness to others, and kindness to the environment. It's great. It gets the students to look beyond our own school walls, our own borders and start to look at how we can be kind to others outside of our own borders. And to know that we are part of a global project that is going on around the world is fantastic."

No act of kindness, no matter how small, ever goes unnoticed as he continues to dedicate his life to random acts of kindness. He writes, "i may not be able to change the world i see around me, but i can change the way i see the world within me."

The Wonderful World of WWOOFers

Living to give is about sharing the magic that Spirit has given us. Our youth of the world, the Kids of the New Earth, are opening to new ways of living on the planet and utilizing the gifts of Living Energy. My sister and brother-in-law offer a place where young adults can learn about organic farming. They also share, with permission, the magic of one's inner connection with Spirit, and how eating organically grown food keeps your body-engine running smoothly.

Dear LifeSpring Farm:

 Before WWOOFers[99] (the members of World Wide Opportunities on Organic Farms) leave to head back home, they write comments in the farm's notebook. Here are a few comments, edited for brevity's sake. The youth of the world truly are lighting up!

I really understand now that everything you need is in the country, in nature. This was my first farming experience. I felt like a whole new world was opened up to me. And it was. Though sometimes I fall back, it's okay because now I have this memory to help me. I remember being scared to even enter the horse yard when I first came. And now I love horses. I now know that if you ask for something, you're given an opportunity.

—**Millie**, age 21, from Vancouver, BC

Here, I remembered that laughing is good for the Soul and that we are always in the right place because we're always learning. It has been very healing and a blessing for me to work outside

with my hands in the dirt every day, and it is a confirmation for me that I have a certain connection with plants.
—**Jaya**, age 23, from Montreal, Quebec

I lost my happiness for a few years and I had forgotten how to feel things around me. These five weeks I spent working on the farm were a rebirth. You opened a window in my mind and I'll never forget that. I learned so much about nutrition, spirituality, how to work with others, how to cook, etc. and above all, I learned about love. You gave me back my smile.
—**Josephine**, age 18, from France

Coming here and staying at your farm, has saved my life.
—**Ben**, age 19, Toronto, Ontario

I wasn't quite sure of what to expect before I came, I only knew that I wanted to be here. I have learned so much and have been made aware of so many things about health, nutrition, spirituality, etc. It has been a life-changing experience for me. Also all the dogs, cats, horses, chickens, ducks, and cows … Please continue on your path!
—**Sally**, age 63, from Ft. Wayne, Indiana

Five WWOOF volunteers making compost tea.
Photo by Anastasia Milne Parkes 2007.

Three WWOOF volunteers bringing in the hay.
Photo by Anastasia Milne Parkes 2007.

These stories make me want to go *walkabout* again, on a spiritual journey to discover what's important to others out there in the world, to once again leave all my material distractions behind. The mass migration to inner wisdom has begun. Accept what *is* in the present moment and ask: "What is *my* reality, not the reality of others?" Go walkabout to see the world or meet your neighbors and help one another. And then return and teach others what you've discovered.

ﾞﾞﾞ★ﾞﾞﾞ

ELEVENTH KEY STORIES

Lesley Punt and her husband Russ Torlage, co-founders of SOTA Instruments Inc., use dreams and waking dreams to make important business decisions.

Dreams as a Guide in Troubled Times
By Lesley Punt

My husband and I had a dream—a dream to build a business to serve others. We got our start as a result of a debilitating fatigue that forced me to resign my position as Vice-President for a clothing manufacturer.

During the seven years I coped with fatigue, I sought help from several natural health practitioners. Each one helped me, but not enough to shed my fatigue. One turning point was the realization that I needed to live from my heart. I wrote in my journal, "I put my heart aside for what I thought was responsibility to earn a living. No more ...."

The next turning point occurred after my husband, Russ Torlage, and I attended a lecture by a physicist who explained how gentle currents of electricity, microcurrents, boost energy and restore well-being. This physicist had a strong desire to serve mankind. He lectured about the technology, selling the instructions for building the units and charging only the cost of photocopying. I am unable to name the physicist because government regulators would interpret that as making a health claim.

Russ has a passion for electronics. He built our first unit for me. When I applied the microcurrents, my initial reaction was to sleep more. After three weeks, however, I noticed I had more energy. After three 3-week sessions, my energy was restored. What a gift!

Russ was able to get one of the units to the physicist. He was so impressed with Russ' design, that he endorsed our company as a manufacturer. He and Russ collaborated on product designs and became good friends.

We realized our mission, and our dream became a reality. We knew that to serve more people, a structure was needed to collect information on how people were helped, as well as manufacture quality units at a reasonable price. Our role was to be stewards for this technology and SOTA Instruments, Inc., was launched (sotainstruments.com). Russ chose the name as it stands for "State-Of-The-Art" to reflect Russ' desire to design cutting-edge products.

As word-of-mouth spread, SOTA soon started to hear from people who had been helped. It was a moving experience that touched our hearts, and continues to do so. We also heard from government regulators. That's when dreams guided us through troubled times. We weathered a difficult four years as government intimidation threatened to shut us down.

We look for guidance from Spirit or God in our dreams as well as from waking dreams. Waking dreams are events and words we observe around us in daily life—signals that Spirit uses to guide us when we ask for help to make decisions.

One waking dream gave us hope. We were flying at night to Los Angeles for a brief vacation, early in our struggles with government agencies. There was a brilliant flash of light in the sky—it was a beautiful sight—and the pilot announced it was a test rocket launched by the government. The next day, we noticed a newspaper headline: "Government Misses Its Target." An anti-missile was not successful in finding its target. We felt that headline was a message from Spirit. The missile represented SOTA, and the message told us the government would miss and not shut us down.

We used our creative faculties to work around government— we called on our customers for feedback, we created relationships with government bureaucrats, and we got our elected representatives involved. We were constantly changing our policies, and Russ changed our website several times as we strove to be proactive. We wanted to keep serving people—people who believed in freedom to choose their health care.

Then I had three successive dreams that told us we needed to change direction.

We had been resisting government demands. The dreams told us we needed to cooperate with government in order to continue to serve those who wanted our products. The dreams made us realize the route offered by government regulators to license our units as medical devices—the route we had been rejecting—would be the shortest and safest.

Several months later, one regulatory hurdle was resolved when the Federal Trade Commission (FTC) in the US informed us they were withdrawing their charges. Russ had spent countless hours on the telephone with the FTC lawyer to create a relationship so they would better understand SOTA. The turning point came when our customers responded to a questionnaire we mailed to them. We are eternally grateful to the customers who responded by letting us know they had not been deceived in making their purchase.

Our hearts had gradually closed as we focused on appeasing governments rather than using our energy to help people. At one point we had most of our units licensed. Once we were licensed, however, regulators constantly demanded more information as they questioned the wisdom of licensing some of our units.

Then I had three more dreams. The message this time was that the medical device licensing route was no longer needed. We would not survive as the regulations were designed for large corporations.

Health Canada officially gave us the option to offer the units as consumer products with no licenses needed. Our dreams and waking dreams had guided us through a difficult four years.

We felt a great sense of relief. Our hearts opened as we could once again put our attention on serving people. We are very grateful to our amazing customers. Through word-of-mouth, they keep us going. The willingness of so many to share their experiences with the units and let others know about us allows us to continue to help others. For our part, we are grateful for the opportunity to be caretakers of SOTA.

✿✖✿

Sharing our spiritual beliefs is a beautiful expression of giving with permission. I asked Reverend Susan Hunt to tell me her story of how she discovered her path and formed a community to share divine love:

Garden of Miracles
By Reverend Susan Hunt

Inquisitiveness, curiosity and a strong desire to learn new ways of doing things have been very prevalent in my life. Asking questions about everything sometimes annoyed my family when I was young. However, my church minister enjoyed my tenacity and need to know what life was about: Why are we here? What's our purpose for being born, living and dying? He took a personal interest in helping me find answers to questions. He took me to the University of Toronto, Ontario, to sit in round-table discussions with theologians. I asked many questions, but one question seemed, somehow, more important.

"What and where is our relationship with God?"

This question seemed to perplex these learned men. Their answers, although appearing to be well thought out, were to me vague and empty and left me confused and even more curious. By my early twenties, I had tired of seeking and finding nothing, so I went in search outside my religion. In fact, I became a skeptic, a non-believer in God's care for me, and at best, just let the whole God thing go and got on with life.

Many years would pass before these early questions would surface again. One evening my girlfriend Annie called me and suggested we visit a fortune teller she had heard about. We ended up off Bloor Street in the middle of Toronto, entering a dark and dingy doorway with a sign that said "Teahouse."

Being skeptical of this new adventure, I looked around and noticed Wicca symbols on the walls, Egyptian hieroglyphics, occult symbols, crystals, brass bowls and a pungent odor wafting through the room. When the soothsayer walked into the room, my curiosity heightened. He resembled an ancient Sage or spiritual master who had lived many lifetimes. He said he read tea leaves, crystals balls, tarot cards and more. I settled for the method that matched the $5.00 in my pocket. And so, he read my tea leaves.

He told me that I would go to the Pacific Ocean; that my destiny lay on the shores of the Pacific. I told him I had no intentions of leaving Toronto. A few years later I found myself flying to Vancouver, not to return to Toronto for twenty-seven years!

Vancouver was a hot bed of the New Age movement and, while I was browsing in a bookstore, a hardcover book fell off the shelf and landed at my feet. The book was *A Course in Miracles* (ACIM). I picked it up and flipped through the pages and was prompted to buy it. ACIM is where I finally found the answers to the questions I had asked so many years before. But it also challenged everything I had been taught. It said my relationship with God had never ended; that there is no separation between God and me; that I had never done anything wrong and I was innocent. Everyone was innocent. The Course said this world is an illusion created by an ego thought system, a system founded in fear. This captured my interest. The word "forgiveness" kept popping off the pages. I was not to understand for quite some time the meaning of forgiveness that ACIM spoke of, but I kept reading. The Course can be summed up very simply this way: Nothing real can be threatened. Nothing unreal exists. Herein lies the peace of God.

One particular holy experience—a rather big nudge—occurred when I was walking at night past a little local church with its lights shining on the cross. Snow was falling. Glancing up at the lights on the cross I found myself on my knees crying. A quiet voice inside me was saying, "You are not alone, choose again."

So I found a Course of Miracles group to attend in order to share my thoughts and also listen. Soon after this experience, I felt compelled to start a community and eventually called it, Garden of Miracles Course Community. It was founded to give each person an opportunity for a deeper understanding of themselves and the Course and to be held in their true identity: a loved thought in the Mind of God. Garden of Miracles provides a safe space to open one's heart and experience inner peace, and to realize that *God is*.

෴✦෴

ELEVENTH KEY EXERCISE

Exercises in Conscious Living

To Share the Magic, Learn to Listen. The secret to practicing the Eleventh Key and sharing the magic is to listen. When you listen to what people need, it moves you beyond your ego-based opinions/judgments and shifts you to a heart-based sphere of consciousness. Listening with an open heart, with compassion, and without judgment, lets you know what *they* need.

Share the Higher Energy. The Eleventh Key points out that the more energy you hold, the more Light Energy you give; and to hold more energy, keep the toxins out of your body, mind, spirit, and environment. If you seek higher energy, and at the same time eat foods or befriend people that rob you of this new energy, your progress is diminished. The toxic cycle perpetuates itself. It is also true that the higher our vibration, the harder it is for toxins to enter.

Notes to Purify Your World. Purifying your world starts with purifying yourself. Find health practitioners in your area who can assist in cleansing, detoxifying, and nourishing your body. We need adequate nutrition, absence of environmental toxins, pure clean spring water, exercise, and joy. It is not necessary to be in perfect physical shape to hold the higher luminous energies in your body; but living a healthy lifestyle helps you to do more service and to live longer. Research the answers to these questions and more:

- What toxins exist in your environment, water, and food? What harmful chemicals are in your carpet, makeup, household cleaners, furniture, and even toothpaste?
- Which foods are over-processed, and contain additives?
- Which prescription drugs are addictive and harmful?
- Which media outlets (television, movies, books, web sites, and music) give subliminal negative messages to keep your mind depressed and suppressed?

Share Joy and Contentment. Do what makes you content. Find what gives you joy and share it. Be around people who nurture you. It's important at this point in your journey to no longer accept coarse influences. You're where you are because you choose to be there. If you're fixated on faults, worry or negativity, instead of virtues and the positives, the cycle continues. If you want to be somewhere else, you'll need to choose something else. Choose joy!

Do a Kind Act for Someone. Kindness brings joy to the giver and the receiver. The Eleventh Key (11:5) points out that the challenge is to remain in the higher frequencies and not let the heavier and coarser energies of your world affect you. Choose conscious freedom and be totally aware of your intentions and other people's intentions in the world around you. We are here to be a vehicle for love and to learn about love. Living your life from your compassionate heart (in the flow of life), as opposed to living in your head (always rationalizing, worrying and thinking), is by far, more advantageous. If you find yourself thinking and worrying too much, do a kind act for someone. A little shift of energy, changes everything!

To Know Joy, Share Joy. For me, contentment means inner peace and doing what gives my life vitality in the present moment. Know your passion and live it in the NOW. Find what you're enthusiastic about, what makes you content, whether it's being with your family and friends, playing with your pet, doing a creative activity, fixing your car, volunteering your time to help others, jogging, playing baseball, dancing, gardening, or reading inspirational books. Soul is a happy being. It doesn't need expensive gadgets to be happy. It only needs you to do what you love and stay present. On the other side of personal joy is the *giving* of joy: To know joy, give joy to the world.

And that brings us to the Twelfth Key.

TWELFTH KEY:
BE A SPIRITUAL WARRIOR

1. Be a Spiritual Warrior!
2. The Twelfth Key leads you to recognize the sphere of consciousness known as *grace,* that which is connected to forgiveness.
3. We are moving from an outer focus to an inner one, to a time when we will rise above the act of using power against another being. Instead, choose spiritual power or the *lack* of power. Spiritual power cannot be controlled or manipulated by any sentient being.
4. The world of two forces (power/fear and grace/love) will unify and be One, becoming the Middle Path. Shift from the mind or will to the heart, choosing to embrace the path of the awakened heart and to live consciously.
5. There will be a critical mass of understanding, and the world will be in a state of grace under the guidance of Living Energy.
6. Until this time, be a Spiritual Warrior, living in conscious freedom.

(12:1 to 12:6)

THE TIME HAS COME TO ACCEPT that you are a spiritual warrior of living energy, living in conscious freedom. The days of the sword have passed. Here are a few observances of a Spiritual Warrior for you to consider:

- A Spiritual Warrior is one who dissolves fear with love.
- A Spiritual Warrior lives a conscious life out in the world.
- A Spiritual Warrior uses the universal energy to heal the body and mind.
- A Spiritual Warrior does not overlook suffering in the world, but will not interfere without permission.
- A Spiritual Warrior practices attentiveness, fully present in the NOW.
- A Spiritual Warrior knows where she or he needs to be.
- A Spiritual Warrior is on an individual path, a living path with no rigid doctrine, ever fluid and ever-changing.
- A Spiritual Warrior keeps the doors to truth open, because truth has no secrets.
- A Spiritual Warrior spreads joy and kindness.

The Path of Grace

What is the Middle Path?

As introduced in the Third Key, a Spiritual Warrior is a being like yourself who has the courage to go on a spiritual quest for the divine consciousness within and to discover Soul—the Grail of legend. The Twelfth Key invites you to be this warrior.

The path of a Spiritual Warrior is different from most. Some people choose the easy road, while others the more difficult one. The Spiritual Warrior chooses the middle path, which is the original nature of a **sentient being**, conscious and awake (12:4). The middle path is easier than the easy path and yet more difficult than the most dangerous road. Does that sound like a contradiction? You must leave behind preconceived notions and attachments to ideologies that no longer serve you on your new path of conscious freedom, and move from an outer focus to an inner one (12:3). That includes letting go of old ego-based mind patterns, plus many beliefs that are in vogue and allow you to fit in with a group mentality. You must go beyond the world of mind to become Source.

Let's say you are a warrior who lives inside a digital computer game. Traveling the middle path in search of the Blue Star, you collect spiritual tools needed to go to the next game level. At each new level the monster-mind Minotaur is bigger, so you need a stronger spiritual "weapon."

Each time you pass a test, your weapon is replaced with one that is more useful. But you've got to let go of the one you have in order to get a better one. The more tests you pass, the more useful the spiritual tool. And so it goes with your worldview. You are being guided to let go of the old way of life you had previously accepted, and to realize there is a totally different way to live that rises above the mind and also above what you've been taught to believe.

This Great Turning—moving away from the mind (with its emphasis on thought-forms and will) to the heart (transformed, and living in Soul consciousness and a state of grace)—is precipitating a physical state of existence we have never known before, and we cannot even guess at the outcome. We have come to the end of our mental belief systems and are leaping across the void into a new way of being.

In order to help us embrace this new path and live consciously in this new world, we have been given not only the 12 Golden Keys, but also the first three Spiritual Warrior Codes.

Recap of Spiritual Warrior Codes

 The weapons of a Spiritual Warrior are compassion, charity, patience, virtue, and selflessness. Being a warrior does not mean you wage war. It means you stand for honor, right action, and humility, living your life with vitality, passion, and purpose to fulfill your inner destiny. It takes due diligence and practice. A true warrior is someone who has learned not to be afraid of struggle, change, and chaos. To recap, the first three codes are:

- Help one another. By example, act, and deed each of us can make a difference.
- We attract to us what we focus on. To change your life, change your attention and your attitude.
- If you live to serve life, you will have lived a life of purpose.

Quest of a Spiritual Warrior

 Many years ago in Manapouri, New Zealand, I sat down to contemplate near a magical lagoon seemingly in the middle of nowhere. Wrestling with feelings of unworthiness and believing I was supposed to be perfect, I sought guidance. These are the words that came through from this powerful sacred place via my inner wisdom:

"We are warriors, you and I, on a quest to lift the veil, the separation between worlds, the Grail of myth in each heart born as Soul. Our one weapon is the desire to know who we are and to know *why* we are .... The Divine Light is within you. It has always been with you. You are eternal; you have no beginning and no ending, for you are Soul. To seek perfection means to search for Soul."

The inner voice continued, "There are many tests on a spiritual quest. Most are tests of courage, but there is nothing to fear. Once the test is won, you will know this. It has taken you eons of time to approach this point. The trials in each of your lifetimes were for one purpose: to reach the golden wisdom of Soul. It is already yours to claim. You deserve to be here now upon this path to the Grail of lore."

I ask YOU now, to claim your seat at the spiritual round table and to continue your quest.

Following the Twelfth Key requires no less than complete surrender to the present moment. (Soul lives in the present.) This can take lifetimes or one second. Open to the path of the heart, and then go on with your life with love and humility, practicing being in a state of grace. No one is meant to be perfect in this physical realm, so forgive yourself as you walk the path and whisper the words "I love you" as often as you can. Underneath your manmade armor you are a perfect Being of Light.

In Closing ...

I hope I have left a light footprint, walking gently beside you. The truth is simply to listen to your breath—the breath of Soul. Once the breath stops, Soul goes on to another adventure. So enjoy this planet. Remember, everything is not as it appears. Look past your thoughts to see Soul. Simply contemplate on the Twelve Keys. Let them flow through you like the river of love, and then begin to discover your own unique way. Simply use your eyes to see and your ears to hear, listening to your breathing. Thus, awakened and empty of all manmade concepts, you will instantly connect to your inner wisdom and be living in conscious freedom.

TWELFTH KEY EXERCISE

Life is a Gift of Love

Contemplate on the words of the Blue Star being:

I want to give a gift to you, the gift of a milieu of stars, of a million universes leavening inside you. The story of the birth of not one child in the manger but thousands in symbiotic communion, of a trillion images which splash the skies like sacred auras, and of the ability to see clearly and not peripherally: The power to be and not merely become. I can show you all of this, beyond the illusion.

—*Utides*, Chapter 25, p. 168

EPILOGUE:
NEW WORLD SPIRITUALITY

TAKE ONE STEP TOWARD SPIRIT and Spirit will take a thousand steps toward you. If you are still a visitor standing at the gateway of Soul, trying to decide whether to enter, know that when you take that first step onto the sacred path, you will embark on your own individual pilgrimage and be part of the new world shift. We are venturing beyond into a more authentic reality, one that uses the Living Energy of divine consciousness, which cannot be written down except in one's own heart. Together we are bringing in the birth of a universal path. It is being brought into this realm for an important purpose and you are assisting in the process.

Doorway to Conscious Freedom

It is of the utmost importance that you follow your own truth, instead of arbitrarily adopting someone else's. Do your own research, make up your own mind, and be responsible for your own knowledge. You must now trust your inner guidance and not that which is outside yourself. You will need to listen and seek within, and then learn how to share your wisdom harmoniously and responsibly.

I am learning my lessons, using my spiritual sight and growing spiritually. We are all *s t r e t c h e d* these days, and it's all part of the evolution of Souls. Life is a daring adventure, said Helen Keller, but many of us never see the world beyond our garden gate. Your gate is wide open. The time has come to make a commitment to yourself, to clear your path toward your spiritual goal of conscious freedom. The path awaits your journey to contentment. Keep putting one foot consciously in front of the other, and you will travel the path of conscious freedom to your authentic self.

A Journey toward Contentment

As mystical travelers on the journey toward contentment and conscious freedom, know that there will always be someone to tell you there's an alternative route. Many people have come forward claiming to have a crystal ball to see into the future. Doomsayers are rampant. Each of us needs to use our own discernment when listening to the theories and supposed solutions from those outside ourselves. We need to ask our own questions and, where possible, go to the primary source. More importantly, we need to ask for our inner guidance to show us the next step, then keep asking and keep moving forward to the next step. These steps will eventually lead us to divine love, of self and others, which is true contentment.

By practicing the 12 Golden Keys I hope you will glimpse what the future holds for you and direct your energies accordingly, so that you will be able to co-create your future, the one that serves you. You will learn ways to prepare your family, friends, and your community for safe passage into the new world consciousness. By using your intuition you are better able to know what to do and how to react. Choices must be made immediately. There is no time to second guess.

Many have declared that the decades after the 2012-shift will be a golden age. Yet many others see catastrophic Earth changes and upheavals, calling it the End Times. Let's just say that the reality is somewhere in the middle. So begin whatever you were going to do anyway, except now do it while living in a state of conscious freedom and, then, see where that takes you. Go on the inner and discern it for yourself; your abilities to do so are now unlimited. Go past the mind-boggling fear that is trying to take over our planet and manifest a life of contentment. Use the 12 Golden Keys and your spiritual sight to help you move beyond the fear. It is essential that you continue the exercises and strengthen your inner connection and abilities, using your personal power.

The Second Key (2:5) points out that when you come upon fear, remember to replace it with love, and the entire world will shift for you. Remember, from the Fourth Key (4:2), that what you pay attention to is what you become conscious of and, thus, attract. Ask yourself: "How do I see myself in relation to this? If it no longer serves me, let it go." If it supports the negative, then shift your energy. See yourself with little shifts of energy, moving toward unconditional love. Then bring it back home to the present moment, listening to the inner breath of Soul. Envision breathing in and out from the heart center, releasing your solar plexus.

Our Spiritual Renaissance

We are in a spiritual renaissance, realizing we are one planet, one spirit, and one family, breaking free of conditioned beliefs. In order to accept the Spiritual (R)evolution and walk together along the path of conscious freedom with awakened hearts, we will need to raise our state of consciousness *en masse* above the material plane (from the Tenth Key, 10:3 & 10:5). Accepting, with the guidance of Spirit, new perspectives and seeing through new eyes is as important as learning how to steer our own boat through rough waters. But to help the planet, we need everyone's participation. To paraphrase Albert Einstein once again: We will never be able to solve the problems facing us from the same level of consciousness that created them.[100]

The human heart has never been more open to accepting a new spiritual paradigm, based on the principles of conscious freedom and divine love, than right now. But will we ever be open to accepting globally a worldwide spirituality based on spiritual diversity?

Let's try asking ourselves a rather elaborate question using the 12 Golden Keys:

If we as Soul with individual creative potential (First Key) can experience other states of consciousness (Tenth Key) by following the Blue Light (Second Key), by looking through the eyes of Soul (Fifth Key) with the help of an inner guide as wayshower (Third Key), immersed in the flow of the life force (Ninth Key), realizing there is no limitation (Fourth Key), then why can't we as a planet lighten up (Seventh Key), let go (Tenth Key) and emerge like a butterfly in a new state of beingness (Twelfth Key) based on the principles of conscious freedom and divine love (Eighth Key), Living to Live in Spirit (Sixth Key) and sharing the magic (Eleventh Key) with all we meet?

As the energies of the new world shift enter our personal spheres, a Spiritual (R)evolution could be one of the only solutions left open to us as a planet. The call is for a dismantling of our beliefs that are based in an old state of consciousness, which is partially embedded in many religious traditions. The call is for an intentional embrace of a new state of consciousness, a symbiotic spiritual union, bringing the followers of Christianity, Islam, Hinduism, Judaism and other faiths together into one spiritual ring, while retaining spiritual diversity—a spiritual round table. We have been taught to be separate. Our tribal divisions are healing and, as they heal, we emerge from our butterfly chrysalis, moving into a new awareness.

We must ask: Can this new awareness of the awakened heart embrace the divine love precepts of each spiritual and religious belief system and merge into one amazingly enlightened ring of spiritual diversity?

When fear—which creates conflict, hate, aggression, and war by using one's will—is replaced with love, then this new awareness will be possible. Using our will to get what we want no longer works in these higher vibrations. We have moved from will to the heart. This is what is meant by the term Shift of the Ages: shifting from using our will to living from the heart. Even now many of our evolved spiritual leaders are gathering together as a think-tank to consider the possibility that with "the development of a new global level of consciousness the world can be constructively changed."[101]

This was proven at the 1986 Summit for Peace in Assisi, Italy, which confirmed that world religious leaders could meet in a symbolic gesture of peace—with no other agenda. There were no politicians present. At the invitation of Pope John Paul II, the 160 religious representatives attending the unprecedented event included Buddhism's Dalai Lama and the Nobel Laureate Mother Teresa of Calcutta. Using no interreligious rite, the various devotees did their own invocations for peace. Hindus and Sikhs prayed in the same church. Buddhists and Shintoists chanted outside under blue skies. Muslims and a Crow Indian medicine man prayed for peace alongside Zoroastrians.[102]

There was no conflict because they came from a state of grace, as opposed to using their will (12:4 & 12:5). The little Italian town of Assisi, dedicated to Saint Francis, was host to a major turning point for an emerging understanding of spiritual harmony and *interspirituality*.

Interspirituality is a term coined by Brother Wayne Teasdale, a lay monk from the Catholic Theological Union, Chicago. He writes in *The Mystic Heart*:

> ... *interspirituality—the sharing of ultimate experiences across traditions—is the religion of the third millennium. Interspirituality is the foundation that can prepare the way for a planet-wide enlightened culture and a continuing community among the religions that is substantial, vital and creative.*[103]

Impossible, you say? Not in our lifetime?

In 2006, when Mayan Elder Don Alejandro met with Sri Bhagavan of India, who is loved by over one hundred million people, it showed us that it is still possible for the spiritual traditions of the West and the East to meet. Even in China, where religion is not allowed under Communist rule, many Chinese practice Daoism (also written, Taoism). *Dao* means "the Way," the principle which creates and guides the universe. Once our enlightened spiritual leaders help to heal our differences, it is then possible for our global consciousness to be raised! Due to world conditions, the people are ready now for one of life's greatest adventures.

An ensuing unfolding of events led me to meet personally with His Holiness the Dalai Lama and other world leaders to discuss what I then called—for simplicity of discussion—"A New Model of Exemplary Global Leadership"...When these highly evolved leaders unify their vision, this higher energy awareness will "lift us up." Like picking a tablecloth up from a single point, the entire cloth rises with it. We are that cloth—you, I, and every human "mind"....It is the beginning of the awakening of mass consciousness, the opening of humanity into a new era of life.

—Ariole K. Alei[104]

What then must we do in order to promote the emergence of the new global shift in consciousness, assisting the spiritual leaders through the "keyhole of Soul" toward the path of conscious freedom?

The basic raw teaching of all the wise prophets of every tradition, without all the modern day trappings, is simply Love. We have now caught up to this path of love because the magnetics of the planet have changed. The old consciousness has come to a close and we, the majority of the population, are now ready to accept our new way of being in the world. This is now quite evident as we look throughout the world, seeing the last vestiges of the use of will to control. It's an outdated system based on fear. When dealing with those still based in fear or will, show them understanding. But remain in your expanded state of consciousness; a hard lesson to accept when being confronted, but a necessary one. And follow the 12 Golden Keys!

The Path Leads to Forgiveness

The path of the awakened heart leads to forgiveness. In order to evolve we need to stop fighting the changes and chaos, stop fighting one another, get on with the adventure of joining together as a unified community, and establish a global heart through forgiveness and reconciliation. But how do we mend the rifts between nations, let alone individuals? If I can forgive you, can you forgive me, so we can survive and work together? We must find a way to break with the past and move toward the future, awakening our hearts to the new shift in consciousness. The Sages believe we can. This is our next step in evolution: to discover the answers on the inner and, then, create them on the outer.

The passage through the Changing Times is upon us. No matter what you are told will herald our transition—an economic collapse, a world war, a solar storm, an asteroid hit, Planet X, a pole shift, earthquakes, the depletion of the Earth's natural resources, the attack of Godzilla and the Sasquatch, or more likely our powerful relationship with FEAR—we have no choice but to accept the NOW *as it is*. There is a bigger purpose afoot and we are being led to help one another live a shared worldview—spiritually, socially, and politically.

The manuscript of the *12 Golden Keys for a New World* began as a simple practical guide with key messages and exercises to assist us in removing the veil over our spiritual eye. It expanded quite naturally. Mankind's evolutionary leap in consciousness from *Homo sapiens* to *Homo luminous* has given us the opportunity to accept how to heal, to create a global worldview by seeing through the eyes of Soul, to feel safe and content, and to grow spiritually in a new world age on the new Earth. Anyone can use the knowledge of these 12 Golden Keys; they are without attachment to any secular path. They are the gateway, not the destination. You can choose to be a co-worker with Living Energy and to pass the message on to someone who may need to hear it, continuing a great mystical tradition.

What Does the New World Look Like?

What does our new world look like? Think of the multicultural intergalactic crew in *Star Trek*, their respectful relationships with one another and with the inhabitants of distant worlds, and you'd be close. But it's much more than that. Living in the new world age includes acting as an Earthkeeper, honoring Mother Earth by showing our deep respect for her bounty. It means raising your consciousness to a higher level. This means living from authentic Soul, being a part of the greater cosmos through conscious dream travel, and thus, existing in different dimensions simultaneously. It means living life with a compassionate heart. When you believe in your relationship with the universal connective life force, you begin to live in a state of grace, under divine influence. Together we shall go through the gateway of the awakened heart to conscious freedom.

We need to surrender and transcend our ego-based perception to accept the new state of consciousness based on divine love. We need to take time to communicate with one another, to have the willingness to understand, and to present ourselves as equals. No matter how little you think another may weigh on the scale of equality, no matter how poor or simple they may appear to you, they are Soul, and therefore, equal. There will come a time when we will need one another to survive.

Although some may try, none can claim to be the figurehead of this new world. When we worship anyone or anything outside our own sacred divinity, it becomes a struggle of will. Keep the dogma and the terminology as simple and clear as possible. Once you put a face or even a name on the field of Living Energy it changes. It is everywhere and everything. It is pure love. It is as it is in the present moment, changing and evolving continuously as we grow spiritually. It is a *Living* Energy. There is no telling where this quantum field of unlimited creative potential will lead us, because we are accelerating and moving forward in quantum time, in leaps and bounds.

We are different in a thousand ways, yet when we look up to the night skies we realize we are a part of the same universal continuum. And we are all a part of the same life energy, living within the very matrix of that which created us. We are not the only ones unlocking the gate to the secret path of Living Energy. There are others in the skies and the Otherworlds who are accepting the new realizations of Soul. The universe is a living organism, interconnective. Look up to the night's sky and watch the stars and planets overhead. Sense how symbiotic it is, and how we are living inside the connective tissues of our living matrix.

It is time to accept your mission, Spiritual Warrior, and go out into your world to lend a hand, to become involved with life, to LIVE TO LIVE, to gather in community, and learn to open your spiritual eye and receive the new shift in energies. Turn off the distractions and be part of the new reality on the new Earth, creating a new world, living in full awareness that you are Soul, a divine Being of Light. It is the most exciting thing you will ever do!

Behold!
This is a time of self-made miracles!
The door to your new reality is unlocked.
It is your choice whether to follow the magic of
the Blue Star that resides inside you.
Walk through the gateway...
Live to Live!

NOTES

Introduction

1. *Alice's Adventures in Wonderland* and *Through the Looking-Glass,* by Lewis Carroll (New York: Penguin Classics, 1998), p. 12; Lewis Carroll's original copyright 1865 and 1872.

2. Pierre Teilhard de Chardin, "The Evolution of Chastity" (Peking, February 1934), in *Toward the Future* (London: Collins, 1975), pp 86-87, as cited on http://en.wikiquote.org/wiki/Pierre_Teilhard_de_Chardin.

3. "God particle" came to me independently as an apt name for these secret life codes. Recently, I learned that "the God particle" is the nickname which physicists have given to the Higgs boson subatomic particle, which they believe could help explain the origin of the universe. The Higgs, as it is also called, is named after Peter Higgs the Scottish theorist who first named it (Stephen Fried, "The Race for the Secret of the Universe," *Parade Magazine*, July 26, 2009, p. 4-5).

4. Joanna Macy, Ph.D., "The Great Turning," at www.joannamacy.net/.

5. The terms *new world, Living Energy, Soul Energy, inner dream travel, 12 Golden Keys,* and *Spiritual (R)evolution* are terminology from the sci-fi novel *Universal Tides® [Utides]* by M. J. Milne (North Vancouver, B.C.: Blue Heron Productions, © 2005); and on the website: www.universaltides.com.

6. The "Ancients" are those wise men and women of both indigenous and cosmic communities who lived in such physical places as Egypt, Greece, the ancient Far and Near East, ancient Britain, Tibet, Peru and the Americas, Lemuria and Atlantis, among others.

7. From the film *The White Road: Visions of the Indigenous People of the Americas* (© 2003 Elke von Linde and Michael Springer); produced by Mexiiico! GbR, Ines Fröschl-Queisser, Elke von Linde, Ph.D., Michael Springer. Website: www.the-white-road.com.

8. For information on the Laika (Q'ero) and the Munay-Ki, go to www.Munay-Ki.org or the book entitled *The Four Insights: Wisdom, Power, and Grace of the Earthkeepers,* by Alberto Villoldo, Ph.D. (Carlsbad, CA: Hay House, 2006).

9. Villoldo, *The Four Insights.* Also, Alberto Villoldo's *Shaman, Healer, Sage: How to Heal Yourself and Others with the Energy*

Medicine of the Americas (New York: Harmony Books, 2000), pp. 46-55.

10. Such films as: *What the Bleep Do We Know?* (Lord of the Wind Films, 2004), *NOVA — Physics: The Elegant Universe and Beyond* (WGBH Boston, 2003) about String Theory, *Cosmic Voyage* (IMAX, 1996), *Leap!* (Leap! Ventures, 2008), and others.

11. "All matter originates and exists only by virtue of a force which brings the particles of an atom to vibration and holds this minute solar system of the atom together.... We must assume behind this force the existence of a conscious and intelligent Mind. This Mind is the matrix of all matter." Planck's speech was entitled "Das Wesen der Materie" (The Essence of Matter). From Gregg Braden, *The Divine Matrix: Bridging Time, Space, Miracles, and Belief* (Carlsbad, CA: Hay House, 2007), Endnotes, p. 216: *Archiv zur Geschichte der Max-Planck-Gesellschaft*, Abt. Va, Rep. 11 Planck, Nr. 1797.

12. Braden, *Divine Matrix*, p. 21, 54-55.

13. Villoldo, *Four Insights*, p. xii.

14. Eric Pearl, *The Reconnection: Heal Others, Heal Yourself* (Carlsbad, CA: Hay House, 2003); www.thereconnection.com/faq. Dr. Eric Pearl is a chiropractor.

15. www.matrixenergetics.com/WhatIs.aspx. Dr. Richard Bartlett, D.C., N.D., is the author of *Matrix Energetics: The Science and Art of Transformation* (New York: Atria Books, 2009).

16. British author and New-Energy researcher John Davidson in *The Coming Energy Revolution: The Search for Free Energy* by Jeane Manning (New York: Avery Publishing Group, 1996), p. 183.

17. Michael Harrington, *Touched by the Dragon's Breath*: *Conversations at Colliding Rivers* (Wilsonville, OR: Susan Creek Books, 2005), p. 20, 24.

18. Chrétien de Troyes, *Perceval, or the Story of the Grail*. Translation copyright 2001 Kirk McElhearn; lines 865 to 870; www.mcelhearn.com/dl/perceval4.pdf.

First Key

19. The wording of many of the Keys differs from the original versions of *Utides*, but the intent remains the same.

20. Harold Klemp, *The Language of Soul: Keys to Living a More Meaningful Life* (Minneapolis, MN: Eckankar; 2003), p. 158; www.eckankar.com; 1-800-LOVE-GOD.

21. "Eileen Caddy and her 'Little Voice,'" on www.skyenergyportal .com/eileen-caddy. See also, www.findhorn.org; and *God Spoke*

to Me by Eileen Caddy (Findhorn, Scotland: Findhorn Press, 1966).

22. Synchronicity is a term coined by C. G. Jung, in collaboration with physicist Wolfgang Pauli, to mean "a causal connecting principle" between events that occur at the same time.

23. Excerpt from Jalal al-Din Rumi, "The Dream That Must Be Interpreted," *The Essential Rumi,* translated by Coleman Barks with John Moyne, A. J. Arberry, and Reynold Nicholson (HarperSanFrancisco, ©1995), p. 112-113.

24. His Holiness the Dalai Lama [Tenzin Gyatso], "Universal Responsibility and Our Global Environment," Address to the Parliamentary Earth Summit (Global Forum) of the United Nations Conference on Environment and Development (UNCED), Rio de Janeiro, Brazil, June 7, 1992; www.dalailama.com/messages/environment/universal-responsibility.

25. "Soul Travel" is a term used in Eckankar, Religion of the Light and Sound of God, www.eckankar.com; 1-800-LOVE-GOD.

26. M. J. Milne, "Dream Travel: 50 Ways to Leave Your Body & Other Stories" © 2000 M. J. Milne, p. 12. Unreleased at time of printing.

27. Darlene Montgomery, "Conscious Women News," December 12, 2007; sign up for this e-letter on www.lifedreams.org.

Second Key

28. Our ancient ancestors were wisdom teachers who taught in ancient Egypt, the Mediterranean, Middle East, Asia, Britain, Peru, the Americas, Lemuria, Atlantis, and other locations. There is speculation by various authors that the Ancients arrived from distant galaxies, namely the Annunaki and the Pleiadians, e.g., in the books of Zechariah Sitchin, Erich von Däniken, Barbara Marciniak, and Paul von Ward. I can only tell you my own experiences.

29. *New King James Version.* (Nashville, TN: Thomas Nelson, ©1982).

30. The Three Initiates, *The Kybalion: A Study of the Hermetic Philosophy of Ancient Egypt and Greece* (Wilder Publications, 2007, reprint of Chicago, IL, The Yogi Publication Society, 1908), p. 15-16.

31. According to A.L. Basham, *The Wonder That Was India,* (Grove Press, 1959), p. 31, the 1st Veda, the "Rg Veda," was probably composed about 1500 to 1000 BCE and the Yajur Veda a century or two later, over 3000 years ago; see www.mandalayoga.net/index-what-en-mantra_om.html.

32. References to Kirpal Singh, Sant Mat, Shabd Yoga, and Light and Sound Current are courtesy of Wikipedia.org: www.wiki pedia.org/wiki/Kirpal_Singh; or, see the glossary at: www. kirpalsingh-teachings.org.
33. From the film *The White Road: Visions of the Indigenous People of the Americas*, www.the-white-road.com/en/film.htm.
34. Quoted on Ruhani Santsang USA: www.ruhanisatsangusa.org/ naam/naam_shabd2.htm.
35. Hazrat Inayat Khan. *The Mysticism of Sound and Music* (Boston, MA: Shambhala Dragon Editions, 1996), p. 64-65.

Third Key
36. Dante Alighieri, *The Paradiso*, translated by John Ciardi (New York: Signet Classic, 2001), p. 339.
37. Basham, *Wonder That Was India*, p. 553.
38. *St. Joseph Edition, The New American Bible,* (Totowa, NJ: Catholic Book Publishing Company, 1992), p. 291, p. 21.
39. Brihaspati, *Mahabharata* (Anusasana Parva, Section CXIII, Verse 8) on Mahabharata Online: mahabharataonline.com/translation/ mahabharata_13b078.php.
40. From IslamiCity: www.islamicity.com/articles/articles.asp?ref= IC0107-322.
41. Calling them "past" lives is actually erroneous because on the *time track* everything is in the present moment. The *time track* is an invisible stream of consciousness that we go to when we dream travel. Wherever you land on the time track is your present moment.
42. Dr. Eugenia Casarin, Ph.D., psychologist and Mayan priestess Nah Kin (Mother Sun); www.the-white-road.com.
43. *On Becoming a Spiritual Warrior* is a collection of e-Zines written by M. J. Milne. When you join the Spiritual Warrior Guild (SWG) you receive codes, current survival tips, ways to connect with other outlanders, and more. www.UniversalTides.com.
44. *Tao Te Ching* by Lao Tzu, translated by Stan Rosenthal; www.vl-site.org/taoism/ttcstan3.html#69.
45. Eckhart Tolle, *Freedom From the World* (Five DVD set), (Vancouver, B.C.: Eckhart Teachings, 2006).
46. *Help One Another* by Hanna Kroeger (Hanna Kroeger Publications, 2007); www.peacefulmeadowretreat.com/hanna _kroeger.php/; www.hannasherbshop.com/content/about _hanna_kroeger/.
47. www.miguelruiz.com, under "Publications."

48. Photographs taken by the Kenya youth: www.mojamojafilm .com. Also: www.doingbusinesswithafrica.blogspot.com.

Fourth Key

49. Harold Klemp, *What is Spiritual Freedom* (Minneapolis, MN: Eckankar, 1995), p. 60. www.eckankar.com

50. Quote reprinted by permission of Abraham-Hicks, © by Jerry & Esther Hicks; workshop excerpt, Seattle, WA, June 20th, 1998; www.abraham-hicks.com; contact (830) 755-2299. www.abraham-hicks.com/lawofattractionsource/index.php.

51. Recorded on Rae Armour's CD *Next Move* (North Vancouver, B.C.: Ocean Pacific Music; 2004); www.raearmourmusic.com.

52. Elke von Linde and Michael Springer made this film with private funds. Part of the income is donated to selected projects in Central and South America. Contact website directly for showings: www.the-white-road.com.

Fifth Key

53. *Soul Awakenings Newsletter* by Nancy and Errol Rubin, Number 43, Fall 2006. Also available at: www.rubinenterprises.info/ insights12.html.

54. M. J. Milne interviewed Nancy Shipley Rubin for a *Shared Vision* magazine article, January 1997; this story is taken from the interview notes. Rubin is a gifted psychic and counselor; www.rubinenterprises.info.

55. A variation of this story, entitled "The Runway" by M. J. Milne is in *Conscious Women Conscious Mothers* compiled by Darlene Montgomery (Toronto, ON: White Knight Publications, 2006); www.lifedreams.org/.

Sixth Key

56. James Redfield, *The Celestine Prophecy* (New York: Warner Books, 1994).

57. *The Age Wave: How the Most Important Trend of Our Time Can Change Your Future*, Ken Dychtwald with Joe Flower (New York: Bantam, 1990).

58. In *Utides* this movement is known as the PPR or the People's Planetary (R)evolution.

59. P. M. H. Atwater, *Beyond the Indigo Children: The New Children and the Coming of the Fifth World* (Rochester, VT: Bear & Company, 2005).

60. Christine Gorman, "The Science of Dyslexia", *Time Magazine*,

July 28, 2003.

61. *Boriska: the Person from Mars,* an article by Gennady Belimov (September 2004); translated from the Russian; www.projectcamelot.org/indigo_boy_from_mars.html. Astrophysicist Dr. Vladislav Lugovenko of the Russian Academy of Sciences, Moscow, studied the boy for several years.

62. Syzygy, a term from astronomy, was first used in this sense by the Russian theologian/philosopher Vladimir Solovyov (1853-1900) (http://en.wikipedia.org/wiki/Syzygy).

63. Frank Waters, *The Book of the Hopi* (New York: Penguin Books, 1977); written with the assistance of thirty-two Hopi Elders in 1963.

64. Milne, *Utides,* p. 42 and 162.

65. "Go as a Sangha" from Thich Nhat Hanh's *Friends on the Path: Living Spiritual Communities*; http://sacredcentre.com/2009/10/15/go-as-a-sangha-thich-nhat-hanh/ [posted on October 15, 2009]. "The next Buddha may not take the form of an individual. In the twenty-first century, the Sangha [community] may be the body of the Buddha."

66. Reprinted by permission of Michael Harrington; November 14, 2007 e-mail included the quote by John Redstone. For info on Michael's books go to www.SusanCreek.com.

67. Reprinted by permission of Joanna Macy. From "Coming Back to Life," written by Joanna Macy and Molly Young Brown; www.joannamacy.net.

68. Based on the author's conversation with Mazie Baker, on November 29, 2007, North Vancouver, BC.

69. Excerpts used with permission of Jane Siberry, April 13, 2008; for info: www.janesiberry.com.

Seventh Key

70. Joseph Campbell (with Bill Moyers), *The Power of Myth* (New York: Doubleday, 1988), p. 123.

71. Don Miguel Ruiz, *The Four Agreements: A Practical Guide to Personal Freedom* (San Rafael, CA: Amber-Allen Publishing, Inc., 1997).

72. "Don Miguel Ruiz about Human Mind;" www.youtube.com/watch?v=tKCWH4KT1Xc&NR=1.

73. "The Nisargadatta Song of Beyond I Am: Selections from The Wisdom of Sri Nisargadatta Maharaj" by Robert Powell on

www.nonduality.com/beyond.htm.
74. Sai Baba, "Have Self-Confidence and Achieve Everything," Tamil New Year Divine Discourse delivered on April 13, 2008; www.saibabaofindia.com/tamil_new_year_discourse_130408.htm.
75. Swami Sivananda, *Essence of Yoga*, www.sivanandadlshq.org/download/essence_yoga.htm.
76. Rick Steves, "The Pilot Said, 'This Plane is Heading for Tehran' ... and Nobody Was Alarmed" (17 May 2008); "Imagine Every Woman's a Nun" (23 May 2008); "Tight Pants, Necklines, Booze ... and Freedom" (20 June 2008) www.ricksteves.com/blog/ (reprinted with permission of Rick Steves).

Eighth Key
77. "Kirpal Singh (1894-1974): His Mission," on Ruhani Satsang USA: www.ruhanisatsangusa.org.
78. See "The Dalai Lama on Compassion" on Dharmakara Net, http://hhdl.dharmakara.net/hhdlspeech.html.
79. Eleanor H. Porter, *Pollyanna* (Boston: L. C. Page and Company, 1912/13). In 1960 Walt Disney Productions released a movie based on this book and starring British actor Hayley Mills.
80. Kahlil Gibran, *The Prophet* (Ware, Hartfordshire: Wordsworth Editions Ltd 1997), from Chapter 3, Marriage, p. 7.
81. W. H. Murray, *The Scottish Himalayan Expedition* (London: J. M. Dent & Sons Ltd., 1951). He quotes Goethe from John Anster's translation of *Faust*, published in 1835.
82. There are many spiritual masters, such as Osiris, Muhammad, Jesus Christ, Krishna, Buddha, the Prophet Elijah, the Mahanta, the Dalai Lama, the Great Spirit, Mother Mary; or a Priest, a Shaman, an Elder, a Yogi, a Guru, i.e., someone who has mastered something that you believe in.

Ninth Key
83. Disclaimer: Due to current government regulations, you need to read this disclaimer: None of the information herein is intended to diagnose, treat, or prescribe; it is for information purposes only. Always seek potentially curative conventional care from a healthcare practitioner. Any person making the decision to act upon this information is responsible for investigating and understanding the effects of their actions.
84. Reprinted by permission of Mary Carroll Moore (May 19, 2009),

American artist and author; www.marycarrollmoore.com.

85. Jerry & Esther Hicks, "Daily Law of Attraction Quotation," Abraham-Hicks Publications: www.abraham-hicks.com; (830) 755-2299.

86. Richard Gerber, M.D., *Vibrational Medicine: New Choices for Healing Ourselves* (Bear & Company, 1996).

87. Reprinted with permission of Adam (Dreamhealer), of Dreamhealer Inc. (July 3, 2008). Visit www.dreamhealer.com for a list of Adam's books and DVDs. Also, his book *Intention Heals* (DreamHealer Inc., 2008).

Tenth Key

88. Kahlil Gibran, "The Crucified," *A Treasury of Kahlil Gibran*, edited by Martin L. Wolf. Translated from the Arabic by Anthony Rizcallah Ferris. (New York: The Citadel Press, 1941), p. 131.

89. New translation and commentary by Doug Marman, *It Is What It Is: The Discourses of Rumi*, (Ridgefield, WA: Spiritual Dialogues Project, *In Press*).

90. "The Extraterrestrial Is My Brother," *L'Osservatore Romano*, May 14, 2008.

91. Alex Collier, *Defending Sacred Ground: The Andromedan Compendium*, www.exopolitics.org/collier-dsg1.pdf/. Revised 1998.

92. Sheldan Nidle, *Your Galactic Neighbors*, (Vancouver: Blue Lodge Press, 2005), Part IV, p. 95; www.paoweb.com.

93. Harrington, *Touched by the Dragon's Breath*.

94. Sheldan Nidle, *Your First Contact*, (Vancouver: Blue Lodge Press, 2000), p. xv.

Eleventh Key

95. Websites: www.findhorn.org; www.eileen-caddy.net/. Eileen Caddy's Daily Guidance from her book *Opening Doors Within* (Findhorn Press, 2007); www.findhornpress.com.

96. Websites: Findhorn.org; Damanhur.org; Keuruunekokyla.fi.

97. http://socialinnovation.ca/; www.lcsi.smu.edu.sg/downloads/MarkSurmanFinalAug-2.pdf.

98. Written with the participation of and reprinted by permission of Brock Tully; information from his websites: www.brocktully.com; and KindActs Coin-spiracy: www.kindacts.net; and his book entitled *Reflections for Living Life More Fully* (Carlsbad, CA: Hay House, 1994).

99. WWOOF or World Wide Opportunities on Organic Farms, a volunteer exchange program. For international programs, visit: www.wwoof.org. For Canadian programs: www.wwoof.ca

Epilogue
100. www.spaceandmotion.com/Albert-Einstein-Quotes.htm.
101. Part of the mission statement from the World Wisdom Alliance (WWA), launched in Toronto, Canada, July 2006; www.wisdompage.com/WWAdec06.html.
102. Info from *A Summit for Peace in Assisi*, by Richard N. Ostling, with Sam Allis/Assisi (Time Inc., Nov-10-1986); www.time.com/ time/magazine/article/0,9171,962783,00.html.
103. Wayne Teasdale, *The Mystic Heart: Discovering a Universal Spirituality in the World's Religions* (New World Library, 2001), p. 26.
104. Reprinted with permission of Ariole K. Alei, *H.O.P.E. = Healing Ourselves and Planet Earth – A Blueprint for Personal and Collective Change* (Vancouver, B.C.: HeartSong Solutions, 2008), p. 4; www.HeartSongSolutions.ca.

GLOSSARY

Words set in SMALL CAPS are defined elsewhere in this glossary.

12 Golden Keys. Keys that unlock gateways to secrets hidden inside each BEING OF LIGHT. By practicing the Key exercises you can discover an inner connection to your true self, SOUL, which will give you the tools to survive in a NEW WORLD.

Age of Consciousness. The NEW WORLD age now beginning with the GREAT TURNING, in which we can live in CONSCIOUS FREEDOM and create a NEW WORLD, living in full awareness of our divinity, knowing we are SOUL, a divine BEING OF LIGHT.

awakened heart. The heart of one who is in an awakened state and open to divine love; a state of consciousness that connects you to divine love.

Being(s) of Light. We are all SOUL beings, some more awake than others. Beings of Light are one with the universal SOUL ENERGY in a cosmic planetary community. You will know them by their positive and gentle influence.

Blue Star or **Blue Light.** A portal of bright light, surrounded by blue; a doorway to SOUL and the OTHERWORLDS, leading to a higher state of consciousness; represents divine love and protection of Spirit.

break free to live free. The process of severing society's stronghold over your mind, body, spirit, so you can gain control and live the life you want. The process is to listen to SOUL's messages, receiving guidance and solutions to life's problems.

compassionate heart. The loving heart or open heart; golden or AWAKENED HEART; having compassion for those who have yet to realize there is more to this life than meets the eye and remain in unawareness.

conscious freedom. The state of being conscious; being aware of your ability to act freely and co-create your life; a state of awareness that allows you the freedom to create and choose how to experience your life and to live in full awareness of who you are and your divinity as SOUL, a BEING OF LIGHT who is here for experience.

consciousness. The state of being conscious; conscious experience of self; different states of awareness; your personal identity compared to your surroundings.

Divine Source. Source, God, or DIVINE SPIRIT; that which is composed of LIVING ENERGY.

dream travel. The art of spiritual sight while asleep or awake; also called soul travel, inner travel, spiritual travel, conscious dream travel. A way of transcending your physical body into different states of expanded consciousness. Experienced by millions of people every day as a natural way to receive spiritual guidance.

eco-spiritualism. A bridge between scientific and spiritual thought; a life-sustaining ecological and spiritual philosophy for the planet.

Great Turning. A term coined by author and activist Joanna Macy to represent "the shift from the industrial growth society to a life-sustaining civilization." www.joannamacy.net.

Help Others Help Others. Also, help others help themselves. A grassroots movement for the purpose of helping people so they can help themselves and then help others, too. Doing kind acts where needed without emotional attachment; sometimes, people need a little kindness to get them going.

HU. *Pronounced "hue" or "Hugh."* A sacred sound; often sung as a spiritual exercise to experience divine love. Used in many of the Key Exercises.

intuition. Intuition is beyond mind; it is using one's inner wisdom to receive a spiritual illumination; an inner knowing about something that is beyond the perception of the mind.

Karma Warrior. A SOUL who has experienced thousands of past lives and is learning to unravel karma with responsibility; assisted by KEY GUARDIANS.

Key Guardian. A spiritual guide and teacher who protects; a co-worker alongside SPIRIT; an ancient spiritual traveler. Ask them to teach you the 12 Golden Keys.

Kids of the New Earth (KONE). A person of the new spiritual-survival age of LIVING ENERGY. The abbreviation "KONE" is pronounced like "cone" as in "Kone Kids," as in a cone that holds the future.

Living Energy. The ocean of Source energy or the life force in all the universes and beyond in the OTHERWORLDS. This unlimited field connects all beings and is the Godforce or Source, having the twin aspects of light and sound. We are immersed in this luminous field of God as a fish in water.

The terms SOUL, SOUL ENERGY, Soul essence, living light energy, golden light energy, Divine Spirit or Source, Godforce, divine consciousness, primal sound current, and the LUMINOUS ENERGY FIELD (LEF) are connected with the LIVING ENERGY.

Luminous Energy Field (LEF). A transformative energy field which can heal the body, mind, and spirit, changing the way we live our lives; flows out of God or the field of LIVING ENERGY.

new Earth. Our changing planet that is rebirthing itself. As the Earth changes, we change, and vice versa, because all is connected. The outer manifestation of the NEW WORLD consciousness. The global habitat in which we assist one another to assimilate the new energies of the NEW WORLD age.

new world. The transformed CONSCIOUSNESS of planet Earth; a complete global shift in how we live our lives; a new world view, or new world age; an evolving social and spiritual consciousness on planet Earth. The world as a result of a new state of consciousness based on CONSCIOUS FREEDOM, the AWAKENED HEART, and the influx and assimilation of new energies. A new type of global society based on one planet, one world, one spirit. Represents a shift of consciousness from a negative viewpoint to a positive one, which will bring us to a new way of living together in the AGE OF CONSCIOUSNESS.

Otherworlds. A term from *Utides* (p.104) referring to "a land where Spirit dwells." Includes the other dimensions and parallel worlds; heaven; the Far Country; and spiritual planes of expanded consciousness. It is a different realm than Earth/Gaia.

outlanders. Humans living on the edge of society, passionate about freedom and their purpose of saving the planet; fringe-dwellers.

portal. An inner gateway that opens into other worlds, the OTHERWORLDS; a pinpoint of bright light or a BLUE STAR when using the THIRD EYE.

sentient being. Something that exists and possesses consciousness, perception, and thought.

Soul. An eternal, immortal, conscious BEING OF LIGHT. One's authentic, higher self which temporarily resides in the physical body and is directly linked to DIVINE SOURCE. It is a part of God, the LIVING ENERGY, yet retains individuality. Soul is the breath in the body. When the breath is gone, Soul is gone elsewhere.

Soul Energy. A part of the universal life force residing in each and every living being; commonly referred to as SOUL; part of the LIVING ENERGY, and then the LUMINOUS ENERGY FIELD (LEF) when it enters the physical realm.

Spirit. That which flows out of LIVING ENERGY; DIVINE SOURCE.

spiritual exercise. An exercise which helps one grow spiritually by providing a means to connect with Spirit in its many different aspects, to learn about the power of advanced spiritual sight, and to DREAM TRAVEL; often done in contemplation.

Spiritual (R)evolution. A revolutionary evolution of the way we see ourselves, our planet, and our spirituality in a NEW WORLD; a spiritual renaissance.

spiritual wake-up call. A conscious message received from one's higher self, Soul, through synchronicity and/or endless ways Source or God uses to get your attention.

Spiritual Warrior. One who follows a spiritual quest; a being who has the courage to go on a spiritual quest to discover Soul and the divine consciousness within—the true legendary quest.

Third Eye. The seat of visionary sight. Also known as the inner eye or the spiritual eye; it is the PORTAL to Soul and the higher worlds; "the immortal portal," located in the pineal gland between the two hemispheres of the brain, between and behind the eyebrows in the middle of the forehead. The ancient Egyptians called it the All-Seeing-Eye, and enlightened seers used it for spiritual sight.

Universal Tides. The *living* body of water that touches every land mass; the action of waves pulling away the old and bringing into shore the new. The title of M. J. Milne's sci-fi/survivalist novel, *Universal Tides®: Barbed Wire Blues*, nicknamed *Utides*—the story of a bounty hunter and an intergalactic Being of Light who rescue a woman scientist and help her save the planet from corporate dictators. The main character receives 12 GOLDEN KEYS that initiate a SPIRITUAL (R)EVOLUTION.

MEET THE CONTRIBUTORS

*Those listed below have given signed permission for
use of their story, poem, artwork, or photographs.*

Rae Armour B.PEd, B.Ed, is a realtor and singer/songwriter who began performing quite unexpectedly when she auditioned for a popular rock band
during a teacher's strike at the Edmonton, Alberta, high school where she
taught. Thus began a thirty-year music career. Her first release, *On Track* (1986),
garnered her double-winner status at the Pacific Songwriters Association
awards; Rae has recorded two more CDs: *Next Move* (2004) and *The Sweetest
Day* (2008) with AUGUST. Websites: raearmour.com, raearmourmusic.com,
augustmusic.net.

Mazie Baker was born in Vancouver, BC. Velma Doreen "Mazie" Baker is a
feisty Great Grandmother, a political activist, and an Elder of the Squamish
Nation who inspires people by telling stories about her large family and her
community. Her famous bannock bread is a highlight at the Squamish Nation
Powwow. She was invited to Ottawa to speak before a Senate Committee on
Native Women's Rights to hold property on Reserves, and Bill C49. Website:
squamish.net.

Aisha M. Davidson, BFA, is a creative artist; born in North Vancouver, she
is a graduate of the Emily Carr University of Art and Design; is a vegetarian;
and has traveled to more places in the world than most. She created the icons
for the 12 Golden Keys, the logo for *Utides*, the Rise Up/Stand Up! poster, and
other artwork for *Universal Tides'* website: universaltides.com.

Mike Dyer, Ph.D., is a retired professor of mathematics, an international
public speaker, and a workshop facilitator. He lives in Quito, Ecuador, with
his wife Evelyn and her four college-age children. He is a spiritual student
of a living master, a writer, a singer/composer, and a lover of the outdoors,
especially mountains. For the last twenty years he has traveled the world
giving workshops on spiritual topics, such as how to use your dreams to
understand your daily life.

Marie Eklund, B.S., of Oregon, USA, a musician, teacher, writer, poet, parent,
public speaker, and clergywoman, accepts life as a great spiritual adventure.
Traveling the globe as a young person, especially to the Far East in times
of political unrest instilled in her a radically changed and open worldview.
History and Spirituality are favorite topics, resulting in the book, *Our Once
and Future World*, to be released online in 2010.

Ken Hancherow, B.M.Ed., earned his music degree from the University of Western Ontario, did post-graduate studies at the prestigious Eastman School of Music in Rochester, New York, and started the Canadian Music School in London, Ontario. He and his partner own the 96-acre organic LifeSpring Farm. He is co-founder of an alternative energy company, a wellness consultant, a sought-after public speaker on dozens of subjects, and has a new CD of improvisational piano music. E-mail: ken@web.net. Websites: kenhancherow. com, and 24hoursolar.com.

Michael Harrington, B.A., A.A., grew up near Colliding Rivers in southern Oregon, USA. He works as a water quality specialist in the Pacific Northwest. He is author of *Touched by the Dragon's Breath: Conversations at Colliding Rivers* (2005), and *Porcupines at the Dance: Parables and Stories from Colliding Rivers* (2008) both by Susan Creek Publishing which he owns. Besides writing, Michael enjoys softball, skiing, Tae Kwon Do, and hiking through old growth forests. Website: susancreek.com.

Marjorie Haynes, R.M.T., a healer in Vancouver, BC, has been in private practice since 1990. During the Harmonic Convergence of 1987, Marjorie had a cathartic experience—leading her to change from being a professional singer/composer to studying medical sciences. While in pre-med to become a registered massage therapist, she met a healer named Gurli Ohm Hernu and became her apprentice. Marjorie established the Open Door Healing Arts Centre and is currently writing a book. Website: opendoorhealingarts.com.

Debra Howell was brought up in Coquitlam, BC, and is a Sound Healer (musician, songwriter, performer) and Matrix Energetics Practitioner. She creates and provides music and projects for all types of mainstream media that are infused with genuine intentions and frequencies based in nature (432hz) to assist humankind and the world to function optimally and harmonize peacefully. Her CD is *Tune In & Be the Change! Chakra Tuning: Guidebook & Audios* (2009). Website: debrahowell.net.

Reverend Susan Hunt was born in Birmingham, England. She moved with her family to Toronto and later to Vancouver, Canada. She founded Garden of Miracles Course Community, dedicated to remembering Peace of Mind by practicing the principles of *A Course in Miracles* (ACIM). ACIM (published 1975) was scribed by Dr. Helen Schucman, assisted by Dr. William Thetford. Susan is currently writing a book. Website: gardenofmiracles.com, or the official Course website: acim.org.

Kay Johnston, B.A., M.Ed, was born in Cumbria, England, and now lives on acreage in the beautiful Shuswap area of BC, where bears, deer, coyote, and cougar visit, knowing they are safe on the land. The bear is Kay's totem and guardian. Kay Johnston is co-author with Gloria Nahanee of *The Spirit of Powwow* (Hancock House, 2003). For information go to the website: spiritofpowwow.com.

Sasha Jordan was born in Prince Albert, Saskatchewan; she now lives in North Vancouver, BC, where she works in a spiritual bookstore and is a Reiki practitioner. Sasha, also a singer, discovered *bhajans* or devotional songs during her first visit to India in 2000. Since then she has devoted herself to mastering this musical genre. Sasha feels a deep connection to India and returns annually. *Awakening* is her CD of bhajans (devotional songs); website: cdbaby.com/sashaj. E-mail: sashaj11@gmail.com.

Denise Kellahan from Vancouver, BC, has a son and a daughter, and grandchildren. Denise is a retired national union representative. She and Richard, her husband, were together for seven years when he was killed instantly in a diving accident while they were on vacation. Since that fateful day, she has been processing her grief and nurturing her spiritual development. Today she believes strongly in living life to the fullest, one day at a time.

Karethe Linaae, M.F.A., is a mother of one, foster parent of two, and co-founder of an organization helping some of the millions of children orphaned due to AIDS. For the past decade she has art-directed TV commercials to pay for her philanthropic endeavors. She has worked as corresponding journalist throughout Europe and written a film script on India. She is currently writing a book on gratitude. Website: snobb.net.

Elke von Linde, Ph.D., scriptwriter and co-producer/director, was born in Austria. A dream led her halfway around the world to the Yucatán Peninsula. The privately funded film *The White Road: Visions of the Indigenous People of the Americas* turned out to be a documentation of the first-ever gathering of people from other cultures who were invited to the reunion of Elders, indigenous Priests, and Shamans from North and South America in the spring of 2003. Website: the-white-road.com.

Jeane Manning, B.A., was born in Cordova, Alaska. Her family moved to Idaho where she graduated from the University of Idaho; she now lives in Vancouver, BC. Her books include *Angels Don't Play This HAARP: Advances in Tesla Technology*, with Nick Begich (Earthpulse Press, 1997); *The Coming Energy Revolution* (Avery Publishing, 1996); *Energie* (Omega Verlag, Germany, 2000); and *Breakthrough Power: How Quantum-Leap New Energy Inventions Can Transform Our World* (Amber Bridge Publishing, 2008), with Joel Garbon. Websites: jeanemanning.com; changingpower.net.

Janet Matthews is an author, editor, professional speaker, workshop facilitator, *Heal Your Life*® facilitator, and co-author of the Canadian bestseller *Chicken Soup for the Canadian Soul*. Janet's stories can be found in six *Chicken Soup for the Soul* titles as well as several other publications. She is a popular radio and TV talkshow guest and speaks to a wide range of audiences, consistently earning rave reviews. Janet lives in Aurora, Ontario. Visit: janetmatthews.ca.

Carol Milne is an entrepreneur at heart. Born in Vancouver BC, she has traveled the world many times over, which has given her a global perspective. Carol is a foster parent, a willing volunteer, a respected TV commercial producer of twenty-five-years (Front Porch Productions), and is the mother of creative artist Aisha M. Davidson. She has a vast social network and is now transitioning to create her next entrepreneurial adventure.

Anastasia Milne Parkes was raised in North Vancouver, BC. She is a photographer, a Certified Nutritional Consultant, and an organic farmer. She and her husband own the 96-acre LifeSpring Farm in Ontario. A favorite pastime is being with her animals. For information on purchasing their organic produce, free range eggs, chickens, plus nutritional and wellness products, a Nutritional/ Wellness Consulting session, or a de-cluttering and Life Cleanse appointment, e-mail: anastasi@web.net. Website: lifecleanse.ca, and, lifespringfarm.ca.

Darlene Montgomery, well-known author and public speaker on inspirational topics, has for twenty-six years dedicated herself to the exploration of dreams and their spiritual application. Her company, Lifedreams Unlimited, sponsors inspirational seminars designed to assist individuals to a more direct path of personal success and fulfillment. Her books include: *Dream Yourself Awake*, and *Conscious Women-Conscious Lives: Powerful and Transformational Stories of Healing Body, Mind and Soul* (White Knight Books; 3 volumes). E-mail: lifedreams@idirect.com. Website: lifedreams.org.

Dr. Ingrid Pincott, N.D., has been practicing naturopathic medicine since 1985. She graduated from the National College of Naturopathic Medicine, practiced in Vancouver for eleven years before moving to Campbell River, BC. She also graduated from the Royal Jubilee Hospital Nursing program in 1979 and completed two years of pre-med at the University of Victoria. She and her husband love spending time in nature, communing with the birds and wild animals, enjoying camping and boating. Website: drpincott.com.

Lesley Punt and her husband, Russ Torlage, are grateful to be operating a business using spiritual principles. In addition to being the visionary for their business, SOTA Instruments Inc., Lesley loves tending her flower garden and playing with Jesse, their Yorkie, who opens their hearts each day. As a member of the Eckankar clergy, she accepts life as a perpetual learning experience, with Spirit always providing stepping stones or opportunities for growth. Website: sotainstruments.com, 1-800-224-0242.

Reverend Sharon Richlark, B.A., B.Ed., a Certified Kroeger Practitioner, resides in North Vancouver, BC, where she educates clients to use their natural and intuitive abilities of well being, employing techniques from homeopathy (including biotherapeutic drainage), bio-resonance therapy and bio-energetic testing, and recommending whole food nutritional concentrates. Sharon is known for her ability to work with impossible situations originating from improbable causes. Her motto: "There is no disease except congestion. There is no cure except circulation." Websites: wholisticallyspeaking.com; healthnanny.com.

Nancy Shipley Rubin and her husband Errol Rubin live in Hawaii, USA, and travel the world giving lectures and workshops. Nancy is a gifted psychic and counselor, providing clear, direct guidance and teaching. Her work has evolved from over twenty years of psychic practice, as well as psychological and contemplative studies. Presenting principles of empowerment in a kind and humorous manner, Nancy encourages each person to access their inner guidance and recognize their unique gifts. Website: rubinenterprises.info.

Eva-Maria Schoen was born in Bad Harzburg, Germany. A member of Eckankar, Religion of the Light and Sound of God, she is a respected artist who focuses on spiritual expression in her digital artwork. Along with art, she loves yoga and is a yoga teacher in a beautiful little town in Lower Saxony near the Harz Mountains. To view some of her original artwork go to picasaweb. google.com/EvaMariaSchoen.

Jane Siberry was born in Toronto, Ontario, and is a poet, artist, and singer/ songwriter. In 1981 she was studying music and microbiology at the University of Guelph when she released her debut album, *Jane Siberry* (1981). She is known for such mega hits as "Mimi on the Beach" and "Calling All Angels." Her recent CDs are *Dragon Dreams* (2008), and *With What Shall I Keep Warm?*(2009) Website: JaneSiberry.com.

Lyvia L. Smith, a mother, author and motivational speaker, was born in Toronto and raised in Beverly Hills. Settling in Vancouver, she and her husband, the late Dr. Allan Smith D.D.S., raised two talented daughters. Lyvia's acute psoriatic and rheumatoid arthritis is one of life's major lessons. Her book, *"The Joy of Positive Thinking: How to Be Up When You're Down"* (2007) is a testament to her belief in living life to the fullest. Email: lyvialsmith@shaw.ca.

Kendra Sprinkling, born in Winnipeg, Manitoba, was raised in BC. Well-known for her deep, raspy R&B voice, Kendra sang in musical groups for twenty-five years. She is now doing what she loves best and is the Founding Executive Director of the Shooting Stars Foundation, a special events company that produces shows raising money for local, direct service AIDS agencies including A Loving Spoonful and The Dr. Peter Centre. For current events, visit shootingstarsfoundation.org.

Susan Standfield was born in Vancouver, BC. In 2001 an idea "sparked" when she taught Fijian children how to take photos. Susan is the founder and creative director of SHINDA: Africa's Youngest Brand, a for-profit company that empowers African youth through their own consumer brand. Their goal is to build SHINDA Design Studios in capital cities across Africa where kids can learn the business of commercial design. Author of "*TRADE, NOT AID: Doing Business with Africa.*" E-mail: jumpstartrevenue@gmail.com.

Cathy Stevenson, a Registered Nurse for over twenty years, was born in Vancouver, BC. Her favorite pastime is traveling. She has visited many remote and exotic places, such as Borneo, Nepal, Peru, Morocco, Israel, Thailand, Vietnam, Cambodia, and India. As a result, traveling taught her to see the beauty behind all cultures, to be non-judgmental, to know that we're all the same, and to realize that the world is a small place.

Rick Steves grew up in Edmonds, Washington, and studied at the University of Washington. His real education came from traveling in Europe. Since 1973 he's spent one third of his adult life living out of a suitcase and it's shaped his thinking. Today he employs eighty people at his Europe Through the Back Door headquarters in Edmonds where he produces European guidebooks, a travel TV series, a weekly radio show, and a weekly newspaper column. Website: ricksteves.com.

Brock Tully, B.Ed., is an internationally recognized speaker and musician; author of the series, *Reflections*; creator of the Cycling for Kindness Tour; producer of Kindness Sings concerts and One of A KIND Stories; he co-founded and is a fundraiser for the non-profit society KindActs, a member of the World Kindness Movement; he runs Kindness Rocks, a fundraiser for the Coin-Spiracy program, affiliated with the Random Acts of Kindness Foundation. Website: brocktully.com.

COPYRIGHT

(These pages constitute an extension of the copyright page.)

Grateful acknowledgement is made to the following for permission to publish their work:

First Key: You Are the Key
   "The Play" © 2008 Michael Harrington
   "Finding My Unique Way to Serve Life"
      © 2009 Jeane Manning

Second Key: Follow the Blue Light
   "The Call" © 2008 Kay Johnston
   "Tuning into Spirit" © 2008 Debra Howell

Third Key: You Are a Key Guardian
   "The Magic of Sharing Music" © 2009 Kendra Sprinkling
   "Six Plastic Cameras" © 2008 Susan Standfield
   "Dream: An Ancient Lifetime" © 2009 Rae Armour
   "Sunset on Grouse Mountain" © 2008 Janet Matthews

Fourth Key: There Is No Limitation
"When Spirit Calls My Name" © 1997 Rae Armour & M. J.
Milne on the CD "Next Move" © 2004 Rae Armour
"Living Life in the Zone" © 2009 Ken Hancherow
"Road to the Mayans" © 2008 Elke von Linde

Fifth Key: Look Through the Eyes of Soul
"Reflections of a Child Psychic" © 2009 Nancy Shipley
Rubin
"A Sign" © 2008 Darlene Montgomery
"I Kept on Singing HU" © 2008 Micheal Neale Dyer
"Soul Messages from Animals" © 2008 Ingrid Pincott

Sixth Key: Live to Live in Spirit
Photograph: "Angkor Wat, Cambodia" © 2003 Carol Milne
Photograph: "Mali, Dogon Country" © 1985 Carol Milne
"Be Proud of Who you Are" © 2009 Mazie Baker
"Poem to a Teenager" © 2008 Jane Siberry
"Angels on the Eastside" © 2009 Carol Milne

Seventh Key: Lighten Up to Light Up
"Trusting in God" © 2008 Sasha Jordan
"Simply Giving Love" © 2009 Cathy Stevenson
"Dear Traveler: *Arriving in Iran*" © 2008 Rick Steves,
*The Pilot Said: This Plane Is Heading for Tehran ...
and Nobody Was Alarmed.*
ricksteves.com/blog/ (17 May 2008).
Reprinted with permission.
"Dear Traveler: *Visiting*" © 2008 Rick Steves
"Imagine Every Woman's a Nun," ricksteves.com/
blog/ (23 May 2008). Reprinted with permission.
"Dear Traveler: *Departing*" © 2008 Rick Steves
"Tight Pants, Necklines, Booze ... and Freedom"
(20 June 2008); ricksteves.com/blog/.
Reprinted with permission.

Eighth Key: Love and Gratitude are Key
"I Am Grateful" © 2008 Karethe Linaae
"Look for the Silver Lining" © 2008 Lyvia L. Smith
"How Love Saved My Life" © 2009 Anastasia Milne Parkes

Ninth Key: Go With the Flow
"Trusting Our Gifts—Brownie's Gift to Me" © 2008
    Marjorie Haynes
"Discovering My Life's Purpose" © 2009 Sharon Richlark

Tenth Key: Let Go and Dream Travel
"Our Once and Future World" © 2008 Marie Eklund
"Messages from the Other Side" © 2010 Denise Kellahan

Eleventh Key: Share the Magic
"Re-Cycling the Heart for Kindness" © 2008 Brock Tully
"Dear LifeSpring Farm" © 2007 Anastasia Milne Parkes
Photograph: "Making Compost Tea" © 2007 Anastasia
    Milne Parkes
Photograph: "Bringing in the Hay" © 2006 Anastasia
    Milne Parkes
"Dreams as a Guide in Troubled Times" © 2008
    Lesley Punt
"Garden of Miracles" © 2009 Reverend Susan Hunt

Twelfth Key: Be a Spiritual Warrior
No stories in this chapter.

LIST OF EXERCISES

 *Key Tips*

Spiritual Key Exercises

Spiritual Experiences

Spiritual Wake-Up Calls

Spiritual Warrior Codes

Stories from the Heart

ACKNOWLEDGEMENTS

My deepest thanks to Rae Armour for her encouragement, devoted friendship, and for the first copy edit, cheerfully calling it "the good book." Thanks to Karla Joy McMechan for her careful editorial review and her inspirational suggestions; and also, many thanks to Clélie Rich.

I am very grateful to all the contributors for their wonderful stories, poems, artwork, and/or photographs. All of you have enriched my life and I am ever so grateful. There are so many stories to tell (too many for my wee book).

In appreciation to a community of friends who helped with design features, my loving gratitude to Jerry Leonard, John Pritchard, Wendy Rosier, artist Eva-Maria Schoen, and Peter Sysoev.

Thanks to Gerry Clow, John Endo Greenaway, Babe Gurr, Michael Harrington, Doug and Karen Marman, Janet Matthews, Dominica Mitrou, Darlene Montgomery, Bonnie Munn, Lynne Pavey, Carole Punt, Lesley Punt, Joanne Sarginson, Veronica Scully, Jodi Smith, and Christine Williams for their suggestions; to Don Macpherson for his gentle legal guidance; to author Jeane Manning for our monthly get-togethers; to my supportive and loving family; and to my mentor Harold. I usually wrote while cat or dog sitting, so my love to Milo, dear Nellie, and the many animal Souls for setting loving vibrations. And a special acknowledgement to the guidance of Spirit, which connects all of us with limitless divine love.

ABOUT THE AUTHOR

M. J. Milne was born and raised near the rainforests of Vancouver, BC. Her writing and artistic abilities, love of travel, and interest in the worlds of Spirit emerged early. She studied at the Emily Carr University of Art+Design, Simon Fraser University, and the University of British Columbia. Later, her imaginative landscape paintings were sought after by art collectors. During her stay in northern BC, working in an isolated gold mine, her connection with nature heightened.

Her search for spiritual answers began soon after a series of profound occurrences transformed her life. Seeking to understand them and their usefulness in her everyday life, she began an intense spiritual journey. Realizing that the answers were not to be found in the experiences of others, M. J. was led along a pathway to find the answers within herself. She is now dedicated to teaching those guided to her how they, too, can remove society's veil to see their own inner truth as Soul.

M. J. Milne has traveled extensively, served as the grassroots publicist for a Canadian music group, and produced and directed several music events. She has published magazine articles, written screenplays and the revolutionary new-age/science-fiction novel *Universal Tides*® in which the 12 Golden Keys are introduced. Milne still resides in the Vancouver area, near a forest.

HERE IS A SAMPLE CHAPTER FROM THE SCIENCE-FICTION NOVEL

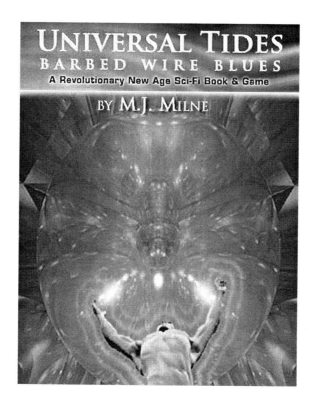

A Galactic Fairytale for Survival

★   Ω   ⊕   ⌘   Δ

by M. J. Milne

ISBN 978-0-9739654-0-7

CHAPTER 1 — The Prophecy

The tide was high, higher than it had ever been. The rays of the setting sun danced across the waves as they broke on the rocks. Below, seaside homes and cabins rotted underneath ten feet of water, now a part of the thousands of lost hectares of land along every tideline of planet Gaia, Mother Earth. On a ridge overlooking this vast ocean, a Native American of the First Nations sat cross-legged in quiet contemplation, waiting.

The day had been long—the longest of his life. He was a big man, and he had traveled far, over land and sea, to arrive at this island. Breathing deep in the silent motionless air, he felt the satisfaction of knowing he had arrived—and was now exactly where he was supposed to be at this moment in time. The fact that he did not know the reason why he was supposed to be here was not relevant. He had heard the Call and he had answered, and now he simply waited for a sign. To comfort himself, he began to sing an ancient chant his Grandmother had taught him when he was a boy:

"Hey—ya—hey—hey—hey—yo—HO! Great Spirit, our guide. I give thanks for all that is. And for the Light in my heart, and within all of us. This Light shines out into the world to light our paths. One day we will all shine within the Light as equals, and fear will not exist. All will be as One."

As the wind rose from the trees, he felt the gooseflesh rise on his arms. The sudden burst of wind fluttered several crows who had been basking in the still burning sun, and as their wings danced they angrily cawed at him, blaming him for the rustle of leaves. He knew that Spirit had spoken. It was a good sign—the birds went back to their resting—because it meant the SuperStorms and Earth's upheavals were also resting; in other words, no massive earthquake or tsunami today. He had lived through the worst. For the past few decades, the massive raising of the Atlantic Ocean bed and the shifting of the Cascadian Teutonic Plates had wrecked havoc and horrific destruction, and the reporting of 20,000 and 30,000 deaths had become standard news. Years passed before the universal population had been told the truth about sunspots on the Sun that caused Solar Flares, and also, about the instability of the Earth's magnetic core. A massive explosion from a solar flare on the Sun could release as much energy as a billion megatons of TNT, and huge X-class flares were now common events.

For the time being the Earth's core and magnetic field had somehow stabilized. There was a time he wouldn't listen for the signs that came from outer messages and vibrations in the miasma of Great Spirit's playground, and messages from his inner guidance had been ignored. Too many years of his life had passed in oblivion, until one day he was led to return to his roots, and like his ancestors, to follow the whispered footsteps of the Great Spirit. And so he had returned to Spirit then, leaving behind the city and a life of drugs, alcohol, and meaningless diversions. The city had been a U-turn, distracting him from his life's purpose. So he left with nothing, and naked, he entered into the great lush rainforests of British Columbia. These mysterious dark forests provided a rich cornucopia for the senses, of rain and green, of smells and feelings and sounds from Nature—Mother Nature, that ever-present watcher in the woods. Frightened at first, he clawed the ground until he learned how to sustain himself and found a new way of life. He knew he had to learn the ways of survival and quickly. Complete immersion was the quickest way.

Now, perched on this cliff at the edge of his time, this big brute of a man waited for an important sign, the most important in his life and for the life of the planet. He knew the sign would be unique. He'd been able to find his way through his own personal horror. He knew he was meant to help bring Earth through a horrific event. Prophesied for centuries in Native American folklore and mythology, his Great Grandmother had told him the prophecy:

"When the Eye above two circles of light opens..." he paused, trying to remember. "From this time onward the world will be as a world upside-down. Where gold will be worthless and water will be priceless. Where religion will be in sacredness to the land. Where we will be as animals, on a quest for survival..."

In the distance, above the horizon line and coming out of the east, he spotted a black cloud. Was this the sign? As it drew closer he realized it was a huge mass of birds, all kinds of birds...

To download the eBook:
universaltides.com/ebooks.php

LIVE-2-LIVE

Help Others Help Others
LIVE-2-LIVE®
In-Spirit-Nation:
inspiring ourselves and others to do
one positive change for the world every day.
Join the movement!

www.12GoldenKeys.com
or e-mail: info@12goldenkeys.com

TO ORDER MORE COPIES OF
12 GOLDEN KEYS FOR A NEW WORLD
visit www.12GoldenKeys.com

E-mail: twelvekeys@shaw.ca
info@12goldenkeys.com

LaVergne, TN USA
02 August 2010
191780LV00004B/14/P